What Binds Marriage?

What Binds Marriage?

Roman Catholic theology in practice

TIMOTHY J. BUCKLEY CSsR

continuum
LONDON · NEW YORK

Continuum
The Tower Building
11 York Road
London SE1 7NX
www.continuumbooks.com

First published 1997 by Geoffrey Chapman
Revised and expanded edition printed 2002 by Continuum

British Library Cataloguing-in-Publication Data
A catalogue record for this book is available from the British Library.

ISBN 0-8264-6192-1

Typeset by Action Typesetting, Gloucester
Printed and bound in Great Britain by
Biddles Ltd, Guildford and King's Lynn

Contents

Abbreviations   ix
Preface   x

1 Catholics adjusting to marital breakdown   1
    Background   1
    A changing world – a changing Church   3
    On consulting the faithful   12
    The problem of language   16
    Focusing on the pastoral   22
    Notes   24

2 The theological history   28
    The biblical vision   29
    The bond in the early Church   40
    The Scholastics and the bond   47
    The teaching of the magisterium   52
    Previous pastoral solutions   58
        The Pauline privilege   58
        Non-consummation   60
        Canonical form   61
        The sacramental question   63
    The practical consequences of the theology of the bond   63
    Notes   68

3 Pastoral options   74
    A divorced Anglican seeks marriage with a Catholic   74
    A remarried mother seeks reception into the Catholic
        Church   79

Summary	83
Notes	84

4 The support groups — 86
The Association of Separated and Divorced Catholics — 86
The Rainbow Groups — 90
The Beginning Experience — 92
Findings from the group meetings and interviews — 93
    Relating within the groups — 93
    Relating to the wider Church — 97
    Relating to the clergy — 104
Special needs and looking to the future — 107
Summary — 110
Notes — 111

5 The opinions of the clergy — 115
Legalism and personalism — 117
The centrality of the Eucharist — 120
The internal forum – a cause of controversy — 123
    Epikeia — 125
    Equity — 125
    Oikonomia — 125
    Conflict and hardship cases — 126
Testing my findings — 134
The initiative of three German bishops — 136
Summary — 138
Notes — 139

6 Irregular marriage situations and RCIA — 143
The pastoral options — 145
    The annulment process — 145
    The internal forum — 146
    Reception into the Church without the sacraments — 147
Looking to the future — 148
Summary — 149

7 The tribunals — 150
Post-Vatican II – tribunals respond to the new situations — 152
Contrasting experiences — 153

Contents

Contrasting annulment and divorce   158
The new grounds for annulling marriages   160
Summary   163
Conclusions from all the empirical data   163
Notes   165

8 The theological future   167
Facing the theological impasse   168
The Orthodox tradition   172
The *sensus fidelium*   177
Final thoughts on the bond and indissolubility   179
Some practical suggestions   180
Notes   182

9 Defending the bond or the indefensible   184
The ongoing doctrinal discussion   188
The ongoing pastoral discussion   189
Annulments: differing perspectives   190
A final prayer   195
Notes   196

Appendix 1 Sample case history for discussion with
                          support groups   197
Appendix 2 Sample case history for discussion with
                          clergy groups   199

Bibliography   201
Index   205

Dedication

I dedicate this book to my mother and sister and to the memory of my father. It was with them that I first learned something about love in the family.

Thanks

I thank all those who guided, supported and encouraged me during the long years of study and research. I extend a special word of thanks to those who so generously and enthusiastically took part in interviews or group sessions, especially my new friends in the support groups. They wait expectantly on the Lord and his Church. May their patience be rewarded.

Acknowledgements

Monsignor Ralph Brown and the staff of the Westminster Tribunal: for providing me with the opportunity to attend a session of first and second instance nullity judgements.

All who replied to questionnaires and requests for information.

Fowler Wright Books, Leominster: for permission to include a lengthy quotation from Ladislas Örsy's book, *Marriage in Canon Law*.

Scripture quotations are taken from the New Revised Standard Version Bible, copyright © 1989 by the Division of Christian Education of the Churches of Christ in the USA, and used by permission. All rights reserved.

Quotations from the documents of the Second Vatican Council are taken from *Vatican Council II: The Conciliar and Post Conciliar Documents*, ed. Austin Flannery OP (Leominster: Fowler Wright Books, 1988).

Abbreviations

ASDC The Association of Separated and Divorced Catholics
BBC British Broadcasting Corporation
BE The Beginning Experience
CCL-GBI *The Code of Canon Law in English Translation*, prepared by the
Canon Law Society of Great Britain and Ireland
CCL-USA *Code of Canon Law: Latin-English Edition*
Translation prepared under the auspices of the Canon Law
Society of America
CDF The Sacred Congregation for the Doctrine of the Faith
CIC *Codex Iuris Canonici*
CLSN *Canon Law Society of Great Britain (and Ireland) Newsletter*
CMAC The Catholic Marriage Advisory Council
(Now renamed: Catholic Marriage Care)
DS Denzinger–Schönmetzer
FC *Familiaris Consortio*
GS *Gaudium et Spes*
IIMSO Her Majesty's Stationery Office
INTAMS International Academy for Marital Spirituality
LG *Lumen Gentium*
RCIA The Rite of Christian Initiation of Adults
RSV Revised Standard Version of the Bible
Vatican II The Second Vatican Council
VS *Veritatis Splendor*

References to papal documents, the documents of Vatican II, the
Catechism of the Catholic Church and Denzinger–Schönmetzer are given
according to their article numbering.

Preface

This book is the result of theological study and social research undertaken between 1990 and 1995. The work was originally commissioned by the Marriage and Family Life Committee for a report to the Bishops' Conference of England and Wales and that report was presented to the Low Week Meeting in 1994. A comprehensive analysis of the data was accepted by the University of London as a doctoral thesis in 1996. This book is an edited version of the thesis.[1] Therefore it must be clearly understood that as author I take sole responsibility for the theological arguments presented. In no way can they be presumed to represent the opinions of the bishops of England and Wales. Indeed the theological argument was developed precisely because I was unable to respond to a key request from the Bishops' Conference: namely 'to suggest a coherent pastoral policy'.

The report to the bishops, then, was a separate document, to which they responded with a press release after the 1994 Low Week Meeting. In their statement they expressed regret for the failings of the Catholic community in regard to the separated and divorced, for it was accepted that many of these feel alienated and ostracized. The bishops further promised to continue to address 'the difficulties of the present system for attending to marital breakdown in the Catholic Church'. That work continues in their conference. In this second edition of the book I have added an extra chapter, reflecting on what little progress has been made in the intervening four years since its first publication.

My conviction is that the problems as explored and analysed in these pages are not peculiar to the Church in Britain. At international conferences I have met moral theologians from all over the world who immediately identify with the issues. Many told identical stories of people struggling to understand the legal maze that surrounds them when they seek an ecclesial solution to the problem of their broken marriages. This was especially true of those from the English-speaking countries of North America, Australasia and Britain, where for some reason the annulment process has been employed more widely than in other parts of the Catholic world. But in the rest of Europe, in South America and Asia the same canonical problems beset theologians and canonists and they too have encouraged me to publish my findings.

Therefore, while the social research was confined to the Church in England and Wales, I maintain that the theological questions it illustrates are common to the universal Church. I am not the first to point the theological argument in the direction of the Orthodox tradition of *oikonomia*, but I believe that by carefully consulting the faithful, unravelling the history of the definition of the bond, challenging the disputable theology on which the present Western discipline is based and seeking a sacramental dialogue with the East, I am offering a serious contribution to the ongoing theological debate in this field.[2]

I ask of the reader only this: please approach this book with an open mind. It is difficult to have a theological discussion today without positions quickly becoming polarized. We all have our in-built prejudices and it is important to be aware of them. I have tried to listen to all sides of the argument and I have no axe to grind. I am not advocating easy divorce or easy annulment, or suggesting that the fundamental Christian belief in the sanctity and permanence of marriage no longer holds sway. I am arguing that the Catholic Church's present discipline in these matters and the theology which underpins it not only leave a lot to be desired, but as a matter of justice should be reformed.

Notes

1   A chapter of the thesis was devoted to an explanation of the methodology employed in the social research, while an appendix detailed the dozens of meetings and interviews conducted, and assemblies attended and addressed. Literally hundreds of people were involved in the research. In this book I have omitted all but a few helpful details so that the reader will not be distracted from the underlying theological argument and the pastoral experiences of the priests and people which have fashioned it.

2   I have used the word 'disputable' advisedly. The relationship between the magisterium of the Church and theology was discussed in an *Instruction on the Ecclesial Vocation of the Theologian* from the Sacred Congregation for the Doctrine of the Faith in 1990 (published by St Paul Books and Media). This began by stating that 'the living Magisterium of the Church and theology, while having different gifts

and functions, ultimately have the same goal: preserving the People of God in the truth which sets them free and thereby making them "a light to the nations"' (21). It concludes the same section:

> It can also happen that at the conclusion of a serious study, undertaken with the desire to heed the Magisterium's teaching without hesitation, the theologian's difficulty remains because the arguments to the contrary seem more persuasive to him. Faced with a proposition to which he feels he cannot give his intellectual assent, the theologian nevertheless has the duty to remain open to a deeper examination of the question. (31)

Theology in the great Scholastic tradition, which is the focus of much of this study, was built around the art of disputation. When I presented my findings to the University of London the examiners concluded that I had been 'overly constrained' by my work for the Catholic Bishops' Conference, concluding that 'the thesis had lamely passed the problem to the Church's magisterium'. In responding to their criticism I have tightened the argument and suggested a way forward. I would humbly suggest it is now the task of the local and universal magisterium of the Church to respond to the arguments in this disputation.

1

Catholics adjusting to marital breakdown

How to respond to the breakdown of marriage is a subject that has pre-occupied men and women of every generation in the Judaeo-Christian tradition. In our own time, the increased incidence of marital breakdown has ensured that separation, divorce and remarriage have become the subjects of constant attention in the Church and in society as a whole.

Statistics reveal that in England and Wales 'four in ten newly formed marriages are likely to end in divorce'.[1] The Catholic community is not immune from the effects of this social upheaval. On the basis of his national survey in 1978, Michael Hornsby-Smith tentatively concluded that 'overall, Catholics are not any less prone to divorce than members of the population at large'.[2]

Background

As the incidence of marital breakdown increased during the 1980s, the Bishops' Conference of England and Wales, confronted with the more and more complex pastoral issues associated with the question, asked its Committee for Marriage and Family Life 'to start an inter-disciplinary study of the various situations of people whose marriages have broken down or who are in second or invalid marriages'.[3]

In the latter part of 1989 I was invited to undertake this research, and, with the permission of my Redemptorist Superiors, was able to begin work in the autumn of 1990, under the direction of Heythrop College, London University.

The Bishops' Conference had specified that 'such a study would involve theology (both dogmatic and moral), law (canon and civil), the human sciences (sociology and psychology) and pastoral theology and practice'.[4] After discussions with the committee three definite objectives were agreed.

a. To get in touch with the experience of Catholics in the breakdown of marriage and family, and discover how the Church in England and Wales responds in such situations.
b. To discover to what degree those in canonically irregular marriages consider themselves to be members of the Church, and what steps the Church takes to integrate such people into itself, with particular reference to sacramental practice.
c. To suggest a coherent pastoral policy based on a sound theology of sacrament and Church.

This has been primarily a qualitative study. The data were collected through fieldwork, a method which of its very nature requires flexibility. Gerry Rose in his book *Deciphering Sociological Research* discusses the importance of understanding what he calls 'the natural history' of a project.

Research based on the fieldwork approach is not tightly structured in advance. Decisions must therefore be made from day to day about the future direction of the project, in the light of the data gathered and the field-work experience so far.[5]

The natural history of this project can be traced back long before the invitation from the Marriage and Family Life Committee. Unlike a researcher approaching a subject from an independent standpoint, I have been conscious of the divorce question in the Catholic Church throughout my life. As a priest I have been pastorally involved with the question for 26 years.

In this first chapter I will chart the background from which the present pastoral problems have emerged, using the perspective of my own growing awareness and involvement. In this way I can introduce the essential topics under discussion, and explain the framework of the study and the focus of each chapter.

I was grateful for the opportunity to study a question which has troubled me consistently during my years of pastoral ministry. I joined the Redemptorists in 1964, was ordained to the priesthood in 1970 and worked for a year on a parish in Plymouth, before being assigned for the rest of the

1970s to the special Redemptorist ministry of preaching missions and retreats. During that period I was also Director of Vocations. Both ministries entailed a lot of travelling and provided me with contrasting experiences of the Church in different parts of Britain. Early in 1981 I was appointed parish priest of the Redemptorist parish in Birmingham and in 1987 to the same post in Sunderland.

Although I was conscious of the complex pastoral problems surrounding marriage breakdown in the earlier years, when I became a parish priest and had to minister to people in these situations over long periods I became more aware of the intensity of their problems.

Even as a child I can recall that the ideal was that Catholics married Catholics in the Catholic Church, and there was no question of divorce. Indeed I can remember my parents refusing to attend the wedding of a cousin who had chosen to marry outside the Church. This was standard practice in the 1950s. If we had attended the wedding we would have regarded ourselves as being guilty of complicity in their sin.[6]

The position on divorce was regarded as uncomplicated. It had been explicitly forbidden by Jesus and was not possible for Catholics. The gospel texts of Matthew (5:31–32; 19:3–9), Mark (10:2–12) and Luke (16:18) were interpreted without qualification.

Occasionally there was news of a Catholic being granted an annulment. We were taught that this was a special process which proved that in fact the person had never been married. It was not to be confused with divorce. People would sometimes express unease that annulments were granted only to important people with influence and money, but most Catholics were very trusting and did not doubt the Church's integrity in this matter.

A changing world – a changing Church

In many ways the Catholic position was not remarkable. Although the divorce rates had risen steadily throughout this century and quite dramatically in the wake of the Second World War, reaching a peak in England of over 60,000 in 1948, the 1950s had seen a gradual decline, levelling out to an average of 24,000 per year at the end of the decade.[7] Divorce was still somewhat frowned upon in society in general and the other Christian Churches were similarly strict on the subject.

Among the social upheavals of the 1960s was a marked change of attitude towards sexual behaviour. The divorce rate in England and Wales soared, increasing by a few thousand each year from 25,000 in 1961 to 51,000 in 1969, the year of the Divorce Reform Act.[8]

During the 1960s the Church too was undergoing an upheaval. Pope John XXIII had called the Second Vatican Council and had set its agenda of *aggiornamento*. It would be difficult to overestimate the significance of that event. Theological and scriptural insights which had been germinating for decades now shaped the formulation of documents which were to give expression to the Church's understanding of itself in the modern world.

It was a remarkable sequence of events. An old man, Angelo Giuseppe Roncalli, had been elected Pope at the age of 77. Virtually everyone regarded his election as a temporary expedient to give the Church time to reflect after the long pontificate of Pius XII. Yet in four years Pope John XXIII had transformed the Catholic Church. The political implications within the Church of what was happening were not lost on him. On 11 October 1962 John XXIII opened the Council with a speech containing some memorable passages. He challenged the pessimists.

> We feel we must disagree with those prophets of gloom, who are always forecasting disaster, as though the end of the world were at hand.
> In the present order of things, Divine Providence is leading us to a new order of human relations ... And everything, even human differences, leads to the greater good of the Church.[9]

His vision was predominantly pastoral.

> The substance of the ancient doctrine of the deposit of faith is one thing, and the way in which it is presented is another. And it is the latter that must be taken into great consideration with patience if necessary, everything being measured in the forms and proportions of a magisterium which is predominantly pastoral in character.[10]

This *pastoral* direction was adopted by the Council. In the Pastoral Constitution on the Church in the Modern World, *Gaudium et Spes*, theologians were advised 'to seek out more efficient ways ... of presenting their teaching to modern man' (62).[11]

> For the deposit and truths of faith are one thing, the manner of

expressing them is quite another. In pastoral care sufficient use should be made, not only of theological principles, but also of the findings of secular sciences, especially psychology and sociology: in this way the faithful will be brought to a purer and more mature living of the faith. (GS 62)

Gaudium et Spes was the final document of the Council and heralded a new era of moral and pastoral theology in response to the vision of Pope John XXIII. One of its most commonly quoted phrases is that which begins: 'At all times the Church carries the responsibility of reading the signs of the times and interpreting them in the light of the Gospel' (4).

It is the pastoral urgency of the situation that has inspired this research. The struggle to distinguish what is 'the deposit of faith' and what is only its presentation or formulation, is at the heart of the debate.

In *Veritatis Splendor* Pope John Paul II drew attention to that opening conciliar address of Pope John XXIII, and noted that 'the development of the Church's moral doctrine is similar to that of the doctrine of the faith'.[12] In this study I will be examining some key doctrinal developments in the theology of marriage as well as their corresponding moral implications and seeking to isolate what is 'the deposit of faith' and what may have been only a 'manner of expressing' it.

Church politics are no different from human politics. Writing to the Corinthians St Paul condemns the factions that have built up and the use of slogans to designate who is supporting whom: '"I belong to Paul," or "I belong to Apollos," or "I belong to Cephas," or "I belong to Christ"' (1 Corinthians 1:12). The same can easily happen today. Those who rejoice in the inspiration of Pope John XXIII may be less ready to acknowledge that the Holy Spirit continues to guide the Church through the leadership of the popes who have succeeded him and vice versa. This study cannot escape the tension that exists in the Catholic Church at present regarding the exercise of authority.

I am writing as a Catholic priest, convinced that the Lord fulfils his promise: 'And remember, I am with you always, to the end of the age' (Matthew 28:20). I believe that the Lord is with the whole Church, the hierarchical Church with its structure and its laws, as well as the grass-roots Church with its saints and sinners. Henri de Lubac S J wrote about his vision of this all-embracing Church as he meditated on *Lumen Gentium,* the Dogmatic Constitution on the Church, the document which was to give shape to the whole of Vatican II.[13] His writings are significant because he was among the theologians whom the Church authorities silenced prior to Vatican II, but whose work was vindicated by the Council itself.

In *Lumen Gentium* the Vatican Council offered the Church a new image of itself and its structure. The hierarchical order was turned upside down. The Council emphasized the importance of the local church, highlighting the role of the bishop as a successor of the apostles, with authority in his own region. Just as he and the pope form a collegial team, so do the bishop and his clergy, called always to be united in the service of their people. And in turn the dignity of all the faithful was recognized; they too are to be reverenced as temples of the Holy Spirit and their voice is to be heard (LG 9–38).

In some quarters there is frustration that this vision of the Church is far from being realized. I believe it would be encouraging to see the voice of the laity carrying greater weight, especially in matters pertaining directly to their way of life. Thus it must be right that married people help to formulate the theology of marriage.

In England and Wales far-reaching developments have taken place. For example, the Committee for Marriage and Family Life, which commissioned this study, comprised one bishop, two priests and three lay people, two of whom were women. Indeed the fact that it was commissioned in the first place demonstrates the determination of the Bishops' Conference to be as fully informed as possible.

The first task of the research was to report as faithfully as possible the opinions and experiences of all who took part. The second was to interpret those opinions and experiences and consider them in the light of the theology and canon law of marriage.

The developments brought about by Vatican II are important because they are based upon the sound insights of learning from a multiplicity of disciplines. Alongside the development of philosophical and theological thinking, Scripture scholarship has opened up the Word of God to us in a new and enriching way. Also the Council was ready to acknowledge how the remarkable advances in the natural sciences, the behavioural and social sciences, and medicine help us understand more fully the mystery of God and his creation.

Gaudium et Spes explored the implications of all these developments. As well as recognizing that 'the Church carries the responsibility of reading the signs of the times' (GS 4), it also insisted that the Church express its teaching in a language which is understandable.

In language intelligible to every generation, she should be able to answer the ever recurring questions which men ask about the meaning of this present life and of the life to come, and how one is related to the other. (GS 4)

De Lubac saw the value of his own experience coupled with that of the Church.

Her [the Church's] experience, she tells me, permits her to grow in the course of the centuries in the perception of the Truth which was revealed to her: my own experience, my modest experience, I can say to her, has permitted me too to grow in the course of my brief years in the perception of what she is for me as for each of her faithful. ('The mystery of the Church', p. 77)

The tension which sometimes arises in the life of the Church between the magisterium and theologians in search of the truth is illustrated at this present time by the encyclical *Veritatis Splendor* and by the reaction to it of another theologian who had a marked influence on the Council, the Redemptorist Bernard Häring. In an article in *The Tablet*, he described the pain he felt at not being trusted.[14]

Away with all distrust in our Church! Away with all attitudes, mentalities and structures which promote it! We should let the Pope know that we are wounded by the many signs of his rooted distrust, and discouraged by the manifold structures of distrust which he has allowed to be established. We need him to soften towards us, the whole Church needs it. (p. 1379)

Introducing him, *The Tablet* described Häring as 'probably the best-known moral theologian in the Catholic Church' (p. 1378). Certainly he has been a major figure for over forty years. He was much involved in the preparation of the text of *Gaudium et Spes* and especially the section on marriage and family life, a subject which had been hotly debated from the very beginning. The story behind this is well documented. In the *Commentary on the Documents of Vatican II*, Bernard Häring himself wrote a chapter on 'Fostering the nobility of marriage and the family'.[15]

Cardinal Heenan, the then Archbishop of Westminster, was very suspicious of the so-called *periti* (experts) at the Council and his biting remark during the debate in the Third Session, 'Timeo peritos annexa ferentes', is quoted by Häring (p. 226), knowing that it was directed especially at him.[16] In his recent book, *My Witness for the Church*, Häring referred to the fact that Cardinal Heenan vigorously attacked his work by name.[17] Later he could not conceal his delight over the remarkable reconciliation which took place between them as a result of *Humanae Vitae*, the papal encyclical of Pope Paul VI on the Regulation of Birth, promulgated in 1968.[18]

Häring wrote:

> Concerning Cardinal Heenan one assumed – presumably also the Pope – that he remained on the old strict line . . . In the Council, in St Peter's, he had taken a hard position against me specifically on account of this question. Nevertheless, Cardinal Heenan not only had completely reconciled himself with me, but had also more or less worked his way through to a conviction which was the same as mine.[19]

This is a significant point of reference. *Humanae Vitae* was a turning point in the moral perception of Catholics because of the introduction into their thinking of the *conscience clause*. There had been a widespread expectation that the Church would relax its ban on artificial contraception. When this did not happen bishops in many parts of the world were engaged in a process that could only be described as damage limitation.

The bishops of England and Wales issued their own statement;[20] but in this connection probably the single event which carried the most impact in Britain was a television interview with the said Cardinal Heenan. Pressurized on the subject by his interviewer he admitted that it was possible for people to disobey this teaching and still be in good conscience. Michael Hornsby-Smith, in a lecture at Heythrop College, drew attention to the importance of this particular interview, not because of what Cardinal Heenan had said, but because of the expression on his face when confronted with the question.[21] And it is the sociological significance of this wider dimension of communication to which Hornsby-Smith draws attention in the introduction to his book, *Roman Catholic Beliefs in England* (p. 6).

> For the first time authority figures, whether cabinet ministers or the Cardinal Archbishop of Westminster, were subject to detailed cross-examination in one's own front room, and in the process became

vulnerable to critical evaluation in a way that had never been possible before.

The climate was slowly changing. Others have carefully analysed the implications of the birth control debate;[22] it is enough for us to note its consequences in relation to the pastoral care of the separated, divorced and remarried.

For many couples the teaching on contraception put an enormous strain on their marriages, especially when one partner was not a Catholic. Today that problem is undoubtedly less acute. Hornsby-Smith states that 'the evidence we have reviewed suggests ... that lay people ... have largely made up their own minds on this matter, and now regard it as none of the business of the clerical leadership in the Church'.[23] Nevertheless, fidelity to this particular teaching still seems to provide a kind of litmus test of orthodoxy for the Roman magisterium.[24]

The question of birth control has been raised repeatedly during this research, especially in the context of authoritative teaching. Many priests and people have expressed the fear that no matter what conclusions this report reaches, unless these conform to the papal magisterial teaching on marriage, at best they will be dismissed, at worst I personally will be subjected to some form of censure. This fear was most powerfully expressed in an anonymous 'Viewpoint' in *The Tablet* entitled 'One *Humanae Vitae* is enough'.

We remember Paul VI's encyclical *Humanae Vitae* reaffirming the ban on contraception. The majority recommendations were based upon sound reasoning; the minority's sole argument was an appeal to the Church's authority. The conclusions of the majority were rejected. The conclusions of any research that seem to threaten church authority will be ignored or dismissed. Rome deals crudely with dissenters ...

We do not want another *Humanae Vitae* – a church teaching proclaimed but not followed. We do not want an official church teaching on marriage that is increasingly ignored by various forms of the internal forum solution.

There is danger of a division between the institutional Church and a popular Church going its own quiet way. This is the way of private conscience. The Mystical Body is rent.[25]

I think the 'Viewpoint' is too simplistic in stating that 'the minority's sole argument was an appeal to the Church's authority'. I believe its argument has more to do with the fear of a break with tradition, the fear that any change of direction might call into question the validity and therefore the authority of the Church's teaching on moral matters in general. It is this question which dominates the encyclical *Veritatis Splendor*.

The use of authority by the magisterium is a matter which will exercise our minds throughout this book.[26] In *Veritatis Splendor* Pope John Paul II asserts that 'opposition to the teaching of the Church's Pastors cannot be seen as a legitimate expression either of Christian freedom or of the diversity of the Spirit's gifts' (VS 113). He appeals to his Bishops 'to act in conformity with their apostolic mission', insisting that *'the right of the faithful* to receive Catholic doctrine in its purity and integrity must always be respected' (VS 113). This call for whole-hearted assent even to non-infallible teaching echoes the profession of faith and the oath of fidelity required of those who have assumed certain ecclesiastical offices since 1 March 1989.[27]

A research project such as this is bound to raise questions regarding the interpretation of theology and canon law. I am aware of the delicacy of the situation. In *Veritatis Splendor* Pope John Paul II expresses appreciation for the work of many theologians, who are encouraged 'to continue their efforts'; at the same time he warns against developments not consistent with 'sound teaching' (2 Timothy 4:3) (VS 29). He acknowledges the value of developments in the behavioural and natural sciences, but warns that moral theology 'does not rely on the results of formal empirical observation or phenomenological understanding alone' (VS 111).

The encyclical examines the fundamental moral issues with which I have been confronted throughout the course of this research. They include the tension between freedom and law (VS 35–53) and the relationship between conscience and truth (VS 54–64). Introducing the discussion on freedom Pope John Paul II notes that 'certain currents of modern thought have gone so far as to *exalt freedom to such an extent that it becomes an absolute, which would then be the source of values'* (VS 32).

The abuse of freedom deprives others of their freedom and must always be challenged by the Church, which is called upon to free people from the slavery of sin. At the same time the primacy of conscience is always to be respected and is reaffirmed in the encyclical (VS 62).

The document pays careful attention to the formation of conscience and explains that 'Christians have a great help for the formation of conscience *in the Church and her Magisterium'* (VS 64). A particular difficulty is how to judge whether people have taken care to inform their consciences. Pope John Paul II reminds us that 'conscience, as the judgment of an act, is not exempt from the possibility of error' (VS 62). He does not address the problem that the magisterium is likewise 'not exempt from the possibility of error'. By not making a distinction between fallible and infallible teaching, he fails to deal with the difficulty that the Church's teaching has not always been consistent and unchanging.

There is a further consideration. The magisterium, the teaching office of the Church, is also exercised by the bishops. Faced with the confusion and unhappiness of so many of their people after the publication of *Humanae Vitae* in 1968, we have seen that many Conferences of Bishops issued their own statements. Commenting on this Austin Flannery concluded that many of these statements actually 'qualify the teaching of the encyclical in its application in the concrete'.[28] In England and Wales, the bishops noted the difficulties of those who had come to expect a change in the Church's teaching.

> Understandably many wives and husbands, anticipating the promised statement of the Pope, have come to rely on contraception. In this they have acted conscientiously and often after seeking pastoral advice. They may now be unable to see that, at least in their personal circumstances, the use of contraception is wrong. A particular difficulty faces those who after serious thought and prayer cannot as yet understand or be fully convinced of the doctrines as laid down.[29]

Does this statement constitute a qualification? How does it measure against the statement in *Veritatis Splendor*, which argues that 'it would be a very serious error to conclude that the Church's teaching is essentially only an "ideal" which must then be adapted, proportioned, graduated to the so-called concrete possibilities of man, according to a "balancing of the goods in question"' (VS 103)?

Seemingly concerned about the negative publicity surrounding the long awaited *Veritatis Splendor*, the bishops of England and Wales issued a pastoral message to be read at all the Masses on 3 October 1993, the Sunday preceding its publication. It included this comment:

> Contrary to some newspaper reports, the Encyclical is not all about sex, nor indeed about any one particular moral issue. For

example, it only makes one or two passing references to contraception and homosexuality, and does not in any way change the Church's position on these matters.

After its publication Cardinal Hume was quick to defuse the debate about the role of theologians (VS 113) and the 'Catholic' status of institutions of learning (VS 116). Interviewed at the launch of the encyclical, he warned that it 'would be a mistake to blow up out of proportion or take out of context' these references.

> We are not engaged in a witch-hunt. We have very good relations with moral theologians in this country. We know our moral theologians are having to deal with problems that are entirely new.[30]

Carefully worded, diplomatic statements such as these are important examples of that broader exercise of the magisterium in the Church. Nevertheless they cannot completely eliminate those feelings of unease among many that the Roman magisterium in particular is out of touch with the experiences of many of God's people.

More and more priests and people are finding the courage to speak openly. Morris West, writing about the magisterium in the same issue of the *Catholic Herald* in which the Cardinal's comments were quoted, provides a good example. He argued that 'the channels by which we may communicate with our pastors and they with us are, at best, sclerotic, clogged with protocols and protective procedures'.[31]

West's comment is a particular challenge in the context of this research, which has sought to communicate with the bishops – with the magisterium – to enable them to hear the experiences of their people.

On consulting the faithful

Social research is treated by the Roman magisterium with caution.

> *Some ethicists*, professionally engaged in the study of human realities and behaviour, can be tempted to take as the standard for their discipline and even for its operative norms the results of a statistical study of concrete human behaviour patterns and the opinions about morality encountered in the majority of people. (VS 46)

Familiaris Consortio is a document of central importance to our study.[32] Addressing the question of research it states:

> The Church values sociological and statistical research, when it proves helpful in understanding the historical context in which pastoral action has to be developed and when it leads to a better understanding of the truth. Such research alone, however, is not to be considered in itself an expression of the sense of faith. (FC 5)

The sense of faith – *sensus fidei* – the consciousness of the Christian community as a whole as to what is right and true before God, is a very delicate theological issue. *Lumen Gentium* explains it as follows:

> The whole body of the faithful who have an anointing that comes from the holy one (cf. 1 Jn. 2:20 and 27) cannot err in matters of belief. This characteristic is shown in the supernatural appreciation of the faith (*sensus fidei*) of the whole people, when, 'from the bishops to the last of the faithful' (See St Augustine, *De Praed. Sanct.* 14, 27: PL 44, 980) they manifest a universal consent in matters of faith and morals. (LG 12)

Social researchers are faced with a dilemma. Pope John Paul II teaches that an essential criterion for the validity of research is that it 'leads to a better understanding of the truth' (FC 5). If the truth has already been formulated by the magisterium, then how can researchers contribute to that formulation? However carefully they may research their subject and present their findings, researchers fear that they may find it difficult to gain a hearing should those findings call into question that formulation.

The tension I have outlined here is not new, but part of an unfolding struggle to determine how to exercise authority in the Church and how to define infallibility. The First Vatican Council defined the nature of papal infallibility, but an understanding of how this is shared by the bishops and all the faithful was not formulated until the Second Vatican Council (see *Lumen Gentium* 12, 25).

Prior to the First Vatican Council, John Henry Newman had contributed to the debate and had suffered for it. An essay in *The Rambler* in July 1859, 'On consulting the faithful in matters of doctrine', was the cause of considerable hostility and meant that in Rome Newman was held in great suspicion for many years.[33]

Newman maintained that the laity have a right to be consulted, 'because the body of the faithful is one of the witnesses to the fact of revealed doctrine, because their *consensus* throughout Christendom is the voice of the Infallible Church' (p. 63). John Coulson explains that Newman understood this in the sense that 'infallibility is not, strictly, *in* that consensus, but rather the consensus is an *indicium* or *instrumentum* to us of the judgement of that Church which *is* infallible' (p. 22). Newman based much of his argument on the experience of the Church during the dark days of the Arian heresy in the fourth century when it was not the bishops who preserved the faith defined at Nicaea, but the laity. He also pointed to the more immediate experience of the Church in 1854 in promulgating the dogma of the Immaculate Conception.

In spite of the adverse criticism Newman did not change his position, he only clarified it. He consistently argued that much of the misunderstanding surrounded the definition of the English word 'consult', which he insisted he was using in a popular and not a scientific way to mean 'inquiring into a matter of *fact*' (p. 54): and that matter of fact was the belief of the faithful (*sensus fidelium*).

This distinction will be important when we come to analyse the results of my consultation with both the laity and the clergy which forms the basis of much of this study. Newman's primary concern was with the dogmatic teaching of the Church. This too is significant because while so much of the discussion regarding marital breakdown focuses on *moral* imperatives, I am convinced that the root cause of most of our present difficulties lies in our understanding or misunderstanding of the *dogmatic* teaching about marriage. I am satisfied that I heard a clear consensus, which might well constitute an expression of the *sensus fidelium* on this matter.

Newman was clear in his own mind that the teaching Church (*Ecclesia docens*) should not cut itself off from the faithful or prevent them from taking part in the study of her doctrines. Thus his essay concluded:

> I think certainly that the *Ecclesia docens* is more happy when she has ... enthusiastic partisans about her ..., than when she cuts off the faithful from the study of her divine doctrines and the sympathy of her divine contemplations, and requires from them a *fides implicita* in her word, which in the educated classes will terminate in indifference, and in the poorer in superstition. (p. 106)

As we have seen this teaching was echoed in the documents of Vatican II, but it may take a long time for some to move beyond a belief that all that is required of them is a *fides implicita*.

An important aspect of this research is the fact that originally it was commissioned by the Conference of Bishops. I am conscious that for many people this has given my work a particular authority. In spite of the changed climate and the new freedoms experienced by a good number of Catholics, the Church's official teaching weighs heavily with Catholics in general. The formation of conscience is a complicated process of discernment and growth. The *conscience clause* is not easily understood or interpreted by many. In Britain there is the added complication that we tend to be somewhat pragmatic and interpret all law in a literal and prescriptive way.

My findings suggest that the challenge for the magisterium is to examine a situation in which its pastoral directives fail to find an echo in the minds and hearts of the body of the faithful.

It is now accepted that in the renewal of the Church the laity have a great deal to contribute. Their opinions are to be sought, their co-operation encouraged, their gifts exercised in ministry.[34] This has called for a radical reappraisal on the part of clergy and laity alike, and it is not surprising that the process of reshaping our thinking has sometimes been slow and painstaking.

When people have been brought up to view the Church in a particular way, it is difficult immediately to transform that view. Clergy trained to believe that they had most of the answers to most of the problems have not always taken kindly to the idea that some of their parishioners may know more about even certain theological questions than themselves. By the same token, parishioners brought up with a deep respect for their clergy have often found it hard to respond to the invitation to assume new responsibilities in areas previously reserved to their bishops and priests.

There is no doubt that some of the laity are disillusioned because of unhappy experiments in consultation or collaboration, and it remains a very sensitive issue in the pastoral care of separated, divorced and remarried Catholics. Of necessity much of the pastoral care has been initiated by the laity. This has created its own tension because the laity look to the clergy to give their ministry its authority, and the clergy's approval is not always forthcoming.

When I was appointed a parish priest in the early 1980s I felt a certain sense of hopelessness in the face of the rising tide of divorce among Catholics. My experience, especially on parish missions, had impressed upon me the seriousness of the situation and I had often drawn the local clergy's attention to specific cases in their parishes in the hope that annulments might be sought.

Although I was aware of the *internal forum* solution, I had always been hesitant to employ it because I remained uncertain about its authority and rarely felt that the fundamental conditions for its use could be satisfied by a peripatetic preacher.[35] Certainly annulments were being granted more freely and on a variety of new grounds. The key development since the Council had been the acceptance by the Roman Rota and the Segnatura Apostolica of new psychological grounds, notably *lack of due discretion* and *inability to assume the obligations of marriage.*[36]

In this development of the tribunal process and the granting of annulments I saw a genuine effort on the part of the hierarchical Church to bring pastoral relief in the face of so much human suffering. However, in spite of increased staffing in many of the diocesan tribunals and a genuine effort to deal with the new caseloads, it was clear that only a small percentage of those whose marriages were breaking down could successfully petition for annulments.

The problem of language

For some time now sociologists and theologians have been paying attention to the tensions which exist between their respective disciplines. While some would hardly see the relevance of the other, there are many who value interdisciplinary discussion, recognizing that both seek to give meaning to human experience.

A symposium of sociologists and theologians met in Oxford in 1978 and 1979 and the papers they produced were edited in *Sociology and Theology: Alliance and Conflict.*[37] In the introduction John Orme Mills notes that 'theology's language and structure of concepts are no longer shared by the academic community' (p. 4). He identifies the gravest threat to theology's status to be 'the spread of cultural pluralism and the associated "privatization" and present extreme subjectivization of religious beliefs'. He concludes:

And, although this is largely an outcome of transformations in society itself, it is the social sciences which have supplied the language and concepts in which it has been possible to describe and explain what has happened and to pose the painful questions. (p. 4)

Certainly I have struggled to find a meeting place for the language and concepts of social research and the languages and concepts of the different schools of theology, canon law and Scripture. Marriage preparation programmes emphasize the importance of good communications between the partners.[38] If it is true that stable human relationships are formed around good communication, it is also true that language barriers have presented me with endless problems in researching the pastoral care of broken marriage relationships in the Catholic Church.

Bernard Lonergan maintains that all our knowledge is derived from a process of reflection on experience.[39] His theory gives me hope that ultimately the search for a coherent pastoral policy, which is one of the main objectives of this study, may not be in vain. As men and women of hope we are constantly searching for meaning in our lives and seeking to interpret our experiences.

Alasdair MacIntyre laments the fact that the moral argument has become interminable because there is no common ground upon which we can have the debate, and in *After Virtue* he illustrates this by pointing out that *emotivism* is now in possession.[40] It is true that the debate becomes impossible if everyone becomes his own authority, a point strongly argued in *Veritatis Splendor* (32), but we must also ask whether this situation is not caused, at least in part, by the failure in Christian moral theology to determine which are the absolutes. For while it is impossible if everyone becomes his own authority, it is equally impossible if the teaching Church tries to maintain positions based on arguments where the logic breaks down.

Theodore Mackin's discussion of indissolubility in marriage exemplifies this well. In an exhaustive treatment of the subject in his book, *Divorce and Remarriage*, he is forced to conclude that while the Church believes that by its very *nature* marriage is indissoluble, it reserves 'really indissoluble indissolubility for a special kind of marriages, for only those that are Christian sacraments, and, among these, for only those that are consummated as Christian sacraments'.[41]

Veritatis Splendor is concerned to defend the notion of *absolute truth*, basing much of its argument on the Thomistic doctrine of 'natural law', defined as the rational creature's participation in the eternal law (VS 43–44). Within this system the Scholastic categories of *objectivity* and *subjectivity* provide the framework for determining the *absolutely objective* norms which must govern the *subjective* behaviour of men and women. Behaviour which is contrary to the natural order is condemned as intrinsically evil (VS 80). The Church's condemnation of artificial means of contraception is based on this natural law argument.

It is essential that the reader understands that this is not the issue in this study. The natural law argument in favour of monogamous, faithful and permanent relationships in marriage is not called into question. Nor is the Church's right to teach authoritatively on these matters. What calls for careful examination is the way in which the Church, in the formulation of its laws and in its exercise of the magisterium, has been able to override the natural law by the use of 'pastoral solutions' *in favour of the faith.*

Although the language of the Scholastics is widely referred to in *Veritatis Splendor*, the Pope explicitly states that 'the Church's Magisterium does not intend to impose upon the faithful any particular theological system, still less a philosophical one' (VS 29).

The language of Scholastic objectivity is not the language of modern social research. Social researchers are concerned to establish the *validity* of their methods of data collection and analysis. In that context much of this study should be assessed on its validity, not its objectivity.

I was led to reflect on the problem of language and its usage, and the very real gulfs in understanding which can exist because of the different languages employed by different disciplines. In an interdisciplinary study such as this, it will be important to bear this in mind.

There is a sense in which all our problems are problems of communication. While sociologists today do not think in the categories of Scholastic philosophy, neither do modern philosophers, psychologists or theologians.

When we fail to understand one another, it is always a problem of language. Either we do not understand the concepts or we are unable to empathize with the other's experience. If the formulation of our doctrine is in a language which cannot be understood by the majority of the people for whom it is intended, then the teaching Church must address that problem. This was precisely the reason for calling the Second Vatican Council; precisely the question to which Pope John XXIII called attention in his opening address.

Sociologists will examine a research project for its validity rather than its objectivity because the latter suggests a notion of the *absolute*, which it might be impossible to establish. Could it be that we can find a parallel in our theological language? Much of our traditional theology has sought to define God and his creation in terms of absolute truths.

Theologians are able to specify the limited number of infallibly defined dogmas, but in the moral sphere the position is far less clear.[42] For example, from the very beginning the magisterium made it clear that *Humanae Vitae* was not an infallible document. Vincent Genovesi writes on this subject.

> It should be noted that neither in recent years nor beyond has there ever been an infallible definition by a pope or an ecumenical council concerning specific moral issues; as a matter of fact, there is a broad consensus among Roman Catholic theologians today that even in the exercise of its ordinary universal magisterium, the Church has never taught infallibly in the area of concrete moral norms.[43]

Catholics often find it difficult to distinguish the import of comparative teachings. Many of the problems in the wake of the Council resulted from the fact that familiar customs and rituals were thought to be part of an *absolutely* unchanging tradition. In its theological search for the truth, the Church might do better to concentrate on *integrity* rather than an *objectivity* expressed in *absolutes*. This is not to deny the existence of the truth, just to recognize humbly that it is often difficult to discern in a complicated and changing world.

'Integrity' is a word which modern men and women readily understand. Nothing causes greater scandal in the Church than a lack of integrity. The furore over Bishop Eamonn Casey in 1992 is a good example and it has been raised by interviewees in this research.[44] It is not for us to judge him personally before God, and the outpouring of forgiveness and understanding from so many in his diocese and in the wider community was a marvellous expression of Christian charity at the time, but the implications of this story warrant some attention.

What seemed to have caused distress was not the fact that he had failed, but that for so many years there had been such duplicity, and that the options for him and for any priest are so dramatically different to those of people who fail to keep their marriage vows.

The explanation is logical in terms of the absolute thinking of the Scholastics. The bond of a sacramentally consummated marriage is absolutely indissoluble in the objective ontological order of supernatural grace, and that bond remains no matter what arrangements we make to the contrary here on earth. The priesthood is also irrevocably sealed in this new ontological order, but the vow of celibacy which accompanies it is a disciplinary decision of the Church, which can be revoked by an authoritative decision because it is not intrinsic to the priesthood itself.

Thus, while priests cannot give up their priesthood, it is sometimes possible for them to obtain permission to give up the *exercise* of that priest-hood and get married. Likewise it is possible for men and women who have taken perpetual vows in religious life to receive a dispensation to leave their communities and be free to marry.

To the outsider and even to many Catholics the logic of this position is not easily grasped. They see people who have made solemn promises to live particular vocations. When things go wrong, as in the human condition they so often do, there is an escape route for some, but not for others. It is not that the Church is trying to make people's lives a misery, but sometimes, when the legal position is clinically presented, it can appear harsh and uncaring. There is a gut feeling among many that it does not correspond to the full gospel message of hope and forgiveness.

What is the difference between the fidelity required of the bishop, priest or the vowed religious and the married person? It is not to be found in the consent to be committed to that way of life: that can be dispensed by the Church. In certain circumstances it can be dispensed for married people: for example for those not sacramentally married or those who have not consummated a sacramental marriage. Furthermore it does not depend on the physical fact that two people have procreated and have responsibility for a child, even though that is the foundation of the natural law governing marriage. The difference is that in certain marriages, those between baptized people who have had sexual intercourse after they have made their marriage vows, an absolutely indissoluble bond has been established, which cannot be dissolved.

It is often said that marriages are made in heaven and broken on earth. The broken marriages on earth are the subject of this research. The brokenness is identifiable in the separation of the partners and the pain of their situations. It is possible for the social researcher to get in touch with this brokenness, gather and analyse data and present conclusions. However the same methods cannot be used to get in touch with the 'heavenly' dimension of this question, and it is here so often that communication breaks down.

The tradition of the Church is that in a sense marriages are made in heaven, blessed by God and sealed with an indissoluble bond. Yet it is also true to say that throughout its history the Church has struggled to determine exactly the circumstances in which that bond is created and becomes wholly indissoluble. Indeed the present discipline has evolved largely as a result of attempts to deal with the pastoral problems of marriages failing, beginning with St Paul and the new pagan converts in Corinth (1

Corinthians 7:10–16) and continuing to our own day with the introduction of the new psychological grounds for annulment in the face of the ever more complex nature of life in the modern world.

Bridging the language gap between the different disciplines in this study will be a constant challenge. However I believe that while MacIntyre argues that it is difficult to find common ground for the moral debate in society in general, the common ground for this research is not in doubt. This research has been carried out, not in society in general, but within the Catholic community, a community which puts its faith in the person of Jesus Christ, who said of himself: 'I am the way, and the truth and the life' (John 14:6). This community proclaims that Jesus is Lord and Saviour, and that through his Holy Spirit he lives among his people, making his salvation present in every age. It is not surprising then that repeatedly people have asked the question: 'What would Jesus say in this situation?'

There is no simpler way of defining the common ground of this study. We will have to contend with contrasting levels of faith in individuals or groups, and we will have to wrestle with how to interpret the meaning of *salvation*, but the beginning and end of this study is a search for what the Lord Jesus wants.

When Catholics proclaim their faith in Jesus and his Church, they are proclaiming faith in a community that has struggled for two thousand years to understand and live out its faith. The dogmas which are professed in the creeds were formulated after centuries of debate, debates that probably seemed interminable to those involved in them. We can understand those dogmas and all that the teaching Church proclaims only in the light of our experience in the world at the end of the twentieth century.

The fundamental belief of the Church is that Jesus is Saviour of the World. How we understand the concept of salvation will certainly depend on how we have experienced life itself. The person whose life has been reduced to a hell on earth in an unhappy marriage will almost certainly have a very different image of Jesus as Saviour from the academic celibate theologian who ponders the mysteries of the theology of marriage in a certain isolation. Both their experiences are valid; both contribute to the debate.

As individuals and as church we proclaim our belief in Jesus as Lord and Saviour, as the *Truth*. This research is now part of the search for truth about the question of divorce, and the pastoral problems of our time call for the prayerful attention of the community of faith. Pastoral problems always call for pastoral solutions.

Focusing on the pastoral

This study will expose many paradoxes and anomalies in the theology and the canon law of marriage. One crucial area of concern is the apparent gulf between systematic theology and pastoral theology. If the ideal is presented in such a way that it is far removed from the lived experience, then of what use is the ideal?

A recent study of the sacramentality of marriage, *What God Has Joined ...* by Peter J. Elliott, touches on this point in the introduction.[45] Elliott is concerned to study the doctrine of marriage, which in his opinion has been neglected in recent times.

> So often the sacramentality of Marriage has been neglected as a focus for theological research and reflection. Study of the sacramentality of Marriage has been overshadowed by the work of specialists in the fields of Canon Law and pastoral theology. However necessary and important such practical work may be, in our times especially there is a great need for a deeper understanding of the sacramental mystery of Marriage. We need a thorough theological investigation of the divine activity at work in this unique and specific union of man and woman. (pp. xv–xvi)

I will argue that just as we should not divorce *the* divorce issue from all the other social and theological issues which confront society and the Church today, so we should not divorce the practice from the mystery, the pastoral theology from the sacramental theology. The alternative is a schizophrenic religious mentality, and indeed the symptoms of that mentality are to be found everywhere in priests and people alike.

The *bond* is central to the theological discussion of marriage. Its importance in determining the limits of pastoral care will be illustrated throughout the reports of the fieldwork of the social research. Chapter 2 will analyse the theological history of the bond, linking it with some of the key pastoral decisions which have led to the present discipline in the *Code of Canon Law*.

Chapter 2 provides us with the framework within which we can present the findings of our consultation with the laity and the clergy.

With the focus firmly directed at the pastoral question, I resolved to avoid the pitfall of trying to offer some quantitative analysis of Catholic opinion, concentrating rather on the people actually involved in ministering or receiving pastoral care. Undoubtedly some measure of Catholic opinion can be gathered from the data in Chapters 3 to 7, but no attempt is made to draw conclusions beyond the evidence of the data presented.

That said, the backdrop to this study is that opinions and behaviour patterns in relation to marriage and family life are rapidly changing in the Catholic community as they are in society as a whole.[46] So this is primarily a qualitative study, seeking to understand the situation by inviting priests and people to reflect on their experiences and share their opinions. Thus I have sought out those groups which have been formed or formed themselves in response to the pastoral needs of those whose marriages have failed.

Chapter 3 is the record of two case histories from my own pastoral experience. During my years as a missioner and a parish priest I was faced with many pastoral problems in the field of marriage breakdown. If there appeared to be hope of reconciliation and if it seemed opportune I would suggest seeking the assistance of the Catholic Marriage Advisory Council (CMAC), now Marriage Care; if not, I would explore the possibility of an annulment, and when appropriate refer the situation to the diocesan tribunal. My memories evoke mixed feelings about the work of the tribunals. I have never had reason to doubt that those who serve on them act with integrity and form their judgements according to their understanding of the evidence before them, but on a number of occasions I was left with the feeling that justice had not been done. The first case history illustrates this problem. The second, which in the event did not involve the diocesan tribunal, is typical of many of the pastoral situations encountered by the clergy. They will serve as a springboard for the wider discussion that has taken place in meetings and interviews across England and Wales.

The early 1980s saw an increase in pastoral activity in the field. At that time the Association of Separated and Divorced Catholics (ASDC) and the Rainbow Groups were formed, and the Beginning Experience (BE) was introduced from the United States of America. Reports on the information gained from many sessions with these groups provides the material for Chapter 4.

The clergy, representing the voice of the hierarchical Church, are at the sharp end of much of what happens. Their opinions and experiences have been sought in a series of meetings around the country and it is this information which is examined in Chapter 5.

A forum in which the pastoral care of the separated, divorced and remarried takes on a special significance is that of The Rite of Christian Initiation of Adults (RCIA). This process is now the approved way of preparing people for reception into full communion with the Catholic Church. Almost inevitably more and more enquirers are coming from a background of divorce and irregular second marriages, often with little or no realization that this may present pastoral difficulties, especially if they have already received Christian baptism in another denomination.

So acute has the problem become that the subcommittee of the Bishops' Conference for RCIA approached me with a view to researching this aspect of pastoral care separately. Accordingly, in the autumn of 1992 I interviewed priests and their RCIA teams in a sample of parishes and the findings of that survey are presented in Chapter 6.

In the work of the diocesan tribunals we find a public forum for pastoral care. A brief summary of my findings is given in Chapter 7.

Chapter 8 offers a final analysis of the findings of this research, isolating the theological impasse and suggesting a theological way forward.

Notes

1   Duncan J. Dormor, *The Relationship Revolution: Cohabitation, Marriage and Divorce in Contemporary Europe* (London: One Plus One, Marriage and Partnership Research, 1992), p. 22.
2   Michael Hornsby-Smith, *Roman Catholic Beliefs in England: Customary Catholicism and Transformations of Religious Authority* (Cambridge: Cambridge University Press, 1991), p. 183.
3   *Briefing*, The Documentation and News Service of the Bishops' Conferences of England and Wales and of Scotland (London: Catholic Media Office), vol. 18, no. 24 (1988), p. 515.
4   *Briefing*, vol. 18, no. 24 (1988), pp. 515–16.
5   G. Rose, *Deciphering Sociological Research* (Basingstoke: Macmillan Education, 1982), p. 115.
6   This strict interpretation of the dangers of giving scandal can be found in the manuals of moral theology. For a typical discussion of *scandalum* and *cooperatio* see: I. Aertnys – C. Damen CSsR, *Theologia Moralis* (17th edn, rev. J. Visser CSsR, 2 vols; Turin: Marietti, 1956), I, pp. 363–86.
7   Lawrence Stone, *Road to Divorce: England 1530–1987* (Oxford: Oxford University Press, 1990), pp. 435–6.
8   Stone, p. 436.
9   Pope John XXIII, 'Opening speech to the Council' in *The Documents of Vatican II*, ed. Walter M. Abbott SJ; translation ed. Very Revd Mgr Joseph Gallagher (London: Geoffrey Chapman, 1966), pp. 712–19 (pp. 712–13).
10 Abbott (ed.), *The Documents of Vatican II*, p. 715. For a freer translation, taken directly from Pope John XXIII's Italian draft, and a discussion of some of the machinations behind the scenes regarding what was finally published in the *Acta Apostolica Sedis* (the official collection of papal documents) see Peter Hebblethwaite, *John XXIII, Pope of the Council* (London: Geoffrey Chapman, 1984), pp. 427–34.

11   *Vatican Council II: The Conciliar and Post Conciliar Documents*, ed. Austin
      Flannery OP (2 vols; Leominster: Fowler Wright Books Ltd, 1987), I, pp.
      903–1014. Further references to *Gaudium et Spes* will be in the abbreviated form
      GS. Number references for the documents of Vatican II and all official Church
      documents correspond not to page references but to the numbering of sections in
      the documents themselves.

12   (Vatican: Libreria Editrice Vaticana, 1993), 53 (footnote 100). Further references
      to *Veritatis Splendor* will be abbreviated to VS.

13   See Henri de Lubac SJ, 'The mystery of the Church', *The Month*, 37 (1967), pp.
      74–82. *Lumen Gentium*: Flannery, *Vatican Council II*, pp. 350–432. Further refer-
      ences to this document will be abbreviated to LG.

14   B. Häring, 'A distrust that wounds', *The Tablet* (23 October 1993), pp. 1378–9.

15   *Commentary on the Documents of Vatican II*, ed. Herbert Vorgrimler and others (5
      vols; London: Burns & Oates Limited, 1969), V, pp. 225–45.

16   Cardinal Heenan was referring to Virgil's famous line *Timeo Danaos et dona
      ferentes* (I fear the Greeks even though they offer gifts) (*Aeneid* II, 49). Thus: I fear
      the experts even though they offer amendments.

17   Bernard Häring, *My Witness for the Church*, trans. Leonard Swidler (New York:
      Paulist Press, 1992), p. 62.

18   Trans. the Rt Revd Bishop Alan C. Clark DD and the Revd Geoffrey Crawford
      (London: Catholic Truth Society, 1970).

19   *My Witness for the Church*, p. 78.

20   'Statement by the hierarchy of England and Wales' in *Humanae Vitae and the
      Bishops: The Encyclical and the Statements of the National Hierarchies*, ed. John
      Horgan (Shannon: Irish University Press, 1972), pp. 112–18.

21   Michael Hornsby-Smith, lecture, 2 October 1991.

22   See Austin Flannery OP, 'Analytic guide' in *Humanae Vitae and the Bishops*.

23   Hornsby-Smith, *Roman Catholic Beliefs in England*, p. 177.

24   It is true that *Veritatis Splendor* explicitly refers to the Church's ban on artificial
      means of contraception only in article 80 by quoting directly from *Humanae Vitae*.
      Nevertheless the publicity surrounding its publication suggested that one of Pope
      John Paul II's prime concerns was the continuing opposition to the teaching on
      contraception. Clearly Bernard Häring considered this to be the case (see the
      Tablet article referred to in note 14).

25   *The Tablet* (9 January 1993), p. 30.

26   In Richard P. McBrien, *Catholicism* (San Francisco: Harper & Row, 1981), the
      magisterium is simply defined as 'the teaching authority of the Church, which
      belongs to some by reason of office (pope and bishops). Others contribute to the
      teaching mission by scholarly competence (e.g. theologians)': p. 1249.
          Lumen Gentium proposes the doctrine of the magisterium in the third chapter
      and especially in articles 24–25.
          A full treatment of the history and theology of the magisterium may be found in
      Sacramentum Mundi: An Encyclopedia of Theology, ed. Karl Rahner SJ and others
      (6 vols; London: Burns & Oates, 1969), III, pp. 351–8.

27   See Ladislas Örsy SJ, *The Profession of Faith and the Oath of Fidelity: A
      Theological and Canonical Analysis* (Dublin: Dominican Publications, 1990).

28   *Humanae Vitae and the Bishops*, p. 366.

29   *Humanae Vitae and the Bishops*, p. 115.

30   Murray White, 'Cardinal says theologians' jobs are safe', *Catholic Herald* (8
      October 1993), p. 1.

31 Morris West, 'A cry from the people of God to their servants', *Catholic Herald* (8 October 1993), p. 12.

32 Pope John Paul II, *Apostolic Exhortation regarding the Role of the Christian Family in the Modern World*, trans. Vatican Polyglot Press (London: Catholic Truth Society, 1981). Further references to *Familiaris Consortio* will be abbreviated to FC.

33 The story of Newman's essay and the conflict it created are presented by John Coulson in his introduction to a reprinting of the same in 1961; it was reprinted again with a foreword by Archbishop Derek Worlock in 1986 (London: Collins).

34 See Pope Paul VI, *The Apostolic Exhortation, Evangelii Nuntiandi*, trans. the Vatican Polyglot Press (London: Catholic Truth Society, 1975), p. 73.

35 The use of the internal forum will be referred to repeatedly in the course of this study and examined in some detail in Chapter 5. From the outset it will be important to note how it is defined by the canonists. The commentary on Canon 130 in *The Canon Law: Letter and Spirit*, ed. Rt Revd Mgr Gerard Sheehy JCD and others (London: Geoffrey Chapman, 1995), states:

> The Church is at once a supernatural mystery: the People of God, and a visible hierarchically-structured society. The exercise of the power of governance within the Church is ordered to a twofold end: the common good of all and the good of each individual. That which is exercised for the common good has to do principally with the social relations between members of Christ's faithful; this must admit of external proof or verification. Accordingly, this canon speaks of the power of governance of itself being 'exercised for the external forum'. What is exercised solely for the good of a particular individual has to do with that person's relationship with God or with his or her own conscience: in this way, the power of governance may also be exercised 'for the internal forum only'. This internal forum may be *sacramental*, i.e. in the context of the sacrament of penance, or *non-sacramental*, dealing e.g. with consultation or advice on any matter of conscience: it could e.g. concern the like of an occult matrimonial impediment, but it is by no means confined to any such a formal juridical situation. (p. 77)

For further discussion of the canonical and theological relationships between the *internal and external fora* read Francisco Javier Urrutia SJ, 'Internal forum – external forum: the criterion of distinction', trans. Leslie Wearne in *Vatican II: Assessment and Perspectives, Twenty-Five Years After (1962–1987)*, ed. René Latourelle (3 vols; New York: Paulist Press, 1988), I, pp. 634–67.

36 For an explanation of the roles of the Roman Rota and the Segnatura Apostolica, see Ralph Brown, *Marriage Annulment in the Catholic Church* (3rd edn; Rattlesden: Kevin Mayhew, 1990), pp. 21–2.

37 *Sociology and Theology: Alliance and Conflict*, ed. David Martin, John Orme Mills OP and W. S. F. Pickering (New York: St Martin's Press, 1980).

38 See *Marriage Preparation: A Practical Programme of Pre-Marriage Instruction* (booklet, questionnaires, six cassettes; Chawton: Redemptorist Publications, 1981), cassette 5.

39 For an introduction to Lonergan's theology see Tad Dunne, *Lonergan and Spirituality: Towards a Spiritual Integrity* (Chicago: Loyola University Press, 1985).

40 Alasdair MacIntyre is an American moral philosopher who has converted to Roman Catholicism. His systematic thinking is a challenge to the moralists of our

day to ensure that their work is the product of sound reasoning and not an undisciplined attempt to cope with the vagaries of human behaviour. Emotivism is defined by MacIntyre in *After Virtue* as 'the doctrine that all evaluative judgments and more specifically all moral judgments are *nothing but* expressions of preference, expressions of attitude or feeling, insofar as they are moral or evaluative in character' (2nd edn; London: Duckworth, 1985), pp. 11–12.

41 Theodore Mackin, *Divorce and Remarriage* (New York: Paulist Press, 1984), p. 543. How the Church reached this position and its significance will be discussed in the theological analysis in Chapter 2.

42 For a summary of the question of *Infallibility* see the article by Henrich Fries and Johann Finsterhölzl in *Sacramentum Mundi*, ed. Karl Rahner SJ and others, III, pp. 132–8.

43 Vincent Genovesi, *In Pursuit of Love: Catholic Morality and Human Sexuality* (Dublin: Gill and Macmillan, 1987), p. 85. He provides a footnote in support of this statement: 'Richard A. McCormick, S.J., *Authority and Morality*, *America*, 142 (1980), 169–71 at 169.'

44 In the spring of 1992 a scandal broke in the media over Bishop Eamonn Casey, the Bishop of Galway, and as a result he resigned. The substance of the case was that in the early 1970s, when he was Bishop of Kerry, he had an eighteen-month-long affair with Annie Murphy, a young divorcee from America, then in her early twenties. A child, Peter, had been born of this union and he, now seventeen years of age, was claiming to be incensed over his father's treatment of himself and his mother. It became clear that the Bishop had tried to cover up the whole affair from the time Peter was conceived and there were reports of substantial financial settlements, some of which, at least initially, had been taken from diocesan funds.

45 Peter J. Elliott, *What God Has Joined ...* (New York: Alba House, 1990).

46 See Kathleen Kiernan and Malcolm Wicks, *Family Change and Future Policy* (London: Family Policy Studies Centre, 1990). See also Michael P. Hornsby-Smith, *Roman Catholics in England: Studies in Social Structure Since the Second World War* (Cambridge: Cambridge University Press, 1987), pp. 89–115; and *Roman Catholic Beliefs in England*, pp. 182–7.

The theological history

The purpose of this chapter is to situate the pastoral problems of today in their theological context. In the Catholic tradition the concept of the 'bond' has emerged as the focus of all marriage theology. How a word which originally was used as a metaphor for marriage came to be defined as an ontological reality, the pastoral circumstances which shaped that definition and the consequences of that definition, form the substance of this chapter.

Addressing the Roman Rota on 28 January 1991, Pope John Paul II said:

> The bond which is created between a man and a woman in the marriage relationship is *superior to every other interpersonal bond*, even the one between parent and child. The sacred author concludes: 'That is why a man leaves his father and mother and clings to his wife, and the two of them become one body' (Genesis 2:24). [The italics are mine.][1]

Pope John Paul II situated the bond of marriage in the heart of the creation narrative. By so doing and by comparing it to other natural bonds he defined the bond of marriage in the natural order as relating to all marriages of all time. However the context of this statement, an address to the Roman Rota, suggests that he was more concerned with the specific Catholic definition of the bond in relation to those marriages which come under the jurisdiction of the Church. This inconsistency is a perennial difficulty when we try to interpret the meaning of the term 'bond' in Catholic theology. Is the Catholic Church concerned to defend the sanctity and permanence of marriage as an institution for all or only for those who are members of the Church? It is a question which the reader will do well to bear in mind as this chapter unfolds, because I believe it is the failure to answer this question which is at the root of so many of our pastoral problems.

The biblical vision

Neither the Old nor the New Testament uses the word 'bond' in relation to marriage, though both consistently call for permanence and faithfulness in monogamous unions.

Before we examine the key scriptural texts on the subject of divorce and remarriage, we must determine our own methodology in using Scripture. Nothing will be gained from simply quoting texts out of context and without any reference to the message of salvation conveyed by the whole Judaeo-Christian tradition.

Since Vatican II Roman Catholic exegetes have had greater freedom to explore the content and unity of the Scriptures.[2] Likewise the relationship between Scripture and tradition has been developed, Scripture being defined in terms of what it *is*, namely the word of God consigned to writing; tradition in terms of what it *does*, namely handing on the word of God.[3]

By avoiding the pitfalls of fundamentalism and prooftexting (the latter still commonly used in the documents of the magisterium) the hermeneutical approach to Scripture provides Catholics with a method consistent with their tradition. It acknowledges that the Scriptures are part of God's living revelation in every generation and must be interpreted within the context of the lived experience.[4] This is at the heart of my theological argument. The authors of Genesis were offering an explanation of their experience of God's world when they wrote their creation stories. It is indisputable that their monogamous interpretation of the human condition has been the consistent belief of the Judaeo-Christian tradition. For men and women of faith in the twentieth century God reveals this truth to us through his sacred Scriptures, through the tradition and magisterium of the Church and through our lived experiences. Only these experiences can validate those teachings which have been handed on to us.

The Book of Genesis teaches us much about the human condition of weakness, failure and sin. It reveals that the harmony of God's plan for creation has been disrupted and that the world is in a mess, a mess created because people in their pride tried to do it their way, to be 'like God' (3:5), and take control of the world (11:4). The mess is always reflected in broken human relationships. Out of jealousy and anger Cain kills his brother Abel: murder becomes the ultimate solution to a broken relationship (4:8).

The story of the people of the Old Testament is the story of their broken relationships with God and one another in this broken messy world. It is also the story of God's desire to save them and restore those relationships, and their desire to be saved. The prophets Hosea, Jeremiah (3:1–5), Deutero-Isaiah (50:1–3) and Ezekiel (16) use the image of an unfaithful wife to describe the people's relationship with God, who, by contrast, always remains faithful to his covenant with them.[5] Like most writers on Christian marriage both Theodore Mackin and Michael Lawler comment on this metaphor as they seek to situate marriage in the Judaeo-Christian tradition.[6] They both stress the significance of God's faithfulness, which is being held up to the people as a possibility both in their relations with God and with each other.

Marital breakdown was a reality among the Old Testament people, and in Deuteronomy, included in the many prescriptions relating to sexual relations, there are those governing divorce (24:1–4). Such behaviour could be justified by their interpretation of the early Yahwist creation account, which gives us the remarkable paradox that the very text which Pope John Paul II cites in defence of the bond of marriage – Genesis 2:24 – is the text upon which it was possible to argue the right to divorce. For man and woman become one body precisely because the woman had been created from the man in the first place.[7] Thus the woman could be seen as the possession of the man, who could issue her with a writ of dismissal if, because of some impropriety, she did not truly complement him.

Modern Christian understanding argues that those Scripture texts give no such permissions, not least because when Jesus was challenged on the divorce question he took his listeners back to Genesis to remind them of the Father's real intention.

Jesus' teaching on divorce is reported five times in the New Testament. In Luke there is the unequivocal statement:

> Anyone who divorces his wife and marries another commits adultery, and whoever marries a woman divorced from her husband commits adultery. (16:18)

Mark deals with the question in the context of a challenge from some pharisees (10:1–12). Jesus coaxes them to tell him what Moses taught, and when they inform him that Moses permitted them 'to write a certificate of dismissal and to divorce her' (10:4), Jesus retorts:

> Because of your hardness of heart he wrote this commandment for you. But from the beginning of creation, 'God made them male and female.' 'For this reason a man shall leave his father and mother and be joined to his wife, and the two shall become one flesh.' So they are no longer two, but one flesh. Therefore what God has joined together, let no one separate. (10:5–9)

The evangelist reinforces the teaching by recording that when the disciples questioned Jesus, he spelt it out by saying:

> Whoever divorces his wife and marries another commits adultery against her; and if she divorces her husband and marries another, she commits adultery. (10:11–12)[8]

Matthew tells the same story of Jesus' confrontation with the pharisees at the beginning of chapter 19, but as in the short teaching on divorce in the Sermon on the Mount (5:32) he includes his celebrated exceptive clause: 'except for *porneia*' (19:9). I have not attempted to translate the Greek because volumes have been written about the origin, meaning and application of this text. Does it translate as 'fornication', 'adultery' or the degrees of consanguinity and affinity forbidden under Jewish law (Leviticus 18:6–18)? Was this an original teaching of Jesus or an addition of Matthew's to deal with a particular pastoral problem among his Jewish converts? After detailing six possible explanations, Theodore Mackin concludes:

> In the end, I think, we simply cannot know exactly the meaning of the exceptive clause in these Matthean passages. We can, however, come to the solidly probable conclusion that the phrase is not Jesus' but a device within Matthew's attempt to interpret Jesus' mind. Whatever his success in interpreting it accurately, he did take up the task – to interpret and adapt – that no one who chooses to live by Jesus' words can escape.[9]

In spite of all the advances of biblical scholarship it seems that it is still not possible to decide this matter simply by scriptural exegesis.

Clearly Matthew was engaged in a dialogue with his readers just as his successors, the bishops, continue to seek a dialogue with their people. There is no doubt that the dialogue which Matthew and Mark record Jesus having with the pharisees was in the particular context of a rabbinical debate that had developed between the schools of Hillel and Shammai over the interpretation of the divorce text in Deuteronomy: 'the unchastity' (RSV translation of *erwat dabar* (Hebrew) – *porneia* (Greek)), which permitted a man to divorce his wife. For the strict school of Shammai this could refer only to some serious sexual misconduct, the most obvious being adultery, whereas for the school of Hillel it was eventually extended to almost anything which a husband found displeasing in his wife.[10] Matthew records Jesus' handling of the challenge as to which school he would support, in a much more subtle way than Mark. For example in Matthew it is the pharisees who claim that Moses 'commanded' a writ of dismissal. Jesus corrects this by insisting rather that he 'allowed' this practice because they were so unteachable. In other words they had misunderstood not only God's will but also the teaching of Moses.[11] Effectively Jesus refuses to be drawn and take sides; rather he seizes the opportunity to correct them all.

I would lay great stress on this because there is no doubt that the context of this teaching gives the context for the Church's fundamental teaching on marriage: namely that it is in the very nature of our human experience that men and women complement one another and are called to lifelong and faithful unions. This message the Church has consistently and faithfully proclaimed to the world. What is at stake is not this fundamental teaching, which is undoubtedly the teaching of Jesus and which remains unchanged, but the language we use to explain it and the means we use to defend it.

Jesus took the argument back to Genesis, so he was talking about marriage in itself, not a special form of marriage for Christians, born again in baptism. If we quote the Yahwist creation text in Genesis to explain the meaning of the bond of marriage, as so many official texts in Church teaching do, we must of necessity be referring to all marriages of all time, because this text is concerned with marriage in the natural order.

Historically what has moved the argument into a different sphere is the teaching of the Church that Jesus raised the natural union of marriage to a supernatural sacramental union for his faithful followers. The understanding and formulation of this teaching took centuries to develop. The twelfth century marked an important stage in the theological systematization of the sacraments and Hugh of St Victor (1079–1141) was instrumental in beginning the process of defining marriage as one of the seven sacraments.[12] This process was carried on by the Scholastics and came to fruition with the decrees of the Council of Trent in 1563. Canon 1 on Marriage states:

> If anyone says that marriage is not truly and properly one of the seven sacraments of the Law of the Gospel, instituted by Christ the Lord, but that it was devised in the Church by men and does not confer grace, *anathema sit*.[13]

This canon was preceded by a discursive statement situating the theological argument in the Scriptures, firstly in Genesis:

> The first father of the human race, inspired by the divine Spirit, proclaimed the perpetual and indissoluble bond (*nexus*) of matrimony when he explained: 'This at last is bone of my bones and flesh of my flesh ... Therefore a man leaves his father and his mother and cleaves to his wife, and they become one flesh' (Gen. 2:23f).[14]

secondly in the Gospel:

> But that only two are united and joined together by this bond [*vinculum*], Christ the Lord taught more clearly when, referring to these words as having been uttered by God, He said: 'So they are no longer two but one' (Mt. 19:6), and immediately confirmed the stability of the bond which was proclaimed long ago by Adam in these words: 'What therefore God has joined together, let no man put asunder' (Mt. 19:6; Mk 10:9).[15]

and thirdly in the writings of St Paul:

> Christ Himself, who instituted the holy sacraments and brought them to perfection, merited for us by His passion the grace which perfects that natural love, confirms the indissoluble union and sanctifies the spouses. St Paul suggests this when he says: 'Husbands, love your wives, as Christ loved the Church and gave Himself up for her' (Eph. 5:25), adding immediately: 'This is a great mystery, I mean in reference to Christ and the Church' (Eph. 5:32).[16]

This image of the Church as the Bride of Christ shapes the sacramental theology of marriage. It is an image first formulated by the prophets when describing God's relationship with his unfaithful people and it complements the Pauline teaching of the Mystical Body, in which we all become one in the second Adam, Christ. The Scriptures conclude with the same image in the Book of Revelation, where the new Jerusalem (the Church) is described as 'coming down out of heaven from God, prepared as a bride adorned for her husband' (21:2): this is 'the bride, the wife of the Lamb' who is Christ (21:9).

As we examine the development of the theology of the bond of marriage we will see that at the heart of the discussion at each stage is how to interpret the passages of Scripture cited above.

The words of Jesus, 'what God has joined together, let no one separate' (Mark 10:9), are often cited as the last word on the subject. But it is clear that they are not the last word because they are not the only words spoken by Jesus that bear upon the subject, and they must be considered in the context of the whole of Scripture, the inspired word of God. The hermeneutical method offers us a way forward precisely because it is concerned with the whole and therefore with integrity. Thus the question that has been asked by so many during my research, 'How do we get round this teaching of Jesus?', becomes a false question, because we are not seeking to get round this teaching, but to understand its true meaning.

We can begin by noting that Jesus did not establish a new code of laws, but proclaimed the law of love, on which depends 'all the law and the prophets' (see Matthew 22:34–40). Matthew introduces us to Jesus' teaching and the new spirit of God's kingdom with the Sermon on the Mount. It is there too he introduces us to the teaching on divorce: 5:31–32. The basis of all this teaching is to be found in the Beatitudes (Matthew 5:3–12; Luke 6:20–23), and the basis of the Beatitudes is poverty: that poverty of spirit which frees people to recognize their need of God. This is the conclusion of Dennis Hamm in his study of the Beatitudes in context.[17] The cry of the poor in our world today is insistent and demands the attention of the Church, and among them are those whose poverty of spirit and accompanying recognition of their need for God have been occasioned by the trauma of marital breakdown.

Just as Hamm seeks to place the Beatitudes in the context of the whole of the Scriptures, we must do the same with the teaching on divorce, and we can begin by putting it the context of the Beatitudes. We find the teaching on divorce in Matthew is immediately preceded by the teaching on adultery, which Jesus reinforces with some suggestions, which, if read out of context, become very alarming (5:27–30).

Today we know that his hearers would have understood that when Jesus spoke about tearing out the eye if it causes you to sin, or cutting off the hand if it causes you to sin, he was dealing with the possibility of the whole person's involvement in sin. The Jews could not conceive of a distinction between body and soul. For them the eyes and the heart represented the knowing and desiring part of a person; the mouth and ears the communicating part; the hands and the feet the acting part. In today's parlance Jesus' 'cut it off' would be translated 'cut it out' – in other words 'stop it'. Yet even without this explanation the Christian community has never been tempted to presume that Jesus was literally telling us to maim ourselves. Indeed moral theologians have always taught that such behaviour itself would be morally wrong.

Of course it does not follow that what Jesus then says about divorce and adultery is not to be taken literally, but it must be taken in context. He is telling his hearers to cut out the scandalous abuse of women that had arisen out of the use and abuse of the Deuteronomic divorce law. Whether that can be taken as a blanket condemnation of all marital breakdown is quite another matter. Indeed taking Scripture and tradition together it is clear that it cannot because, as has already been noted, in certain circumstances the Church has seen fit to dissolve the kind of marriage to which Jesus was addressing himself, namely the marriages of non-Christians. And this practice too finds its justification in Scripture through the Pauline privilege, which is based on the text of 1 Corinthians 7:10–16, and the extension of this, called by some the Petrine privilege, which finds its scriptural justification in the exercise of the power of the keys, given to Peter and his successors (Matthew 16:18–19). The focus of this part of the Church's discipline is faith, and so the Church speaks of dissolving a marriage 'in favour of the faith'.[18]

Paul's letters pre-date the Gospels, yet the Lord's precept is proclaimed as authoritatively and as unequivocally as in the Synoptic Gospels:

> To the married I give this command – not I but the Lord – that the wife should not separate from her husband (but if she does separate, let her remain unmarried or else be reconciled to her husband), and that the husband should not divorce his wife. (1 Corinthians 7:10–11)

If the origins, authority and interpretation of the exceptive clauses in Matthew are difficult to determine, there is no doubt about who is authorizing the exception in the first letter to the Corinthians. Paul continues: 'To the rest I say – I and not the Lord' (7:12). This is enough to tell us that however strictly we interpret the Lord's teaching – 'What God has joined together, let no one separate' – it was not held by the apostolic Church as so absolute a prohibition as to admit of no exceptions.

Paul resolves the problem in the community of faith *in favour of the faith*. I think this gives us a clue as to how important it is for the Church in any generation to recognize that the word of God cannot be interpreted or make sense outside a living community of faith. The teachings of Jesus turn our human way of thinking upside down and can only be grasped by the 'poor in spirit' who recognize their need of God. Only in such a community of faith can people accept that the last will be first (Mark 10:31; Matthew 19:30, 20:16), that those who lose their life will save it (Mark 8:35; Matthew 16:25), that there is no limit to forgiveness (Matthew 18:21–22), that we must love our enemies (Matthew 5:44), that we must not judge (Matthew 7:1) and that the ordering of the community is to be achieved not in domination but service (Mark 10:42–45).

In his book *Jesus and Community*, Gerhard Lohfink argues that it is understanding this call to service that gives us an insight into the Church as a 'contrast-society' and ultimately 'the sign to the nations'.[19] He claims that the New Testament communities clearly understood themselves 'as a fundamental *contrast* to paganism, as a holy people which had to be different from pagan society' (p. 124). However he concedes:

> On the whole the consciousness of churches in Western Europe has become assimilated in a disturbing way to the rest of society and its structures. *Resistance* or *refusal* has occurred only sporadically. Western European Christians are no longer aware that the church as a whole should be an alternative type of society; at most this has again slowly penetrated their consciousness in the past few years. (p. 125)

I would like to emphasize the community dimension because this research has forcefully reminded me that gospel values can have meaning only in a community of faith. And if it is possible to consider Christianity in contrast to the surrounding society, it is also possible to contrast the ways different Christian communities embrace gospel values and resolve their problems.

We know that the most effective preaching is always by example: 'By this everyone will know that you are my disciples, if you have love for one another' (John 13:35). In the Acts of the Apostles we see how attractive the early Christian community was: 'having the goodwill of all the people' (2:47). Only in such communities can the whole gospel message begin to make sense.

Love which finds its expression in unconditional forgiveness and a willingness to leave the judgement to God is not society's way of coping. The human way of establishing order in the face of disorder is to use force or the threat of force. There can be no greater contrast than this to the Christian way. Jesus taught that he is 'the way, the truth and the life' (John 14:6), and his way is the way of service which leads to the way of the cross. It is of the very nature of this way that it cannot be imposed: you cannot force people to love and forgive. But herein lies one of the great tensions for every Christian community since those apostolic times: the tension of how to maintain the unity of the community in freedom and love, and how to exercise authority in the form of service. Lohfink comments on this:

> It is one of the church's tragic blind spots that it again and again seeks to protect its authority (which is certainly necessary and legitimate) through *domination*. In reality it undermines its authority in this way and does serious harm to the gospel. True authority can shine forth only in the weakness of renouncing domination. True authority is the authority of the Crucified. Paul knew this better than anyone else; for this reason he constantly connected the paradox of his apostolic authority with the paradox of the Crucified and Risen One. It is astonishing how intensely the substance of Mark 10:42–45 reappears in Paul. (p. 120)

Before proceeding to a review of how the post-apostolic communities confronted the divorce question, we must examine from a scriptural point of view one further area of tension. It was discussed by Pope John Paul II in *Familiaris Consortio* under the heading 'Moral progress', as the difference between 'the law of gradualness' and the 'gradualness of the law'. He argued that 'what is known as "the law of gradualness" or step-by-step advance cannot be identified with "gradualness of the law", as if there were different degrees or forms of precept in God's law for different individuals and situations' (FC 34).

In virtually every other area of the moral life this principle is more easily applicable than in that of divorce and remarriage. The reason for this is that most other failures to achieve an ideal are readily identifiable as sins committed in another set of circumstances. The sins may be forgiven and the person converted to live in a new set of circumstances which will nurture growth in the spiritual life. Thus the common comparison is used that a murderer may be absolved and go to Communion, while a divorced and remarried person may not. At the theoretical level this can be explained if we follow the literal interpretation of Jesus' teaching that those who divorce and remarry inevitably commit adultery.

Although murder is commonly regarded as the ultimate offence against another person, a murderer can repent of the sin and seek forgiveness. In such circumstances there is no suggestion that murder is any less wrong or sinful than it was before; the murderer has repented and seeks a new way of life. However, even though both parties in a divorce may repent of the failure of their marriage and the sins they have committed against one another and the family in the marriage, if it is an absolute principle that other partnerships will be adulterous, to enter such a partnership is to enter a permanent state of sin, and while in that state, repentance is made impossible. *Familiaris Consortio* is ambiguous in its response to this problem. On the one hand it calls for 'careful discernment' of people's situations, on the other it refuses admittance to Holy Communion no matter what the result of that discernment (FC 84).

It was truly remarkable how often those who contributed to the discussions, both priests and people, used the analogy of murder to demonstrate what they perceive to be a failure on the Church's part to realize the gospel call to unconditional forgiveness.

Most areas of the moral life have their grey areas. Moralists therefore ask the question: Is it ever legitimate to kill deliberately? The traditional answer is that it can be, for example when an assailant threatens one's own or other people's lives.[20] Beyond that there will be a host of situations in which it is accepted that extenuating circumstances lessen or nullify the guilt. Yet the teaching of Jesus in the Sermon on the Mount was as uncompromising on this matter as it was on divorce, reminding his listeners that even to be angry would render them liable to judgement (Matthew 5:22). Jesus goes on to recommend reconciliation if only to avoid judgement and sentence.

It is precisely in this grey area of seeking to repair broken human relationships that many people find it hard to come to terms with the uncompromising discipline on divorce that has evolved in the Western Church.

In some relationships it is possible to argue that the stress of the marriage was so great that it could easily have led to murder but for the fact that the couple had the wisdom to part.[21]

What is it then that singles out the situation of the divorced and remarried as beyond full reconciliation with the Church? Why should failure to achieve this high ideal alone be the one which debars people from the Eucharist? While 'the two becoming one body/one flesh' is a key factor, it cannot be argued that the physical union of two people in sexual intercourse is the sole factor in this discussion, because fornication or adultery, like murder, are sins which can be forgiven, situations from which people can recover and begin again.

Jesus had pointed to the Father's will in recalling Genesis, but the scriptural texts which have determined the absolute nature of the Church's teaching on the marriage bond are those which compare marriage to the union of Christ and his Church, above all Ephesians 5:21–33. In the Letter to the Ephesians, the writer incorporates Genesis 2:24 (5:31) and comments: 'This is a great mystery, and I am applying it to Christ and the church' (5:32). This is the text upon which the sacramental theology of marriage is based and which makes the circumstances of the divorced and remarried different from any other moral condition.

For the followers of Jesus marriage cannot be viewed simply as the natural union of two people in the order of creation, but also as a reflection of Christ's love for and union with his faithful people, the Church. It is a recognition that just as God remained faithful to his marriage with Israel in spite of the infidelity of so many of the people and now in Christ remains faithful to the Church, so Christians are called upon to mirror that fidelity in their marriage relationships and thus be 'the sign to the nations'. But because fidelity is the vocation of all Christians in every aspect of their lives, we are bound to ask why the ideal of marriage fidelity remains the only gospel ideal which in certain circumstances has to be achieved from the very beginning, why it does not allow of degrees or progress, and why it does not admit of failure. The Scriptures themselves do not answer these questions. If they did we would have to look no further. But, like every preceding generation, we wrestle with the paradox of the gospel, and the eschatological struggle to bridge the gap between the *now* and the *not yet*, between the ideal and the lived experience.

In Matthew's Gospel, at the end of his teaching on the love of enemies, Jesus calls upon his followers to be 'perfect' as their heavenly Father is 'perfect' (5:48). Luke, however, ends the same teaching with the emphasis on 'mercy': 'Be merciful, just as your Father is merciful' (6:36). At first sight perfection and mercy may not appear analogous, at least not to the person who tends towards perfectionism. Yet that is the paradox of the gospel. They are the same, for perfection in gospel terms is the perfection of love, which is always merciful and forgiving. There are many gospel imperatives, but it is important to discern which are fundamental and which are relative. Jesus came that we might have life, 'and have it abundantly' (John 10:10). When we read of Jesus offering this life to the Samaritan woman by the well at Sychar (John 4:14), we want to know how to share it with people whose relationships are similarly in disarray today.[22]

Inevitably we are brought back to the question of why the Church, in the name of the merciful Christ, cannot find a way of forgiving those in irregular marriage unions and admitting them to the Eucharist. Why should a kind of perfection be required of them which is not required in any other area of failure or weakness? Why should the teaching of Jesus on divorce be interpreted in literal and absolute terms, when his teaching on the Eucharist is not? Jesus did teach quite explicitly: 'Unless you eat the flesh of the Son of Man and drink his blood, you have no life in you' (John 6:53), yet in *Familiaris Consortio* it is argued that there are other ways, apart from the Eucharist, in which God gives his life and grace to those in canonically irregular marriages:

> Those who have rejected the Lord's command and are still living in this state will be able to obtain from God the grace of conversion and salvation, provided that they have persevered in prayer, penance and charity. (FS 84)

The answer to these questions can be found only in the unfolding story of how the bond of marriage came to be defined in the Latin Church.

The bond in the early Church

I have mentioned that the word 'bond' was not used in the Scriptures in relation to marriage. The Jewish mind would not have conceived of the kind of metaphysical definition which the Greek and Western mind was able to conjure up later. We have seen that for the people of Israel there was no distinction between body and spirit: their understanding was rooted in the experience of this world and so was their understanding of salvation. Salvation for them was the preservation of the race, the continuation and triumph of the nation, not everlasting life elsewhere. Only in the later writings of the Old Testament is there even a hint of the possibility of an afterlife.[23]

In the New Testament the potential is there for a developing theology of the metaphysical nature of the bond, but although the writer of Ephesians theologizes about marriage and compares it to the Mystical Body of Christ, he reserves his use of the word 'bond' for 'the bond of peace' which maintains the unity of the spirit (Ephesians 4:3).[24] For St Paul and the New Testament writers, this was the work of salvation in every situation: restoring everything and everyone to unity and harmony in the peace of Christ.

During the patristic period and the centuries that followed immediately upon it, it is fair to say that the principle of the permanence of marriage remained undisputed, but uncertainty about how to deal with infidelity and marital breakdown remained. Mackin and others give detailed accounts of the progression of the debate, focusing on the decisions of local synods and general councils to illustrate their findings.[25]

Essentially the problem was always the same: how to reconcile the teaching of Jesus on the permanence of marriage with the teaching of Jesus on forgiveness, growth and conversion. Inevitably developments took place in response to real pastoral needs in the societies in which the Church found itself. Roman law was very tolerant of divorce. Thus when the empire became Christian it certainly took a long time before the Christian discipline on this matter took hold.[26]

Parallels can be drawn with the missionary experience of the Church in every age. In some of the group meetings priests spoke of their experiences of cultures where the women must prove themselves to be fertile and the bridal price must be paid before a marriage can be solemnized. In such situations it is impossible immediately to impose the Christian ethic on sexual morality and marriage. A time of accommodation and adjustment is always necessary.

It was during the patristic period that differences developed between the Eastern and Western Churches, differences that are still in place today. The differences were born of different spiritualities, founded on different metaphysical outlooks. We will be concentrating on the outcome for the Latin Church, but to ignore the discipline in the Eastern Orthodox Churches would mean overlooking part of the painful struggle that took place long before the schisms between East and West over quite different issues.

The *oikonomia* of the East can be traced above all to Basil of Caesarea and John Chrysostom. They were responding to the circumstances of the Church as they found them, seeking pastoral solutions to pastoral problems. In the course of time Basil's canons became the basis of a universal law for Eastern Christendom.[27]

In the West it was Jerome and Augustine who had the major influence in those formative years, but as in the East it took centuries before a settled tradition was established. The difference between the two traditions centres on the interpretation of the key scriptural passages. In the Roman West, the conclusion was reached that, while non-sacramental and unconsummated marriages were subject to dissolution, Jesus' prohibition of divorce applied absolutely to marriages which were Christian sacraments and which had been consummated. Thus any civil arrangements regarding divorce and remarriage were considered null and sexual relations by a partner in such an arrangement were regarded as adulterous. By contrast in the Orthodox East even a consummated sacramental marriage could dissolve in its own failure. Such a dissolution could be acknowledged by the Church and a second union permitted, though the latter would not be considered a sacrament.[28]

The crucial difference in these two disciplines lies not in the fact that one accepts divorce and the other does not, but that the latter approaches the reality of human failure in this area from a biblical, personalist, human point of view, while the former approaches it from a biblical, legalist point of view, trying to apply the perceived law of God.

It is ironic that a Greek philosopher, Aristotle, had such an influence on the development of thinking in the Western Church and the systematization of theology by the Scholastics. This was the great period of revival after the Dark Ages and it would be impossible to overestimate the contribution of men like St Thomas Aquinas to the development of learning and the spread of civilization.

Meanwhile in the Byzantine East, which had escaped the ravages of the invaders, they had already developed their own theology, based more on that mysticism which reverences a God who is beyond human knowledge than on an attempt to define God within the language of human understanding. They avoided the trap of having to employ casuistry to bridge the gap between dogmatic and pastoral theology. They simply accepted that there was much that they did not know and much that they had to leave to God.

Örsy addressed this problem at the beginning of his study, *The Church: Learning and Teaching, Magisterium, Assent, Dissent, Academic*

Freedom, and began by referring to another Greek philosopher, Socrates. He wondered whether contemporary theologians might follow Socrates' example:

> Socrates spent a life trying to find out how much he did not know; ...
> One wonders if a courageous soul should not attempt a similar venture in the field of contemporary theology.[29]

We have noted that the marriage theology of the West was founded on Jerome and Augustine. Jerome used *vinculum* to define the bond of peace in St Paul, but when speaking of the bond of marriage he used *conjugium*, the specific description of wedlock as the coming together of the spouses. Like the Greek Fathers Jerome and Augustine concluded that according to the exceptive clause of Matthew it is permissible in the case of adultery for a couple to separate. They differed by refusing to accept that such separations may lead to second unions. Thus the concept of 'separation from bed and board' became part of the Western tradition.[30]

The movement towards a theology of the bond began in earnest with St Augustine. Augustine does not receive a good press today when it comes to sexual ethics. Some popularist modern writers have attributed all the woes of the Western Church regarding sexual morality to the inhibiting teaching of St Augustine.[31] This is a grossly unjust and inaccurate reading of history. Augustine was a giant in the history of theological thinking and by comparison with the writings of many of his predecessors and contemporaries his writings on sexuality were a tremendous advance in Christian understanding. For example, Augustine did acknowledge the presence of love in marriage:

> You (the Catholic Church) subject women to their husbands in chaste and faithful obedience not for the satisfying of passion but for the procreating of children and for their sharing in family life. You set husbands over their wives not to demean the weaker sex, but themselves ruled by the law of genuine love.[32]

Commenting on this passage, Lawler said of Augustine:

> He has falsified in advance the claim of those who say that only in modern times has sexual intercourse and marriage been seen in relation to the relationship and love of spouses.[33]

The context of Augustine's teaching is important. He was under attack from the dualism of the Manichees and the self-justification of the Pelagians.[34] He strongly resisted the teachings of the former and did not fall into the trap of Gregory of Nyssa and teach that sex itself was the result of the Fall.[35]

However, he struggled in responding to the Pelagians and it is in these writings that we find him asserting the dangers of concupiscence.

To understand Augustine's teaching on sexual ethics it is necessary to recall that his writings were the fruit of his own bitter struggles.[36]

The problem for him centred on the tremendous force of the sexual appetite, a force which had a will of its own. Augustine therefore reasoned himself into the position where he could not see how an act of sexual intercourse, even within marriage, could take place without venial sin being committed because of concupiscence.[37] The positive aspect of Augustine's teaching was that the sexual appetite was in itself good and therefore in marriage men and women could engage in sexual relations for the procreation of the race in spite of the risk of sinning through the concupiscence of their fallen state.

Augustine posited three *goods* of marriage: *fidelity, offspring* and *sacrament*. 'Sacrament' in his context is not equivalent to the later Scholastic definition of marriage as one of the seven sacraments. Indeed it was a way of defining the permanence of marriage and Augustine interchanges the words *sacramentum* and *vinculum* (bond). In chapter 11 of Book 1 'On marriage and concupiscence', he gives us a detailed definition of the bond in relation to his *goods*.

> It is certainly not fecundity only, the fruit of which consists of offspring, nor chastity only, whose bond is fidelity, but also a certain sacramental bond in marriage which is recommended to believers in wedlock. Accordingly it is enjoined by the apostle: 'Husbands love your wives, even as Christ also loved the Church.' Of this bond the substance undoubtedly is this, that the man and the woman who are joined together in matrimony should remain inseparable as long as they live ... And so complete is the observance of this bond in the city of our God ... – that is to say, in the Church of Christ – by all married believers, who are undoubtedly members of Christ, that, although women marry, and men take wives, for the purpose of procreating children, it is never permitted one to put away even an unfruitful wife for the sake of having another to bear children.[38]

Two points should be noted. Firstly the context is that of the community of believers. Secondly the bond is concerned with the permanence of the relationship 'as long as they live'.

However, it is not at all clear how Augustine defines the nature of the bond. In the same chapter he acknowledges that this world's rule about divorce is different from the Christian rule, and refers to the fact that Moses extended this concession. In reiterating Jesus' teaching that those who enter such relationships commit adultery, however, he proceeds with a classic example of traditional logic.

> So enduring, indeed, are the rights of marriage between those who have contracted them, as long as they both live, that even they are looked on as man and wife still, who have separated from one another, rather than they between whom a new connection has been formed ... Thus between the conjugal pair, as long as they live, the nuptial bond has a permanent obligation, and can be cancelled neither by separation nor by union with another.
>
> But this permanence avails, in such cases, only for injury from the sin, not for a bond of the covenant. (p. 268)

The final sentence is interesting. It clearly indicates that Augustine has not developed the concept of the bond as an ontological reality in the way the Scholastics will later: it is 'not a bond of the covenant'. This is reinforced by the preceding sentence where he refers to the obligation arising from the bond, thus focusing on the people rather than the idea. He concludes the chapter by comparing the marriage *sacramentum* with the baptismal *sacramentum*:

> In like manner the soul of an apostate, which renounces as it were its marriage union with Christ, does not, even though it has cast its faith away, lose the sacrament of its faith, which it received in the laver of regeneration. It would undoubtedly be given back to him if he were to return, although he lost it on his departure from Christ. He retains, however, the sacrament after his apostasy, to the aggravation of his punishment, not for meriting the reward. (p. 268)

Augustine's primary concern was marriage in the Christian context and he sees the character imparted by baptism as having a comparable reality to the bond of marriage. Mackin concludes that according to

Augustine what remains after a separation is not the bond in itself, but something in the individual spouse which compares with the baptismal bond and has to do with the individual's commitment to God.[39]

In chapter 12 of the same work, bearing in mind the conclusions the Church will reach some seven centuries later, Augustine makes the following remarkable statement:

> But God forbid that the nuptial bond should be regarded as broken between those who have by mutual consent agreed to observe a perpetual abstinence from the use of carnal concupiscence. Nay, it will be only a firmer one, whereby they have exchanged pledges together, which will have to be kept by especial endearment and concord. (p. 268)

He reasons in this way so that he can explain that the marriage of Mary and Joseph was not lacking in any of the three *goods*. We can deduce that for Augustine the permanence of marriage arises from the consent of the couple, not as a result of physical consummation. However, he introduces a note of uncertainty when summing up the situation of the Holy Family at the beginning of chapter 13:

> The entire good, therefore, of the nuptial institution was effected in the case of these parents of Christ: there was offspring, there was faithfulness, there was the bond. As offspring, we recognize the Lord Jesus Himself; the fidelity, in that there was no adultery; the bond, because there was no divorce. (p. 269)

Augustine helps us further with a definition of the bond in chapter 23. There he asks the *goods* to speak for themselves and he makes it abundantly clear that he equates the bond with the third *good*:

> this will be the answer of the sacramental bond of marriage, – the third good: 'Of me was that word spoken in paradise before the entrance of sin: "A man shall leave his father and mother, and shall cleave unto his wife; and they two shall be come one flesh."' This the apostle applies to the case of Christ and of the Church and calls it then 'a great sacrament.' What, then, in Christ and in the Church is great, in the instances of each married pair it is but very small, but even then it is the sacrament of an inseparable union. (p. 273)

What is particularly interesting here is that Augustine, by returning to Genesis 2:24, uses the word 'sacrament' in relation to marriage from the very beginning and before it became part of the Christian dispensation. For him the 'sacramental bond' is not an exclusively Christian phenomenon. We are forced to conclude, therefore, that Augustine's definitions of the bond do not relate to, nor support, the later theological distinctions which determine the pastoral practice of the Church, namely that only the consummated sacramental marriages are irrevocably indissoluble.

Mackin concludes his discussion of Augustine thus:

> One would call it his theology of the *sacramentum* of marriage except that he never worked carefully enough to settle a consistent meaning for the key terms, to forge a catena of reasoning and to verify his conclusions rigorously enough to form a true theology.[40]

He concedes, nevertheless, that Augustine derived his theology of the radical indissolubility of marriage from his theory of the *sacramentum*. Centuries later when the Scholastics began to theologize about marriage they inherited Augustine's teaching. For them, however, *sacramentum* would have a different, precise and technical meaning, describing marriage as one of the seven sacraments, so they used *vinculum* (the bond) to describe the indissoluble nature of the union. How they fashioned that definition of the bond is the key to understanding the discipline which obtains in the Church today.

The Scholastics and the bond

By the twelfth century we see a polarization on the crucial question of when the bond comes into existence. Effectively there were two schools: Gratian's at the University of Bologna and Peter Lombard's at the University of Paris. Both had gathered collections of theological statements issued by the Fathers and other celebrated teachers of previous generations, as well as by councils and popes. Gratian's *Decretum* is regarded as the first compilation of canon law. Peter Lombard's *Sententiae* were so celebrated that great Scholastics, like Thomas Aquinas and Albert, wrote commentaries on them.[41]

Gratian and Lombard, however, were not mere compilers; they also offered their own opinions in their commentaries. At the heart of the debate was whether a marriage bond came into existence as a result of the *consent* (*ratum*) of the couple or as a result of its *consummation* by sexual intercourse (*consummatum*). Gratian was influenced by the Germanic customs of the north European tribes, for whom fertility and the wider social issues of relating to the extended family played an important part. Therefore he favoured the opinion which suggested that intercourse was integral to the consent and the establishment of a true marriage bond.

Lombard and the Paris School followed the traditional Roman position and taught that a marriage existed solely from the consent of the couple. In the event the teaching Church sought a compromise and tried to marry the two positions.

Pope Alexander III, whose own position had vacillated between the two opinions, made some celebrated pastoral decisions towards the end of his pontificate, from which it was deduced that a marriage bond is truly established as a result of the *consent*, but it becomes wholly indissoluble only after the first act of intercourse following the consent, whereby it is *consummated*.[42]

This teaching directly contradicted Augustine's teaching on the permanence of all Christian marriages, even those where the partners agree to abstain from sexual relations, a situation which Augustine maintained actually made the *sacramentum* (the bond) firmer. I make this point simply as a reminder that we are not going to find a clear unbroken tradition of teaching in this field as some would have us believe.

Peter Lombard developed the Augustinian notion of the *sacramentum*. Where Augustine equated it with permanence, Lombard regarded it as a *quality* whose presence made a marriage permanent. This was because for him the *sacramentum* was a specifically Christian concept, imaging the union of Christ and the Church in Ephesians.[43] It was part of the process of theologizing about Christian marriage that would eventually lead to the defining of marriage as one of the seven sacraments and the teaching that absolute indissolubility is strictly applicable only to consummated sacramental marriage, though Lombard himself did not regard marriage as a sacrament properly so-called because he did not believe it actually conferred grace.

St Thomas Aquinas' *Summa Theologiae* has stood until our own time as the touchstone of Catholic orthodoxy. Aristotelianism was the prevailing thinking which underpinned his work and the writings of the Scholastics in general. It was from Aristotle that the Scholastics inherited the concepts of 'matter' and 'form' to explain the relation between the passive continuum and the active principle in sentient and intellectual life.[44] Aristotle made a clear distinction between physics and metaphysics, the latter constituting the science of being as being, a science which also extends to that realm of being which is beyond the senses and which includes the notion of God.[45] This too the Scholastics inherited. In this system it was possible to distinguish between the 'substance' (the essence of something) and the 'accidents' (that by which the essence is recognized). Then, applying the Aristotelian deductive logic of the syllogism, the Scholastics sought to establish absolute principles in every field of theology, dismantling all the opinions which were contrary to their main hypotheses. Many of these principles have remained unchallenged until modern times. How this systematization developed the theology of marriage and especially the definition of the bond is important.

Aquinas began with Augustine's three *goods* or *values* of marriage and 'transformed them into the three *ends* of marriage'.[46] He taught that there is an inherent order in nature according to the divine plan and that it is possible for men and women to discern the natural order. Examining the nature of sexual relations, he concludes that they are directed towards the procreation of the race and therefore he posits offspring as the primary end of marriage. This end we have from our *animal* nature; the secondary end, fidelity, arises out of the mutual *human* support that a man and woman give to one another, and the tertiary end, the *sacramentum*, arises out of our *religious* nature and relationship with God.

Applying the theory of matter and form to the sacramental system, Aquinas and the Scholastics were able to define how the natural order gives way to the supernatural order in the new creation of Christ's grace. Applying Aristotelian metaphysics they pointed to the reality of entities in an order beyond the experiences of the human senses. Thus the revised edition of the old 'penny catechism', adhering to this teaching, defines a sacrament as 'an outward sign of inward grace, ordained by Jesus Christ, by which grace is given to our souls'.[47] For most of the sacraments this was more readily applicable than for marriage. For example in baptism, the washing with water constituted the 'matter' of the sacrament, while the formula 'I baptize you in the name of the Father, and of the Son, and of the Holy Spirit' constituted the 'form'. In marriage, determining the matter and form was much more complicated.

Before the Council of Trent no set formula or rite within the Church was required to determine the validity of a marriage. The requirements of canonical form would be put in place only at that council.[48] Theologians were still struggling with the problem that marriage is a natural state, only later sanctified by Christ, and were at pains to defend the natural right to marry.

In the decree *Tametsi* of the Council of Trent which introduced canonical form, the Council Fathers insisted that even 'clandestine marriages created by free consent of the parties are true and ratified marriages as long as the Church does not invalidate them', which it then went on to do.[49] In this sacrament alone the Church did not visibly confer a sacrament through one of its ministers. Different Scholastics offered different solutions, but 'both Albert and Thomas stood by their conviction that they (the matter and form) are the spouses who create the sacrament by making their reciprocal consents'.[50] The matter was identified as whatever acts the spouses used to express their consent, and this matter was *informed* by the expressed reciprocal consent of each spouse. Thus the spouses were also understood to be the ministers as well as the recipients of the sacrament.

Here the Western tradition parted company with the East, where the priest was seen as ministering Christ's grace to the spouses, just as he did in each of the other sacraments. This is not just a fine point of theology. It will deeply affect the later discipline of the Catholic Church.[51] The problem with this position is that it does not situate the sacrament in the community of faith, but it was the inevitable conclusion from the philosophical principles on which it was based.

Each of the sacraments is defined by the Scholastics as an outward sign of inward grace. Again, this process is more easily identified in the other sacraments, but in marriage it is of a different order because of the nature of the sign: the Christ–Church union. Peter Lombard did not believe that marriage was strictly a sacrament because he did not believe it actually conferred grace, but it was not to this position that Aquinas and the later Scholastics arrived. They taught that marriage was truly a sacrament and that the grace to image the Christ–Church union was granted in the sacrament.

With this teaching in place, the application of another key Scholastic concept regarding the sacraments – *opus operatum* – will be seen to have far-reaching consequences. *Opus operatum* refers to the fact that the sacrament is valid and efficacious in itself and does not depend on the disposition of those giving or receiving it (*opus operantis*).[52] Thus the minister of baptism does not even have to have faith, but is required only to do and intend what the Church intends, for the sacrament to be valid and efficacious. It will be helpful to bear this in mind when we come to examine the way in which the Church finally determines how the sacramental 'bond' of marriage is established.

With Thomas Aquinas we can go so far, but it would seem that he never fully resolved some of the ambiguities arising from his systematic theology and the Church's pastoral practice. Mackin, in a section on Thomas Aquinas, compares his earlier marriage writings, *Commentarium in IV Libros Sententiarum,* with his later ones, *Summa Contra Gentiles,* and finds both a continuity and some missing links.[53] The issue from our point of view is certainly clouded because Aquinas focuses his attention on the Christian sacramental nature of the third end/good of marriage, the *sacramentum,* as the deciding factor in defining indissolubility. He is certain that marriage is a permanent union because in the natural order it is clear that offspring need the nurturing, care and protection of both parents. He seems conscious of the weakness of the argument that this relationship with their children remains until the end of their lives, and for good measure he adds the human dimension of the mutual support of the spouses in fidelity (what came to be defined in the law as the secondary end) to reinforce the natural law argument for permanence. Then the sacrament takes marriage on to a new plane for Christians:

> Therefore because the union of husband and wife images the union of Christ and the Church, the image must correspond with that which it images. Now the union of Christ and the Church is a union of one person with one person, and a union that is perpetual ... for Christ will never be separated from his Church. As he himself says in the last chapter of Matthew, 'Behold, I am with you even unto the end of the world ...' It follows necessarily then that a marriage, in so far as it is a sacrament of the Church, must be of one man and one woman, and must be a union that is indissoluble. And this belongs to the fidelity by which the husband and wife are bound.
>
> Thus the goods of marriage are three in so far as it is a sacrament of the Church, namely the offspring (which are to be accepted and nurtured for the honor [*sic*] and worship of God); fidelity, in that the man is bonded to one wife; and the sacrament, in that the marital union is indissoluble for being an image [*sacramentum*] of the union of Christ and the Church.[54]

With Aquinas we are moving towards the definitive theology that would govern the decrees of the Council of Trent and ultimately become enshrined in the canon law of the Church. The above quotation was among his later writings and gives the clue as to how he tried to integrate his vision: the bond is seen as 'belonging' to the end (good) of *fidelity*, but for the Christian is reinforced in the *sacrament*. His difficulty lay in trying to accommodate the prior decisions of the magisterium with his natural law vision and his theology of the sacraments. It would seem from a purely logical point of view that he would have preferred to declare unequivocally that the natural bond of marriage was absolutely indissoluble because it is enshrined in the natural law, but because the Scriptures and the tradition of the Church had found ways of dissolving certain marital unions, he could not. His conclusions were not wholly satisfactory and never resolved the issue of why intercourse after the marital consent makes the Christian bond irrevocably indissoluble.[55]

The last crucial development was to come with Bonaventure and John Duns Scotus. Bonaventure does not deal with marriage as a natural state and marriage as a sacrament separately, but in contrasting the character of baptism with the bond of marriage he develops the notion of the bond further than Aquinas. Mackin comments as follows on Bonaventure's position:

> As there is in baptism both an exterior and temporary reality which is the washing with water, and an interior and lasting reality which is the baptismal character in the soul, so too in marriage there is the passing exterior reality that is the *coniunctio* or joining in marriage effected by the mutual consent, and also the lasting interior reality, which is the *vinculum*, the marital bond. Both the joining and the bond, he adds, are called marriage.[56]

Scotus also makes a distinction between the *coniunctio* and the *vinculum*, and proceeds to situate the indissolubility in the bond (*vinculum*) created by the contract, another development which will take root in the official teaching of the Church.[57]

The various components of the teaching on the bond which will eventually become enshrined in the 1917 Code of Canon Law are now in place.

The teaching of the magisterium

From the twelfth century onwards we can gain a clearer picture of what the Western Church taught because we see a development of official pronouncements in Council. Even before Aquinas the Second Lateran Council (1139) had anathematized those who 'condemn the bonds of legitimate marriage'.[58] At the Council of Verona (1184) marriage was listed as one of the sacraments and this was confirmed at the Council of Florence (1439), which listed the seven sacraments which we acknowledge today. The Florentine decree is important:

> The seventh is the sacrament of matrimony which is the sign of the union of Christ and the Church according to the saying of the apostle: 'This is a great mystery, and I mean in reference to Christ and the Church' (Eph. 5:32). The efficient cause of matrimony is the mutual consent duly expressed in words relating to the present. A triple good is found in Matrimony. The first is the begetting of children and their education to the worship of God. The second is the faithfulness which each spouse owes to the other. Third is the indissolubility of marriage, inasmuch as it represents the indissoluble union of Christ and the Church. But, although it is permitted to separate on account of adultery, nevertheless it is not permitted to contract another marriage since the bond of a marriage legitimately contracted is perpetual.[59]

Two points are worth noting. Firstly, in spite of Aquinas the decree refers to the *goods* rather than the *ends* of marriage; secondly the bond is not linked specifically with any of the goods in particular but with marriage itself.

The Council of Trent was concerned to defend the teaching of the Church against Luther and the reformers. Two *anathemas* are of particular importance.

Canon 5.
If anyone says that the marriage bond can be dissolved because of heresy, or irksome cohabitation, or because of the wilful desertion of one of the spouses, *anathema sit*.

Canon 7.
If anyone says that the Church is in error for having taught and for still teaching that in accordance with the evangelical and apostolic doctrine (cf. Mk 10; 1 Cor. 7), the marriage bond cannot be dissolved because of adultery on the part of one of the spouses, and that neither of the two, not even the innocent one who has given no cause for infidelity, can contract another marriage during the lifetime of the other;

and that the husband who dismisses an adulterous wife and marries again and the wife who dismisses an adulterous husband and marries again are both guilty of adultery, *anathema sit*.[60]

Denzinger-Schönmetzer add a footnote to Canon 7, explaining that this form of condemnation was chosen so that the Greeks would not be offended, because while they followed a contrary practice, they did not condemn the practice of the Latin Church.[61]

The definition of the bond in the 1983 Code of Canon Law provides a helpful starting point in trying to determine precisely how the Scholastics understood this notion.

> From a valid marriage there arises between the spouses a bond which of its own nature is permanent and exclusive. Moreover, in christian marriage the spouses are by a special sacrament strengthened and, as it were, consecrated for the duties and the dignity of their state. (Canon 1134)

By defining the bond as having 'its own nature' the Church would seem to be giving it an existence in its own right. This interpretation is reinforced by Thomas P. Doyle in his commentary on the 1983 Code.[62] He defines the marriage bond as 'the ontological reality which exists between two persons who have exchanged marital consent' and says that 'it is a reality that comes into existence with consent and no longer depends for its continued existence on the will of the spouses alone' (p. 766). He speaks of it as 'an integral and not a partial reality' (p. 808) and he leaves us in no doubt about his interpretation of how this definition evolved historically:

> When the Church acquired competence over marriage in the Middle Ages (the authority to declare when marriage began or ended), the understanding of the bond shifted from that of its being purely a moral obligation to that of its being a separate reality. It was something that *could* not be terminated or dissolved rather than a relationship that *should* not be terminated. (p. 808)

By contrast Ladislas Örsy in his book *Marriage in Canon Law* offers a very different interpretation. In a series of footnotes on Canon 1134 he examines the Scholastic notion of the bond and concludes that philosophically it cannot be said to have an existence in its own right:

Bond is often spoken of as if it had an autonomous existence in itself as physical substances have. In reality it is the creation of the law, human or divine, as the case may be; cf. the famous definition of Justinian *obligatio est vinculum iuris* (Inst. 3.13), 'obligation is a legal bond.' The nature of the bond, *vinculum*, is determined by the law (human or divine, secular or sacred) that creates it. (p. 203)

He bases his argument on an analysis of Scholastic philosophy and directly challenges Doyle's position. Because this is so central to the argument of this book I believe it warrants quoting in full:

It [the bond] is not any kind of substance, or *esse in se*; it is an accident that belongs to a substance; the substance in question being that of a human person. The bond is the specific marital relationship of a man to a woman and vice versa, an *esse ad*; that is, a general orientation in the world of their intentionality; an orientation that permeates and dominates their judgments and decisions. Quite appropriately it could be called 'conversion' (turning to in a radical sense) to another person. In the case of a sacramental marriage God himself grants a special grace-filled dimension to this bond.

We use this scholastic terminology to convey a point: no new physical or spiritual substance is created either in a natural or a sacramental marriage. If it were so, it should follow that whenever the church dispenses from a natural or a sacramental marriage, this physical substance is 'annihilated' – a patently absurd proposition.

Marriage is not one of those sacraments that have for their effect what traditionally has been described as 'character', an indelible sign on the soul; baptism is the obvious example. Precisely, because such sacraments bring about a permanent transformation in the person, they cannot be repeated. Although some theologians tried to apply the same doctrine to marriage (e.g. Hugh of St Victor, †1141), their opinion never gained acceptance (see DTC 9.2:2144–2147).[63]

Thomas Doyle in COM-USA uses the following expressions to describe the nature of the bond: an 'ontological reality' (766), 'an integral and not partial reality', 'a separate reality' (808). A way of testing the meaning and correctness of these expressions is to try to locate the bond within the categories of being as they are referred to in nearly every of work of Aquinas. Can the bond be a substance? Certainly not, it has no autonomous existence. So it must be an accident. Among the accidents, a rapid survey of the categories shows that the only one that can accommodate it is relation, *esse ad*.

Now a relation can most certainly be an ontological reality, as long as it remains attached to a substance. No relation can, however, have a separate existence from the substance, not even in the Trinity – if we may go that far.

It follows that the bond is a relationship of obligation. But, due to the sacrament such a relationship is sealed by God's grace and his commitment to the spouses. Therefore, it should not be described in terms of merely natural obligations; it is a grace-filled obligation in the Kingdom.

When the church terminates such a grace-filled obligation through dispensing from the bond of a sacramental non-consummated marriage, it simply frees the person *in the name of God*, on the strength of a power of divine origin, from a *vinculum*, 'chain', that is binding him or her.

Although we used the categories of scholastic philosophy and theology to explain the nature of the bond with some clarity and precision, the essential validity of our explanation does not depend on that system. It could be expressed in other ways.

Be that as it may, in this matter one should aim for the greatest precision obtainable – for the sake of those who eventually will have to carry in real life the burden of our theoretical conclusions. (pp. 204–5)

For our purposes it is not essential to determine the merits or otherwise of these two positions. What they show us is that, although Örsy believes the validity of his explanation does not depend on Scholasticism, it was Scholasticism which shaped the definition of the bond and the absolute principles that arise from it. These continue to determine the pastoral parameters in which we are able to work. Örsy is correct in insisting that the bond of marriage does not confer a 'character' on the soul of the spouses, but I believe it is by concentrating on the definition which makes the bond analogous to this 'character' (an idea formulated by Augustine and taken up by the Scholastics) that we will be able to understand how the consequences of this tradition have left the Church faced with its present impasse. Canon 1055 holds the key.

1. The marriage covenant, by which a man and a woman establish between themselves a partnership of their whole life, and which of its

own very nature is ordered to the well-being of the spouses and to the procreation and upbringing of children, has, between the baptised, been raised by Christ the Lord to the dignity of a sacrament.

2. Consequently, a valid marriage contract cannot exist between baptised persons without its being by that very fact a sacrament.

The theology underpinning this position is that the 'character' of baptism makes the radical ontological difference. Thus, when two Christians marry they form a bond which is radically different from the natural bond because it is formed in the order of God's new creation in Christ. It does not matter whether you adhere to the theory that the bond is an entity in itself or simply an attribute of the spouse, the consequences are the same: because the bond is formed in this new ontological order its effects are as absolute as the character of baptism and cannot be removed or dissolved.[64]

The bond dissolves only on the death of one of the partners.[65] Here we come to the nub of the argument. The sacramental bond is defined as of a totally different order to the natural bond. Yet neither the theologians nor the magisterium have ever been able to clarify the distinction entirely satisfactorily when it comes to indissolubility because of the fundamental belief that all marriages are ordained by God to be indissoluble. Thus the most that can be said about the indissolubility of sacramental marriage is that it is 'strengthened' by the sacrament (Canon 1134). The difficulty with this whole position is that in fact the only indissoluble marriages according to the Church's pastoral practice and tradition are the sacramental ones, and of those, only the ones that have been consummated.

This is an acutely sensitive issue and surfaces whenever the Catholic Church addresses the question of the permanence and sanctity of marriage. The discussion of marriage in *The Catechism of the Catholic Church* illustrates the problem.[66] This document explains how the Church seeks to promote marriage and family life and situate them in the natural order of creation (1601–1605). There is a recognition that disorder comes, not from the *nature* of man and woman, nor from the *nature* of their relationships, but from sin (1607). The subject of the 'indissolubility of the matrimonial bond' is introduced in the section 'Marriage in the Lord' (1612–1617), stating that Jesus, in teaching unequivocally the *original* meaning of the union of man and woman, declares it to be indissoluble (1614) and provides the strength and grace to live marriage in the new dimension of the Kingdom of God (1615).

What the Catechism and other magisterial documents fail to explain is why sin, the cause of the disorder, and the reason Moses gave permission for divorce in the face of the people's hardness of heart (1614), no longer features as an issue in the sacramental order of marriage. Instead, in this one area of the Christian life, the redemptive work of Christ is presumed to have taken complete effect and the sacramental bond (between baptized people), which results from the free human act of the couple and the consummation of the marriage, is defined as a *reality* henceforth irrevocable and guaranteed by the fidelity of God (1640).[67]

Accompanying the speculative theology in every age was the pastoral theology which sought to address the particular pastoral problems of the day. They have not always complemented one another.

Previous pastoral solutions

The Pauline privilege

The first recorded pastoral solution was Paul's for the early Christian community in Corinth (1 Corinthians 7:10–16). Paul takes responsibility for the situation and decides that if a marriage fails because one of the partners joins the community of faith and the unbelieving partner wishes to separate, then 'the brother or sister is not bound'. His reason is that God has called them to peace. In other words Paul seems to be suggesting that the bond of peace is more important than the bond of marriage in these circumstances. It is important to note that Paul does not reach this decision lightly. He begins by quoting the Lord's teaching on the permanence of marriage (vv. 10–11), and he insists that the unbelieving partner should not be sent away, but will be made one with the saints through the believing partner, and there is no problem regarding the children (vv. 12–14). It is only when the situation is not resolvable that the break-up is permitted.

Paul says nothing about remarriage and it was a matter of dispute over the centuries whether he intended to permit remarriage in such situations. Jerome Murphy-O'Connor argues that Paul permitted a full divorce, which in both Jewish and pagan law would have included the right to remarry.[68] Richard Kugelman accepts that from the fourth century 'Christian tradition, with some hesitation, has concluded from this passage that the Christian convert is free to contract another marriage'.[69] Some might consider the phrase 'with some hesitation' to be an understatement. Thomas P. Doyle writes:

There are occasional references to the Pauline saying in the patristic writings in conjunction with the dissolution of marriage, yet there is no conclusive evidence that the Pauline privilege was understood then as it is now. By the high Middle Ages, Gratian and Peter Lombard both spoke of the right of remarriage of the convert if the non-baptized party remarried after separation. The Pauline privilege became part of the Church's canonical legislation in 1199, yet the way in which and the time when the first marriage was dissolved were only clarified in the 1917 Code (CIC 1126).[70]

This pastoral decision of Paul's has been an important part of the equation. It demonstrated, at the very least, that there could be circumstances in which it is better for a couple not to live together. The reason in this instance was that the greater imperative – *peace* (which is the fruit of God's saving work in Christ, who is restoring unity to his broken creation) – could not be maintained.

For Paul it was probably inconceivable that such a situation could arise for a couple both of whom were Christian and living by the power of the Spirit. As in every other situation, including the threat of martyrdom, God's power could and would overcome every opposition of our nature and the forces of evil outside us (Romans 8:35–39). Thus the image of the Christ–Church union for marriage (Ephesians 5:32) was very appropriate in the context of this living community of faith.

However the consequences of this Pauline theology and this Pauline pastoral decision for the subsequent debate cannot be exaggerated. Herein lie the roots of so many of our pastoral difficulties today. Once the Church had finally accepted that the Pauline privilege included the right to remarry, the principle was established that the natural bond of marriage was not indissoluble. Greater goods: the work of salvation and the bond of peace could override it. The reason for demanding indissolubility had to be situated elsewhere and so it was sought in the sacramental sign of the Christ–Church union. Thus only sacramental marriages would be regarded as absolutely indissoluble because in the community of faith it could not be otherwise.

Canons 1143–1147 determine the circumstances in which the Pauline privilege may be applied today.[71] These deal with the specific situation in which someone is baptized into the community of faith and the non-baptized spouse departs, in other words the circumstances envisaged by Paul. The law states that the marriage 'is dissolved ... by the fact that a new marriage is contracted by the party who has received baptism' (Canon 1143.1). According to the law both parties should be questioned and a dispensation granted, but as Örsy points out, 'there is a slight inconsistency in the legal system: the baptized person has a right to contract a new marriage when the earlier one is still good and valid'.[72]

The Church is defining what happens in terms of the ontological reality. A dispensation does not dissolve the former bond, nor is there a declaration of dissolution. The former bond is dissolved by the new bond, but what is truly remarkable, in view of the fact that this privilege is *in favour of the faith*, is that this new bond does not have to be with a believer, and therefore does not have to be sacramental (Canon 1147).

Once the principle that the natural bond could be dissolved was established the way was open to further extensions of the law *in favour of the faith*, and the necessary provisions in law are found in the subsequent canons (1148–1150). These were based on pastoral decisions in the sixteenth century, largely as a result of problems arising from the slave trade, including Christian converts from societies which accepted polygamy and polyandry.[73]

The final canon of this section, 1150, provides the Church with the scope it requires to permit the dissolution of virtually any non-sacramental marriage bond, a process still reserved to the pope alone and therefore sometimes called the Petrine privilege.

We can measure the limits set for granting the dissolution of marriages through the exercise of papal authority by noting how far popes have actually gone in exercising their power. The boundaries have been stretched even during this century, notably by Pope Pius XII.[74] In effect the Church has reached a position where the marriage bond which is not a sacrament can be dissolved to enable a Christian, whether one of the partners of the marriage in question or another party, to live at peace in marriage. The norms governing this exercise of papal authority are not in the Code of Canon Law, but in the Instruction of the CDF *Ut notum est* of 6 December 1973.[75]

Non-consummation

The second example, while hardly likely to be a major issue in today's climate, marked an important stage in the development of the theological thinking of the Church. It is also enshrined in the Code of Canon Law (Canon 1142).

Among the decisions which decided the great debate in the twelfth century about when marriage and the bond actually came into existence was one by Alexander III in 1179. He permitted a wife to enter religious life, provided she had not had intercourse with the husband to whom she was married. He ruled that the wife's pronouncing of religious vows would dissolve the marriage. He justified this and similar decisions on the grounds that a couple could not be said to have 'become one flesh' if they had not had intercourse with one another.[76]

Thus the sacramental bond was said to be established in the consent of the couple, but only became absolutely indissoluble after the first act of intercourse, following the consent.[77] This was duly included in the decrees of the Council of Trent.

> If anyone says that marriage contracted but not consummated is not dissolved by the solemn religious profession of one of the spouses, *anathema sit*.[78]

Two points are worth noting. Firstly, the decision in favour of religious life was taken because of the clear conviction that this was a superior state to marriage.[79] This does not sit easily with the renewed vision of vocation and the common call to holiness presented by the Church today,[80] although Pope John Paul II reiterates this teaching in *Familiaris Consortio* (16) by speaking of 'the superiority of this charism' and quoting Pope Pius XII's encyclical *Sacra Virginitas* as his authority.

Secondly, in spite of the fact that the natural bond of marriage was deemed to be dissoluble, and absolutely indissoluble marriage was reserved for the consummated sacramental union, the Church has returned to nature – the act of sexual intercourse – as the deciding factor regarding the indissolubility of sacramental marriages.

Canonical form

Canonical form is the name given to that form of marriage in canon law which is required of a Catholic for the validity of the marriage. Its origins are in the Decree of Trent *Tametsi*, and the specific pastoral problem addressed by this decree was that of clandestine marriages. Although religious ceremonies to solemnize marriages can be traced back many centuries, and the nuptial mass is first mentioned in the fifth century, the Church's ritual involvement in marriage took centuries to develop, particularly in the West.[81]

The East, where the theology of the sacrament was much more closely linked with the visible sign of being members of the eucharistic community, understood the priest to be the minister of the sacrament. The West had settled for a theology which situated the sacrament in the baptismal character of the spouses who thus became the ministers of the sacrament to each other. The natural state of marriage was sanctified by their Christian character.[82]

The consequence of this theology in the days before society or the Church kept careful records was that an array of pastoral problems accrued around the growing practice of clandestine marriages. With no proof to confirm a couple's consent to marriage, abuses crept in.

For centuries the Church had forbidden the practice of clandestine marriages, but had failed to make an impact, and because of its theology still considered them valid if illegal. The Church tried to deal with this matter definitively at Trent. It insisted that for validity marriages must in future be celebrated before a minister and two or three witnesses.[83] However, the decree was qualified by a crucial provision relating to promulgation, which meant that in practice it did not take effect in many parts of Christendom.[84] This matter was largely resolved with the decree *Ne Temere* of 1909, which extended the obligation of canonical form to the universal Church.[85] The 1917 Code duly included the provisions of canonical form in its marriage law,[86] and although the 1983 Code allows exceptions and dispensations in view of the new ecumenical climate, the substance of the teaching remains the same.

The particular importance of canonical form is centred on the fact that the Church has decreed that it determines the validity, not just the legality of a marriage. In other words if canonical form is lacking, the bond is not established. Theological opinion has differed over whether all baptized people are under the jurisdiction of the pope, but this problem was obviated by the fact that in the 1917 Code non-Catholic Christians were explicitly exempted from canonical form.[87] What is also interesting is that the same canon of the 1917 Code also exempted those baptized in the Catholic Church but not brought up in it. However, because it proved so difficult to determine what constituted 'upbringing in the faith', Pope Pius XII abrogated that section of Canon 1099 on 1 August 1948.[88] From that time until now, Catholic baptism has been the sole criterion governing canonical form.

The sacramental question

In the centuries following the Council of Trent the Church's struggles with the political powers of Europe served to sharpen the theological argument over what constitutes a sacramental marriage. Having decreed that marriage was truly a sacrament of the New Covenant, the Church claimed jurisdiction over the marriages of Christians and argued that it was not possible to separate the secular and sacramental realities.[89] The Church refused to accept that the religious element in marriage was simply an accessory and insisted that for the faithful only one bond was possible and that was a sacramental one. This is a perfectly logical position and is consonant with the Church's teaching throughout history, that the marriages of the faithful are caught up in the mystery of Christ.

Nevertheless the difficulty the Church faced was linked with the perennial problem of defending the natural right of all people to marry and its right to govern the marriages of the faithful. In other words: who are the faithful whose marriages are sacraments? The decision to define the faithful as 'the baptized' in the 1917 Code settled the issue so far as the discipline was concerned.[90] However the discipline was now informing the theology. The argument was simple if disputable. If baptism confers a character which cannot be destroyed and is eternal then when two baptized people marry they can only create a bond which is caught up in that same ontological order, that is a sacramental bond.

The practical consequences of the theology of the bond

Successive popes during this century have striven to arrest the rising tide of divorce. Pope Pius XII regularly referred to the question, appealing through the Catholic community to the wider community. Often he made no distinction between the marriages of the baptized and the unbaptized. In an allocution to the newly married he actually linked the two.

> But what does nature say about this perpetuity? While grace with its salutary action does not change nature, even if it always and in every case perfects it, would it perhaps encounter an enemy that hinders it? No: God's art is wonderful and gentle; it is always in accordance with nature, of which he is the author. That perpetuity and indissolubility, which the will of Christ and the mystical signification of the Christian marriage require, is required by nature also. Grace fulfills [*sic*] the

desire of nature and gives it strength to be that for which it greatly longs.[91]

The same is true of the writings of Pope John Paul II. Echoing the sentiments of *Gaudium et Spes* he says in *Familiaris Consortio* that 'the Church offers her services to every person who wonders about the destiny of marriage and the family' (1) and 'once again feels the pressing need to proclaim the Gospel ... to all people without exception, in particular to all those who are called to marriage and are preparing for it, to all married couples and parents in the world' (3). In his section on 'Indissolubility' he writes:

> Being rooted in the personal and total self-giving of the couple, and being required by the good of the children, the indissolubility of marriage finds its ultimate truth in the plan that God has manifested in his revelation: he wills and he communicates the indissolubility of marriage as a fruit, a sign and a requirement of the absolutely faithful love that God has for man and that the Lord Jesus has for the Church. (20)

John Paul II opens the way to ensure that his teaching will embrace the sacramental theology of the bond, which we have so carefully traced, but it is interesting that again he begins by rooting indissolubility in the personal and total self-giving of the couple.

Dr Jack Dominian has analysed the changing social attitudes towards marriage and sexuality. He has provided us with a useful reference point, not least because he has been able to relate these social attitudes to the developing theology of the Catholic Church and the demands they have made on the Catholic community. He has been able to see the consequences in the Church of the shift from a contract-centred theology to a covenant and love-centred theology of marriage and the new expectations this brings with it to the men and women of our day. Similar expectations have arisen in the secular world where the social role contract of marriage has given way to an egalitarian union of man and woman, largely made possible by the emancipation of women. Sadly the widening gap between the rising expectations and their fulfilment is filled by an ever increasing number of broken marriages.

Today it is readily accepted that civil divorce in itself is not the issue and spouses who are deeply unhappy should not be dissuaded from parting. The pastoral problem facing the Church is that many of these people do not feel able to spend the rest of their lives without a partner.

As we discover more and more about the psychology of sexual relationships and the stages of human growth and fulfilment, the Church is reviewing its teaching on sexual ethics in every sphere of human life.

It is an established fact that the majority of young people are sexually experienced before they get married. This is a situation which the teaching Church remains unhappy about, but largely powerless to influence. In general there is an uneasy silence about the matter. On the one hand many young Catholics believe that it is morally permissible though they know the Church condemns the practice. At the same time the Church senses that much of the teaching or lack of teaching about sexual ethics in the past was very repressive and left many people ill-prepared for a fulfilling sexual relationship in their marriages.

There is a recognition that the new openness and honesty about the subject is valuable and that we have much to learn.[92] Thus, although premarital sex remains a critical issue for the teaching Church, it is a moral problem which it is able to tolerate more easily than remarriage because until marital consent is given the question of an irrevocable bond does not arise.

The reason that a broken marriage is unique among moral problems, including all other serious sexual problems, in the Catholic Church is the theology of the bond.

I believe the time has come to ask for the systematic theological position enshrined in the law to be reviewed. It is inoperable at a pastoral level, and if pastoral and systematic theology become divorced then there is something seriously wrong with the one or the other.

What then are the objections to the theology of the bond and to the annulment process as it stands today? I will use the case history of Julie (Appendix 2, p. 186) to demonstrate the inconsistencies of the present discipline.

In Julie's story we are faced with two previous marriages, hers and her present partner's. As well as examining the problems in the story as it stands, we will also consider the added complications of further hypothetical situations.

Julie, a Catholic, had married in a register office, but the marriage had lasted only a few months. We are not told whether she married another Catholic, a non-Catholic Christian or a non-Christian. However, none of this is relevant because the marriage lacked canonical form. We must note the anomalies.

If in the ontological order *ipso facto* the marriage of two baptized people constitutes a sacrament, how can a piece of purely disciplinary legislation affect that ontological fact? And if we accept that the Church does have the power so to legislate, is it just that someone who is not practising the faith, or even someone who has no knowledge of having been baptized a Catholic, should be deprived of the right to marry validly in another Church or in a register office? A further anomaly arises when we analyse the adjustments made to this law during this century. As we have seen, the decree *Ne Temere* determined baptism as the sole criterion for canonical form, but the 1917 Code modified this position to the extent that those not brought up in the faith were excluded from its jurisdiction. When this was abrogated on 1 August 1948 it meant that someone, baptized a Catholic, could unwittingly form an ontological sacramental bond on 31 July 1948 by marrying in a register office, but in an identical set of circumstances could not do so 24 hours later. To say the least it is hard for the modern mind to conceive of a God whose action is controlled in this way by human legislation.

Julie then is free to marry, though had she originally married in the Catholic Church she would not be. Had she married in the Catholic Church, it would be necessary to establish whether her former husband had been baptized or not. If he had not been baptized, then there would be the possibility of a dissolution of the bond in favour of the faith. If he had been baptized then the only option open would be the annulment process to determine whether they had truly formed a sacramental bond. They had a child, so if it was a marriage it had been consummated.

One is forced to ask at this point: what difference any of these various scenarios would have meant to Julie herself? Clearly she was someone for whom the faith had meant little up to this point in her life. Where she actually married and the religious commitment of her former partner were matters of sheer chance. Yet the Church, amidst its complex web of law, attempts to state definitively whether or not she has established a bond which is absolutely binding or not. Lost in the maze of all this, the majority of priests and people in their frustration ask: how can we be so sure?

Now we must consider Julie's new partner. In the story as it stands, he is the problem. He had been baptized in the Anglican Church and had married a baptized Methodist in the register office. Although the first canon in the 1983 Code states 'the canons of this Code concern only the Latin Church', in certain circumstances, by association, they extend beyond it. Again we are caught up in the ontology of the bond, formed through the baptisms of the spouses (Canon 1055.2). The Church does not impose canonical form on non-Catholics, yet it accepts their baptisms as valid: therefore they have formed a sacramental bond. There is no mention of children, so there might be a slim chance that the marriage was not consummated and therefore the bond could be dissolved under Canon 1142. However, since this is so uncommon, we can presume that the only avenue open will be that of the annulment process.

We must ask in what way the Church regards this marriage as a sacrament. Neither of the partners was a practising Christian and their wedding was not in a church, and therefore they did not in any way demonstrate a commitment to Christian marriage. Neither considered their marriage to be a sacrament. Yet, not being bound by canonical form, the Church considers their union to be valid and therefore a sacrament. We are back to the metaphysics inherited from the Scholastics and used to determine that such a marriage must be a sacrament because both partners had received the sacrament of baptism and neither had formally apostatized. To most people this is a patently absurd position to hold. Many canonists and theologians have challenged the underlying theology of Canon 1055.2.[93]

The argument reaches into the whole question of what degree of faith is required of the recipient and minister of a sacrament. When the theology and even the law were first being formulated it is reasonable to suppose that the phenomenon of the baptized unbeliever was a rarity and possibly even hard to imagine. Today such people abound and it is difficult to believe that God is burdening them with obligations of which they are unaware and which they would certainly refuse to undertake. Elliott discusses the issue in response to its presentation by the International Theological Commission.[94] He offers a vision of hope in God's power to convert every situation:

> People can marry with weak or faithless motives and later be subject to a conversion, which enriches their Marriage so that the reality of the bond is able to be lived in such a way that they become ministers of Grace to one another. But their weak or faithless motives or vague or confused intention did not invalidate their Marriage. God, who is greater than our hearts, is able to bring to fruition what he begins in even his most 'unpromising' children. (p. 197)

What this approach fails to explain is what happens when God is apparently moving a person to the fruition of a faith commitment in the midst of an irregular marriage situation? In the succeeding chapters we will see multiple examples of this and many other anomalies.

Notes

1 *L'Osservatore Romano*, English edn (4 February 1991), p. 3.
2 See article 12 of *Dei Verbum*, the Dogmatic Constitution on Divine Revelation, Flannery, *Vatican Council II* (Leominster: Fowler Wright, 1987), pp. 750–65 (p. 758). See also Alois Grillmeier, 'The divine inspiration and the interpretation of sacred Scripture' in *Commentary on the Documents of Vatican II*, gen. ed. Herbert Vorgrimler (5 vols; London: Burns & Oates, 1969), III, pp. 199–246 (p. 246). See also The Pontifical Biblical Commission, *The Interpretation of the Bible in the Church* (Libreria Editrice Vaticana); reprinted in *Briefing*, vol. 24, no. 4 (1994), pp. 2–19; vol. 24, no. 5 (1994), pp. 20–33.
3 See Joseph Ratzinger, 'The transmission of divine revelation' in Vorgrimler, III, pp. 181–98 (p. 194). A series of articles at the end of *The New Jerome Biblical Commentary*, ed. Raymond E. Brown SS, Joseph A. Fitzmyer SJ and Roland E. Murphy OCarm (London: Geoffrey Chapman, 1989), offers a balanced and up-to-date review of progress in the different fields of biblical scholarship. I would draw special attention to the following: Raymond E. Brown and Sandra M. Schneiders IHM, 'Hermeneutics', pp. 1146–65; Raymond E. Brown and Thomas Aquinas Collins OP, 'Church pronouncements', pp. 1166–74; Robert North SJ and Philip J. King, 'Biblical archaeology', pp. 1196–218.
4 Sandra M. Schneiders deals with these questions in her article 'New Testament reflections on peace and nuclear arms' in *Catholics and Nuclear War*, ed. Philip J. Murnion (New York: Crossroad, 1983), pp. 91–105 (pp. 91–4).
5 The whole of the Book of Hosea is based on this symbolism, probably resulting from the prophet's painful personal experience of an unfaithful wife.
6 See Theodore Mackin, *What Is Marriage?* (New York: Paulist Press, 1982), pp. 50–2; Michael Lawler, *Secular Marriage, Christian Sacrament* (Mystic, CT: Twenty-Third Publications, 1985), pp. 8–11.
7 So the Lord God caused a deep sleep to fall upon the man, and he slept; then he took one of his ribs and closed up its place with flesh. And the rib that the Lord God had taken from the man he made into a woman and brought her to the man. (Genesis 2:21–22)
8 Many commentators are quick to point out that the inclusion of women in this context was notable and shows that Mark was not writing for the Jewish community, where it was inconceivable that a woman could put away her husband. Matthew does not include that sentence (see *The New Jerome Biblical Commentary*, p. 617).
9 Theodore Mackin, *Divorce and Remarriage* (New York: Paulist Press, 1984), p. 66. See pp. 56–66 for the argumentation. For further discussions on the meaning of the Matthean exception clause, see *The New Jerome Biblical Commentary*, pp. 642–3. That this is a debate common to the whole Christian community is well illustrated by a meticulously researched book: William A. Heth and Gordon J. Wenham, *Jesus and Divorce* (London: Hodder and Stoughton, 1984). Heth and Wenham come from the evangelical tradition of Protestantism and challenge the more liberal Erasmian interpretation of all the relevant biblical texts with the

interpretation of the early Church.

10 For a detailed explanation of this tradition see Mackin, *Divorce and Remarriage*, pp. 24–8.

11 Modern theologians and Scripture scholars would be quick to point to the radical nature of Jesus' teaching in the strongly patriarchal society of his day. Women could not be regarded as the possession of men, to be dismissed at will. With society as a whole becoming more and more conscious of the dignity and rights of women, the Church itself is beginning to adjust to the fact that it has a long way to go to redress the balance and heal the hurt of many past injustices in this field. That our perceptions are changing and our horizons broadening is evidenced by the fact that even the general sensitivity to inclusive language would have been inconceivable ten years ago.

For an interesting study of the sociology of the sexual contract in relation to the emancipation of women see Carole Pateman, *The Sexual Contract* (Cambridge: Polity, 1988).

12 See Peter J. Elliott, *What God Has Joined* ... (New York: Alba House, 1990), p. 87; and Theodore Mackin, *The Marital Sacrament* (New York: Paulist Press, 1989), pp. 299–301.

13 *The Christian Faith in the Doctrinal Documents of the Catholic Church*, ed. J. Neuner SJ and J. Dupuis SJ (Glasgow: Collins, 1983), no. 1808, p. 529.

The corresponding reference in H. Denzinger – A. Schönmetzer, *Enchiridion Symbolorum, Definitionum et Declarationum de Rebus Fidei et Morum* (23rd edn; Freiburg: Herder, 1965) is 1801. Further references to this volume will be in the abbreviated form DS.

14 Neuner and Dupuis, no. 1804; DS 1797.

15 Neuner and Dupuis, no. 1805; DS 1798.

16 Neuner and Dupuis, no. 1806; DS 1799.

17 Dennis Hamm in *The Beatitudes in Context: What Luke and Matthew Meant* (Wilmington, DE: Glazier, 1990) offers this conclusion to his study of who the poor of the Beatitudes are: 'In short, "the poor" of the first beatitude are those "true Israelites" who know their need of God. The physically and socially needy have the advantage of experiencing that need most directly' (p. 50).

18 *The Code of Canon Law in English Translation*, prepared by the Canon Law Society of Great Britain and Ireland (London: Collins, 1983), Canon 1143. When canons are quoted in English, it will be according to this translation. Further references to this volume will be abbreviated to CCL-GBI.

19 Gerhard Lohfink, *Jesus and Community: The Social Dimension of Christian Faith* (New York: Paulist Press, 1984). Lohfink reaches the heart of his argument in the last three sections of his third chapter, 'The New Testament communities in the discipleship of Jesus' entitled 'The renunciation of domination', 'The Church as contrast-society', and 'The sign for the nations' (pp. 115–47).

20 Bernard Häring writes in *The Law of Christ* (3 vols; Cork: Mercier, 1963), I:

> Killing of a man is not an unconditionally evil action because the bodily life of one's neighbour is not a value which must be preserved under all circumstances. Only the unjustified attack on the life of one's neighbour is always evil. (p. 288)

21 The connection between divorce and murder is not new. In a chapter note on Theodore of Mopsuestia, Mackin writes:

> Commenting on Chapter 2, verse 16 of the prophecy he said, '"But if you (the husband) have come to hate her, dismiss her," says the Lord God of Israel.'

Taking this literally as God's command Theodore must account for it reasonably. He tries to do so by appealing to divine prudence in permitting the lesser sin in order to avoid the greater. Because of the hardness of husbands' hearts, as Jesus pointed out, God gave them this permission to dismiss their wives lest they do violence to them, even to the point of murder. Theodore was convinced that in offering this counsel through the mouth of Malachi, God made clear why Moses (in Deuteronomy 24:1) allowed Israel's husbands to dismiss their wives. (*Divorce and Remarriage*, p. 164)

22 Jesus banters with the Samaritan woman about her situation and 'her five husbands'. Pheme Perkins in her commentary on 'The Gospel according to John' in *The New Jerome Biblical Commentary* says: 'No completely satisfactory explanation has been offered for the "five husbands"' (p. 957). It is generally accepted that they had something to do with the old pagan gods of the Samaritans (see *The Jerusalem Bible*, St John's Gospel, chapter 4, note e). However it is a text which many divorced people naturally point to as an example of how Jesus meets people in the situation in which he finds them. Whether her situation was complicated by personal relationships or the worship of false gods, her life was in a mess and Jesus offers her the water that will gush up to eternal life (v. 14).

23 See the article by Ingrid Maisch in *Sacramentum Mundi*, ed. Karl Rahner SJ and others (London: Burns & Oates), V, pp. 409–10.

24 The Latin *vinculum* is the word enshrined in Catholic theology and Canon Law for the *bond*. When Jerome translated the Scriptures into Latin this was the word he used to describe the bond of peace in Ephesians.

25 See Mackin, *Divorce and Remarriage*, pp. 90–223.

26 See *Divorce and Remarriage*, p. 117.

27 See *Divorce and Remarriage*, p. 147.

28 See *Divorce and Remarriage*, p. 187.

29 Örsy, *The Church: Learning and Teaching* (Leominster: Fowler Wright Books, 1987), pp. 17–18.

30 See Mackin, *Divorce and Remarriage*, p. 220.

31 Extreme examples of this attitude are to be found in writers like Uta Ranke-Heinemann. In *Eunuchs for Heaven: The Catholic Church and Sexuality*, trans. John Brownjohn (London: André Deutsch Limited, 1990), she writes:

> To speak of sexual hostility … is to speak of Augustine … He was the theological thinker who blazed a trail for the ensuing centuries. (p. 62)

See also Kate Saunders and Peter Stanford, *Catholics and Sex: From Purity to Purgatory* (London: Heinemann, 1992), p. 37.

32 Augustine, 'On the traditions of the Catholic Church' in *De Moribus Ecclesiae Catholicae*, Book 1, chapter 30: cited by Mackin, *What Is Marriage?*, p. 141.

33 Lawler, *Secular Marriage, Christian Sacrament*, p. 32.

34 The Manichean heresy was based on the teaching that the material and physical world was evil as opposed to the spiritual world which was good. The Pelagians on the other hand believed that original sin had not affected human nature and that it was possible to be saved without the help of God's grace.

35 See 'On the fashioning of Man' in *De Opificio Hominis*, ch. 17 (PG 44:87, 190), cited by Mackin, *What Is Marriage?*, pp. 91–2.

36 See Jack Dominian, *Christian Marriage* (London: Darton, Longman and Todd, 1967), p. 27.

37 For a detailed analysis of Augustine's position see Mackin, *What Is Marriage?*, pp. 127–42.

38 'St Augustine's anti-Pelagian works', *A Select Library of the Nicene and Post-Nicene Fathers of the Christian Church* (First Series, ed. Philip Schaff, 14 vols; Grand Rapids: Eerdmans, 1956), V, trans. Peter Holmes and Robert Ernest Wallis, rev. Benjamin Warfield, p. 268. The subsequent quotations from St Augustine are from the same volume.

39 Mackin, *Divorce and Remarriage*, p. 215.

40 *Divorce and Remarriage*, p. 220.

41 For a discussion of the development of the law through the thirteenth century with reference to Gratian and Peter Lombard, see Mackin, *Divorce and Remarriage*, pp. 274–99. For a guide to the influence of the *Sententiae* on the medieval theologians' discussion of marriage, see Mackin, *The Marital Sacrament*, pp. 325–79.

42 See Mackin, *Divorce and Remarriage*, pp. 300–22.

43 See Lawler, *Secular Marriage, Christian Sacrament*, pp. 104–5.

44 For definitions of *matter*, 'the sustaining ground of being', *form*, 'the determining reality of a "subject"', and *hylomorphism*, 'the doctrine of Aristotle, supplemented by the Scholastics, that every physical being is essentially constituted of matter and form', see Karl Rahner and Herbert Vorgrimler, *Concise Theological Dictionary* (2nd edn; London: Burns & Oates, 1983), pp. 179, 222–3, 299.

45 See discussion of 'Aristotelianism' in *The New Encyclopædia Britannica*, gen. ed. Robert McHenry (29 vols; Chicago: Encyclopædia Britannica, 1992), XIV, p. 61.

46 See Lawler, *Secular Marriage, Christian Sacrament*, p. 34.

47 *A Catechism of Christian Doctrine* (London: Catholic Truth Society, 1985), no. 249, p. 42.

48 The Canon Law of the Church would determine that the only legal and valid form of marriage for a Catholic would be in a Catholic Church before a priest (or deacon) and two or three witnesses.

49 Mackin, *What Is Marriage?*, p. 196.

50 Mackin, *The Marital Sacrament*, p. 346.

51 Lawler in a section on 'The minister of Christian marriage' argues that there is room in the Western Church for a development of theological thinking in this matter. Basing his argument on Canon 1108 which states that the priest or deacon 'receives' the consent 'in the name of the Church', he proposes:

> While I do not believe that we need to go all the way to the position of the Eastern Church, which views the priest as the sole minister of the sacrament of marriage, I do believe that we need to go beyond the established Western position, which sees the priest or deacon as merely a legal witness. We need to see him as a *co-minister* ... Such a development I believe is legitimate. It is also necessary to proclaim that Christian marriage is not just a private matter for the intended spouses, but is also a public matter for the entire Church, whose covenant with Christ they are to symbolize in their marriage. (*Secular Marriage, Christian Sacrament*, pp. 78–9).

52 See Rahner and Vorgrimler, *Concise Theological Dictionary*, pp. 350–1.

53 Mackin, *Divorce and Remarriage*, pp. 335–48.

54 *Summa Contra Gentiles*, Book 4, chapter 78, cited by Mackin, *Divorce and Remarriage*, p. 347.

55 See *Divorce and Remarriage*, pp. 347–8.

56 This is based on the *Conclusio* of Distinction 27, Question 1, Article 1 in Bonaventure's *Commentary on the Sentences*: Mackin, *What Is Marriage?*, footnote 16, p. 184.

57 Mackin quotes Scotus' *Commentary on the Sentences* (Distinction 26, Question 1, Article 8):

> Marriage is an indissoluble bond between a man and wife arising from the mutual exchange of authority over one another's bodies for the procreation and proper nurture of children.
> The contract of marriage is the mutual exchange by a man and wife of their bodies for perpetual use in the procreation and proper nurture of children. (*Divorce and Remarriage*, p. 355)

58 See Lawler, *Secular Marriage, Christian Sacrament*, p. 37.

59 Neuner and Dupuis, no. 1803; DS 1327.

60 Neuner and Dupuis, no. 1814; DS 1807.

61 Haec mitior damnationis forma electa est, ne Graeci offenderentur, qui etsi contrariam praxim sequebantur, tamen doctrinam Ecclesiae Latinae ipsis oppositam non reprobabant. (Denzinger–Schönmetzer, p. 416)

62 *The Code of Canon Law: A Text and Commentary*, ed. James A. Coriden and others (London: Geoffrey Chapman, 1985). See Doyle's comments on Canons 1085 (pp. 766–7) and 1134 (pp. 808–9). Further references to this volume will be abbreviated to CCL-USA.

63 DTC: *Dictionnaire de théologie catholique*.

64 Augustine had certainly laid the foundations for this teaching, but he had located the indestructible nature of Christian marriage in the baptisms of the spouses rather than in the bond itself. See Mackin, *Divorce and Remarriage*, p. 180.

65 There is a certain irony in the fact that the Eastern Churches, retaining a belief that the sacramental bond might be eternal and thus obviating the possibility of a second sacramental marriage, permit second non-sacramental marriages.

66 *The Catechism of the Catholic Church*, English translation for United Kingdom (London: Geoffrey Chapman, 1994).

67 In dealing with the question of divorce the Catechism surprisingly designates a remarried spouse as being 'in a situation of public and permanent adultery' (2384). Such uncompromising language seems to run counter to most of the statements of the magisterium in recent years, most notably those in *Familiaris Consortio* (84), which acknowledge that some people enter further relationships for understandable reasons. I can only invite the reader to note the tension.

68 See 'The First Letter to the Corinthians' in *The New Jerome Biblical Commentary*, 49:38. (References to this work in this form are to chapter and section numbers.)

69 See 'The First Letter to the Corinthians' in *The Jerome Biblical Commentary*, 51:40.

70 See 'Marriage' in CCL-USA, p. 814. (CIC: Codex Iuris Canonici.)

71 For a commentary, see Ladislas Örsy, *Marriage in Canon Law: Texts and Comments; Reflections and Questions* (Leominster: Fowler Wright, 1988), pp. 215–23.

72 *Marriage in Canon Law*, p. 222. Örsy adds his own footnote: 'There is a classical description for such occurrences: *inelegans lex*, the law lacks elegance.'

73 See Örsy, *Marriage in Canon Law*, pp. 223–8.

74 See Kevin Kelly, *Divorce and Second Marriage* (London: Collins, 1982), pp. 34, 46–8.

75 For the full text and comments, see *Marriage in Canon Law*, pp. 229–31.

76 See Mackin, *Divorce and Remarriage*, pp. 303–5.
77 To see how Aquinas tried to theologize this concept, see Elliott, *What God Has Joined* ..., p. 16.
78 Neuner and Dupuis, *Catholic Church*, no. 1813; DS 1806.
79 The Council of Trent stated:

> If anyone says that the married state surpasses that of virginity or celibacy, and that it is not better and happier to remain in virginity or celibacy than to be united in matrimony (cf. Matthew 19:11f; 1 Corinthians 7:25f, 38, 40), *anathema sit.*

See Neuner and Dupuis, no. 1817; DS 1810.
80 'It is therefore quite clear that all Christians in any state or walk of life are called to the fullness of Christian life and to the perfection of love' (LG 40).
81 See Mackin, *The Marital Sacrament*, pp. 161–4.
82 This tradition is powerfully expressed in the letter of Diognetus (second or third century):

> Christians do not live apart ... nor are they, like some, adherents of this or that school of human thought. Like other men, they marry and beget children. (Cited in *The Divine Office: The Liturgy of the Hours According to the Roman Rite* (3 vols; London: Collins, 1974), II, p. 590)

83 The decree *Tametsi* concluded:

> The council declares and makes incapable of contracting marriage any persons who attempt to do so without having as witnesses the pastor of the place, or some priest delegated by this pastor or by the ordinary, along with two or three other witnesses. The council declares marriages attempted without these witnesses to be null and void. (Cited in Mackin, *What Is Marriage?*, p. 197)

84 See Mackin, *What Is Marriage?*, pp. 197–8. See also the interesting footnote 5, which highlights a loophole in the law that did not require prior notification of the marriage and was not rectified until the 1983 Code. Örsy in *Marriage in Canon Law* also deals with the history of canonical form, pp. 156–60.
85 See CCL-USA, p. 793.
86 Canons 1094–1103. CIC 1917.
87 CIC 1917. Canon 1099.
88 See CCL-USA, p. 793.
89 The details of this debate are documented in Mackin, *The Marital Sacrament*, pp. 450–515.
90 CIC. Canon 1012.2.
91 Pope Pius XII, 29 April 1942 (in *Papal Teachings: Matrimony*, p. 347), cited by Mackin, *Divorce and Remarriage*, p. 448.
92 Much of the new sexual freedom has been linked with the availability of relatively safe contraceptives. It is interesting that in spite of the Church's continuing condemnation of the use of contraceptives, the statistics indicate that the majority of Catholics have made up their own minds on this matter. See Michael Hornsby-Smith, *Roman Catholic Beliefs in England* (Cambridge: Cambridge University Press, 1991), pp. 168–77.
93 See Örsy, *Marriage in Canon Law*, pp. 54–8, 268–70; Lawler, *Secular Marriage, Christian Sacrament*, pp. 61–8.
94 Elliott, *What God Has Joined* ..., pp. 192–9.

3

Pastoral options

In this chapter I will present two case histories from my pastoral experience. In doing so I will be able to introduce many of the current pastoral questions which will be addressed in the chapters which follow.

The first case introduces the annulment process and the work of the diocesan tribunals. It will refer to the grounds for annulling marriages, including the psychological ones covered by Canon 1095. It will also refer to the circumstances in which the Church authorities can dissolve a marriage, namely when it is not a sacrament and when it is not consummated.

The second case introduces the problems which arise when someone wishes to become a Roman Catholic, but being divorced, would be barred from Holy Communion.

Both case histories raise questions of justice and legal equity, and also the possibility of pastoral solutions in the *internal forum* when the *external forum* of the Church tribunal is unable to resolve the problem.[1]

A divorced Anglican seeks marriage with a Catholic

Some years ago Susan, a student nurse, 20 years of age, married David, a young doctor, aged 25. They married in an Anglican church, though neither was a committed churchgoer. They had known one another for 18 months and had lived together for some time prior to the wedding. The marriage lasted two years and the parting was not amicable. There were no children of the marriage. The divorce was granted on the statutory grounds of irreconcilable differences following a two-year separation. Susan met Patrick, an unmarried Roman Catholic, and they wished to marry in the Catholic Church.

The only way of resolving the situation officially was if it could be established that Susan's marriage to David was either invalid or non-sacramental in the eyes of the Catholic Church. In the majority of cases this can be achieved only by lengthy nullity procedures, which require evidence from witnesses and if possible both partners of the failed marriage.

However, given certain sets of circumstances it is possible to escape this lengthy process, and it was those circumstances which I sought to check first, hoping that one or other legal solution would be available.

The most easily resolvable situation is that which entails *lack of canonical form*.[2] If it could have been established that either Susan or David had by chance been baptized in a Catholic church, even though previously they might have been quite unaware of the fact, then their marriage, without permission of the Catholic authorities, in a church of another denomination, would have been rendered invalid.

In such circumstances the only requirements are certificates to prove a Catholic baptism and a copy of the registration document, followed by an investigation that the marriage had not been convalidated in the Catholic churches where the couple had lived during the time of their marriage.

Such declarations of nullity can be speedily processed through a diocesan office, because they do not require a judicial process, but merely an administrative one.[3]

Unfortunately neither Susan nor David had been baptized in the Catholic Church.

The second possible solution was that the marriage might have been *non-sacramental* if either Susan or David had not been baptized. This would not be as straightforward a process as lack of canonical form, because the Church would not be declaring the marriage invalid, but, through the exercise of either the Pauline or Petrine privilege, dissolving the existing bond in favour of the faith on the grounds that it was not sacramental.[4] Such cases can take time and have to be processed through Rome, but do not require the extensive collection of evidence from witnesses, which the ordinary annulment process requires.

Both Susan and David had been baptized and therefore the Catholic Church did regard their marriage as sacramental.

In today's society it is exceptional but not unique for a marriage to remain unconsummated by an act of sexual intercourse. Since the twelfth century *non-consummation* has provided grounds for the dissolution of the bond of marriage.[5] Susan and David's marriage had been consummated.

Having determined that none of these solutions was available, the only alternative was to explore the possibility of *an annulment* according to the usual procedures.

The annulment process is designed to determine whether there is anything defective in the consent of the couple, which would render their marriage invalid.[6] Susan was informed that if she considered this was the right course to follow it would entail the taking of lengthy evidence from her as well as from witnesses whom she would be asked to nominate, and that her former husband would be asked to co-operate as well.

Initially Susan seemed bewildered that the Catholic Church demanded so much information about a marriage which of itself had no Catholic connections. She accepted and agreed with the fundamental concern of the Church to protect the institution of marriage and its permanence. She could not understand why the Church regarded her marriage as a sacrament, when neither she nor her husband had understood it to be one or intended it to be one, and nor had the denomination in which the marriage had taken place regarded it as one.

I recall that Patrick was as bemused as Susan when we first began to explore the possibilities of resolving their problem. It is understandable that people fail to understand why certain actions create certain effects which were not the intentions of the participants nor anticipated by them.

At least with the annulment process the intentions of those involved are examined. Susan could see that if there was something defective in that original consent, then the contract had not been truly effected. She decided to petition the tribunal.

Susan's story revolved around two crucial factors. One was that during the time she and David were living together she had suffered a miscarriage, and this left her with a deep sense of loss and guilt: psychological problems that seemed not to have been resolved. She spoke of feeling frightened within herself and said she felt she owed it to this child to have something tangible to mark what would have been its birthday.

The other factor was Susan's uncertainty prior to the wedding about her decision to marry. She declared that she felt bemused at the way things took off until in the end it all seemed unreal and remote: she found herself mentally disengaged from the proceedings. Her anxiety was such that she made a verbal pact with David that if the marriage did not work out, divorce would be an option.

I was moderately confident that these two factors coupled with the fact that she was still a young student at the time of the marriage would provide sufficient grounds for the tribunal to come to a decision in her favour.

However there were difficulties. Susan had indicated that her former husband almost certainly would not be co-operative and this proved to be so. His interpretation of events revolved around a belief that Patrick was the cause of the breakdown, something which Susan strenuously and consistently denied. At first David refused to be associated with the annulment process, but later he responded to a formal citation from the tribunal with an angry letter.

A further difficulty was that Susan's witnesses did not add much weight to her cause. Susan was a young woman who did not easily share her innermost thoughts and feelings, and her family and friends would not necessarily have been in a position to corroborate her story at that level. For example, her own father, when questioned about her anxiety on the day of the wedding, explained that he presumed that she had suffered a normal attack of nerves and so persuaded her to go ahead. However, all Susan's witnesses testified to the fact that she was 'honest, reliable and truthful'.

In the event the tribunal judges argued that they did not have the moral certainty they required to grant an annulment under the heading of *an intention against the permanence of marriage*, and the plea also failed under the heading of *lack of due discretion*.[7] In coming to that verdict they argued that they could not ignore the evidence that meeting a fellow student a year or so after her wedding led Susan to leave her husband.

Although no further evidence was asked for, the tribunal granted that the case was worthy of an appeal to another tribunal. An appeal was lodged, but it failed.

During the period in which the annulment was being processed Patrick and Susan regularly attended Mass and they continued to attend after the appeal had failed. I look back on that period and wonder about the pastoral opportunities missed. Patrick admits that he had not been a totally committed Catholic, but the ties were strong enough for him to want what was right, and it was important for him to be at peace with his family. For her part, Susan could not have been more co-operative.

Here are some of the questions which the process could not resolve.

(a) *After the tribunals had made their decisions, could we be absolutely certain that Susan's first marriage was a valid marriage?* Of course we could not. Tribunals accept that their decisions are fallible and open to human error.

(b) *Even if it had been a true marriage, what good could be served now by refusing to let Patrick and Susan share their lives together?* Their love for one another had grown and matured through the experience of co-operating with the Church. At the same time there was no possibility that Susan and David could be reconciled.

(c) *How could the marriage of Patrick and Susan cause a scandal in the Catholic community?* There had been every reason to hope that an annulment would be granted, so no one would have been surprised if it had been granted, and subsequently they had married in the Catholic Church.

(d) *Did the Church require Patrick and Susan to go their separate ways?* In view of the fact that Pope John Paul II calls upon 'pastors and the whole community of the faithful to help the divorced' (FC 84), and acknowledges the presence of people in irregular unions in the Catholic community, we can conclude that such a drastic step could not be demanded.

It remains a great dilemma for pastors to know what to say to young people in such situations. Most of the available advice given by theologians and spiritual advisers and even by the magisterium relates to couples already in established second unions, evidently living a life of fidelity and bringing the children up in the faith. Little is said about how to help people at the time when they are entering into a so-called irregular union.

(e) *Since Susan had acknowledged throughout that the difficult situation of her first marriage was partly, perhaps even largely, of her own making, how could the Catholic Church offer her the opportunity to repent of that failure?*

(f) *Would the only way she could validly repent in the eyes of the Catholic Church be through a life of celibacy?*

When this research was being planned I made arrangements to interview Susan and Patrick.[8] Subsequently they had married, finding 'a young open-minded Anglican priest' to officiate at the ceremony.[9]

Patrick feels bitter about what happened and cannot understand the reasoning behind the Church's position. Susan too fails to comprehend why it did not work out for them.

Eventually they adopted their first child, and he was baptized in the Catholic Church.[10] The occasion was more than the baptism of a little child, it was also a service of reconciliation. For the first time Patrick and Susan and their families had been brought together for a public celebration in the Catholic Church. Their relationship is growing and maturing; indeed gradually it is falling into the category of those which Pope John Paul II and the bishops urge the whole Church to support. It is to be hoped that they will experience that support and strength, and that Andrew and any future children will bind them together in faith and love.

The final questions that demand our attention as we close this story must be: *Was this a missed pastoral opportunity for the Church? Is it possible that had there been another forum in which from the very beginning the Church could have ministered to Patrick and Susan, their faith could have been nurtured and they could have been spared the burdens which have been placed upon them?*

A remarried mother seeks reception into the Catholic Church

The second case history concerns a family who became involved with the Catholic Church through the Rite of Christian Initiation of Adults (RCIA). The mother was the first to enquire about becoming a Catholic.

RCIA was in its third year in her parish. In those early days the parish had no system for determining the marital status of enquirers or candidates: it was presumed that such information would be forthcoming in the normal course of events.

Pauline was part of an enthusiastic group, five of whom asked to be received into full communion the following Easter. The parish in general was becoming familiar with RCIA as the welcoming of new members became more a community and therefore public event. This was particularly significant in Pauline's case because she was a well-known public figure.

The marital complications of Pauline's past life did not come to light until a few days before she was due to be received into the Church at the Easter Vigil. To understand the pastoral complexity of this situation it will be helpful to summarize her story as she described it in an interview for this research.[11]

Formerly Pauline had been an active member of the Church of England, but when she married Michael after her first marriage had failed, she consulted her Anglican vicar about the possibility of receiving Holy Communion and was told that this would not be permitted.[12] Michael had also been divorced, but he too was a religious person and they looked for a church where they would be made welcome and where they could fully participate. For some years they were active members of the local Methodist Church, but after the death of the minister they found it difficult to relate to his successor.

At the same time Pauline began to experience a deep spiritual darkness partly connected with her career and what she described as the amoral behaviour of those with whom she was working. It was at this time that she had an intense awakening and approached the Catholic Church. She recalled being confused about the Catholic Church's position on divorce.

> I had thought that I would not be allowed into the Church as a divorced person except that I had previously ... in about three or four different places read about people – ... and I cannot quote you chapter and verse now – who were quite prominent members of the Catholic Church who had had previous marriages.

It was encouraging to hear her speak of the welcome she experienced and her sense of belonging: it seems as though RCIA did accomplish in her much of what it was designed to achieve, and her enthusiasm was soon to influence other members of her large family. The two younger sons regularly went to Mass with her and subsequently attended catechism classes and were received into full communion. The following year Michael, her husband, asked to be received into the Church. At the time of the interview Pauline's eldest daughter was engaged to a Catholic and was herself under instruction at university. All the evidence pointed to Christ's presence in the home, nurturing and deepening the faith of this family.

Pauline's situation came to light only in the internal forum of sacramental reconciliation. The pastoral problem was immediate and acute.

It could be argued that such a situation would not have arisen if discreet enquiries had been made early in the RCIA process, but, as will be evident from the data in Chapter 6, this problem is often addressed by RCIA teams only after they have had to deal with it at first hand.

It is already evident from our first case history that Catholic procedures can be lengthy and complicated and they do not guarantee a positive judgement. Even a straightforward documentary case of lack of canonical form cannot be processed in a few days. The only possible solution was in the privacy of the internal forum.

The supreme law of the Church is the salvation of souls (Canon 1752) and where a specific situation is not legislated for then it may be necessary to invoke Canon 19.

If on a particular matter there is not an express provision of either universal or particular law, nor a custom, then, provided it is not a penal matter, the question is to be decided by taking into account laws enacted in similar matters, the general principles of law observed with canonical equity, the jurisprudence and practice of the Roman Curia, and the common and constant opinion of learned authors.

Firstly we should note the legal anomaly. Pauline was not yet a Catholic, yet she had been invited to celebrate the Catholic sacrament of penance in accordance with the official directive of the Church.[13] In that sacrament the priest was strictly bound to secrecy by the seal (Canon 983) and therefore could say or do nothing which might betray her situation. Had she not been received into full communion with the Church at the Easter Vigil, this could have aroused suspicion and been interpreted as such a betrayal. Also, as a development she was wholly ill-prepared for, it might have left her in bad faith for the rest of her life.[14]

Pauline later explained that she did not confess her marital situation as a sinful situation, but included it as part of her story by way of putting her confession into context. RCIA is designed so that people can see the grace of God working in their lives: they learn to understand and tell their stories.

According to Urrutia the criterion of distinction between the *external forum* and *internal forum* 'is seen to be the hidden or public manner of acting'. He explains: 'The forums are not separate spheres without any mutual relationship, and therefore a solution given for the internal forum can be based on the norms for the external forum.'[15] Pauline's case can hardly be said to have been resolved according to that criterion. Faced with the immediacy of the problem the question of the validity or invalidity of Pauline's first marriage was irrelevant.

However, the delicacy of her position and the Church's teaching especially in regard to the dangers of misunderstanding and scandal were discussed with her during the sacrament of reconciliation. She was absolved of her sins and received into full communion with the Catholic Church. This pastoral solution was based on the fact that she was in good faith and her ignorance was not culpable. St Alphonsus de Liguori, the founder of the Redemptorists and the patron of confessors and moral theologians, teaches categorically that in cases of invincible ignorance liberty is in possession.[16]

Michael was deeply moved by the reception of his wife and the commitment of his younger children. He became involved in RCIA the following autumn and in due course sought reception into the Church.

This new development also required prudent handling. It transpired that Michael had also been married before, but ironically he had been baptized a Catholic, though never brought up in the Faith. It would have been possible to resolve his situation on the grounds of lack of canonical form without difficulty. However he was so inextricably caught up in Pauline's pastoral solution that it was necessary for them to be taken into each other's confidence before progress could be made.

Pauline gave permission for the resolution of her situation to be explained to Michael. Michael then became an extension of that pastoral solution. It is a measure of how conscientiously they co-operated that to the best of my knowledge no one knows anything of their circumstances to this day.

Were those the right decisions? Since receiving the permission of Pauline and Michael to share this story, I have consulted many canonists and theologians. I have met a variety of opinions, but most have agreed that the pastoral solutions arrived at are defensible.

Canon 19 offers the necessary criteria. In the first place the matters under consideration were not *penal*: they did not incur the penalty of excommunication.

Regarding the existence of laws enacted in similar matters, Canon 1080 concerns the dispensation from impediments when all is prepared for a wedding. The comparison I am drawing is not in the field of marriage law or the impediments to marriage, but where there would be danger of grave harm in postponing a ceremony.

Furthermore it is reasonable to invoke St Alphonsus and those who follow his moral imperatives as providing the required authority of learned authors.

Canonical equity demands that a just solution be found and there is certainly a probable argument that any solution other than the one arrived at, would have caused a grave injustice.

This leaves only the jurisprudence and practice of the Roman Curia. No official directive has yet been promulgated for these situations which remain under review. To date we have only a private directive to a particular hierarchy.[17]

I concede that there may still be those who would consider that the pastoral solution offered to Pauline and Michael, although in good faith, was actually incorrect. In the face of such a judgement, what would be the consequences regarding their full participation in the life of the Church today? Would it be necessary to inform them of such a mistake and deprive them of the sacraments? Such a decision is surely unthinkable, yet if we concede that they should be left in good faith, we must ask why so many others in comparable situations may not be admitted to the sacraments?

In the course of this study this is the kind of question which will be asked repeatedly. The questions arise not because the Church is harsh in its judgement of individuals, but because two ideologies are in conflict. On the one hand there is the interpretation of the Scholastic theology of the bond, designed to defend the indissolubility of marriage and guide people to a right way of living in conformity with God's will as reflected in the natural order and revealed in the Scriptures: a static and principled way of interpreting and directing people's lives. On the other hand there is the existential situation of people's lives which includes the experiences of failure and sin, and calls for the forgiveness and hope also revealed in the Scriptures.

If the Lord taught that the Father's will is that men and women should remain faithful to one another in permanent marriages (Luke 16:18), he also taught that there is no limit to forgiveness (Luke 17:4). Furthermore we contemplate that at the heart of the gospel is the mystery that through death we come to resurrection (John 12:23–25). It would seem that at the experiential level many people only begin to understand the mystery of the death/resurrection theme when they themselves have suffered some traumatic loss, sometimes in the form of the *death* of a marriage.

Summary

In the two case histories recorded in this chapter we have been able to reflect the experiences of people, struggling to understand themselves and seeking to find Christ in their lives. There is no doubt that the Church, the official magisterial Church, wants to reach out to them and lead them to Christ, which is why so many pastoral solutions have been sought in the face of marital breakdown since the time of the apostles. At the same time the Church wishes to remain faithful to Christ's call to fidelity and permanence in marriage, fearing that any relaxation in the law may be a cause of scandal and lead others into error. The tension is severe because the two ideals are the expressions of different philosophies and therefore are couched in different languages. Part of the work of this study is to seek a meeting place and a language which can unite them.

Notes

1   The substantial details of the two case histories are factual, though pseudonyms have been used and other details changed to protect the anonymity of those concerned. The tradition of the Canon Law Society of Great Britain and Ireland in their annual publication for private circulation only, *Matrimonial Decisions of Great Britain and Ireland* (gen. ed. Mgr Ralph Brown, Westminster Matrimonial Tribunal, Vaughan House, 46 Francis Street, London SW1P 1QN), is to 'camouflage' the Decisions (see Preface of vol. 26 (1990), p. i).

2   Canonical form refers to the *form* of marriage required for validity of all those baptized in the Catholic Church or received into the Catholic Church (Canons 1108–1123; note especially Canon 1117).

3   See Canon 1086 and the commentary in CCL-USA, p. 1015.

4   The canons relating to the Pauline privilege are 1143–1150. The Petrine privilege is not legislated for in the Code of Canon Law. The directives governing its use were revised by the Sacred Congregation for the Doctrine of the Faith and promulgated in a *motu proprio*, 6 December 1973 (CDF *prot. no.* 2717/68): see Brown, *Marriage Annulment in the Catholic Church* (3rd edn; Rattlesden: Kevin Mayhew, 1990), pp. 193–9. For explanations of both the privileges see pp. 171–81.

5   See Canon 1142.

6   Brown, *Marriage Annulment*, explains that 'the essence of marriage is the consent of the parties' (p. 13) and that 'consequently, when grounds for nullity are dealt with in the code they are placed in the chapter dealing with "Marital Consent". Each ground concerns some aspect that would take away, in whole or part or affect, the consent required to marriage' (pp. 19–20).

7   For an explanation of these grounds, see Brown, *Marriage Annulment*, pp. 51–7, 92–100.

8   The interview took place at their home on 1 February 1990.

9   In *Anglican Marriage in England and Wales: A Guide to the Law for the Clergy* (London: The Faculty Office of the Archbishop of Canterbury, 1992) it states:

> The Church of England follows the law of the land as regards capacity to marry. The fact that a clergyman may be free from any obligation to solemnize the marriage of a person whose marriage has been dissolved by a Court in the United Kingdom does not alter the fact that such a person is, in law, free to marry. The Church will recognise the validity of such second marriages and clergy are legally free to solemnize them, even though the Convocation of Canterbury expressed the view in 1957 that the Church should not allow the use of the Marriage Service in such cases, and many clergy consequently decline to officiate. (p. 27)

> This is cited by Edward Hone in an unpublished master's thesis, 'Divorce and remarriage in the Church of England: the contemporary debate in context' (Kent University, 1986). Hone examined the deep divisions in the Church of England on this question; divisions which, despite the directive above, remain unresolved.

10   Canon law insists that for lawful infant baptism, it is required

> that there be a well-founded hope that the child will be brought up in the
> catholic religion. If such hope is truly lacking, the baptism is, in accordance
> with the provisions of particular law, to be deferred and the parents advised of
> the reason for this. (CCL-GBI, Canon 868.1.2)

This law leaves room for manoeuvre and, although Patrick was no longer practising regularly, with the support and encouragement of the extended family, there
remained every hope that the child would be brought up in the Faith.

11   Interview with Pauline and her husband Michael at their home on 4 January 1991.

12   Hone states:

> In 1982 the General Synod rescinded the Convocation regulations of 1957
> (Canterbury) and 1938 (York) which made it the responsibility of the diocesan
> bishop to admit (or refuse to admit) to Holy Communion any person who had
> remarried after divorce. (General Synod, *Report of Proceedings*, 13:3
> (November 1982), pp. 770–7.) ('Divorce and remarriage in the Church of
> England', p. 135)

Pauline had consulted her vicar before this change in the discipline.

13   'If the profession of faith and reception take place within Mass, the candidates,
according to their own conscience, should confess their sins beforehand':
International Commission on English in the Liturgy, A Joint Commission of
Catholic Bishops' Conferences, *Documents on the Liturgy, 1963–1979: Conciliar,
Papal, and Curial Texts* (Collegeville, MN: The Liturgical Press, 1982), p. 760.

14   During the interview Pauline said:

> I have to say that if at that point I had been told that I could not have been
> received into the Catholic Church, I think I would never have set foot inside
> the door of a Christian church again.

15   Francisco Javier Urrutia SJ in *Vatican II: Assessment and Perspectives, Twenty-
Five Years After*, ed. René Latourelle (3 vols; New York: Paulist Press, 1988), p.
634.

16   See the discussion of St Alphonsus' teaching on *equi-probabilism* in Bernard
Häring, *Shalom:Peace: The Sacrament of Reconciliation* (New York: Image Books,
Doubleday and Company, Inc., 1969), pp. 56–9.

17   See pp. 147–8 below.

4

The support groups

I will begin this chapter by giving a brief account of the history of the three main support groups, the Association of Separated and Divorced Catholics (ASDC), the Rainbow Groups in Liverpool and the Beginning Experience (BE).

The Association of Separated and Divorced Catholics

In the spring of 1981, a layman, Joe McClelland, responded to an anguished letter in the Catholic press by inviting the separated and divorced Catholics of Manchester to meet and discuss their situations. A public meeting was attended by 120 people and compassionately addressed by Fr Bernard Gardiner, a Jesuit.

A pioneer group of ASDC was formed and by the end of that same year the Bishops' Conference had given the Association its blessing, entrusting it to the care of the Bishop of Salford.

There followed a gradual expansion. By March 1986 30 groups were running in different parts of the country and by the end of 1994 the number had increased to 64, with a total membership of nearly 700.

In a moving article in the *Catholic Herald* to mark the tenth anniversary of ASDC, Cecilia Hull (now deceased), who was the founder of the London group, described the purpose of the organization, not in terms of an agreed objective, but rather as a lived experience:

> It immediately became obvious that the main causes of distress for the divorced Catholic were isolation, guilt, and a widespread ignorance of the real teaching of the church on divorce and annulment. The best way to alleviate this pain, the fledgling organisation found, was for fellow sufferers to meet together in self help groups, and to discover,

through sharing experiences, that they were not unique, that as many Catholic marriages break up as those of other denominations or none, that it is possible to live through such a disaster and come out stronger and wiser people. It was important to recognise that few people wilfully and cynically walk out of marriages, that many people struggle on in hopeless situations which simply cannot be described as that of man and wife, and that those who do break apart may well qualify for an annulment.[1]

Today the Association is a registered charity (No. 701160) and is able to describe its aims precisely:

To provide spiritual and practical support through self help groups. Members are committed to help others especially those in the early stages of separation or divorce.

Through talks on such topics as separations, divorce, annulment, indissolubility of marriage, second marriages, internal forum and sacraments for the remarried, members are informed of the Church's teaching.

To emphasise that the Catholic although divorced is not alone, is not a failure but is still an equal member of the Church. Through his/her experience the divorced Catholic can emerge with greater personal strengths, a more profound faith, a deeper compassion and a determination to build life contributing positively to the life of the Church and society.

To converse with the Church.

To establish the ASDC as an active organisation within the parish.

To permit membership to all separated and divorced Catholics whatever their circumstances.

To help members to come to terms with being on their own, to gain confidence and to face the world again.

To encourage the Association to grow through the formation of local branches.[2]

From the outset ASDC has sought to establish good relations with the hierarchy. The presence of Cardinal Hume at the 1986 Conference in London is still remembered as a significant moment of recognition. In his address he spoke of *the soul* of the association and his comments are now included in their prayer card:

In every human life there is a story, which no-one knows or fully understands, not even ourselves; but THAT story IS KNOWN and entirely UNDERSTOOD by God . . . never forget that. The counsel that he gives is direct to those who open themselves up to see it, and the comfort that he gives to those who can't do that, is the support and understanding that you give each other, and THAT, as I understand it, is the SOUL of your association ... it is a beautiful and simple thought ... THE COMFORT OF GOD IS COMPLETED IN EACH OF YOU BY THE OTHERS AROUND YOU.

There is a genuine concern within the executive that the Association should maintain its good relationship with the hierarchy and not develop into some form of pressure group, lobbying the bishops for change. The majority want to keep the original vision of providing mutual support and encouragement within the Catholic tradition.[3] This is easier said than done. If one of your stated aims is 'to permit membership to all separated and divorced Catholics *whatever their circumstances*' [the italics are mine], at the very least you are inviting to come forward those who may have deep grievances with the Church and who may feel the need to express them.

A non-judgemental openness to everyone is a characteristic hallmark of all the support groups, a hallmark which does not sit easily beside the Church's refusal to readmit to eucharistic Communion divorced persons in irregular second unions. The fact that this issue keeps surfacing should be no surprise, for around it much of the tension exists.

At the 1992 ASDC National Conference in Wolverhampton Bishop Christopher Budd praised the non-judgemental approach as the 'best in the repertoire of the pastoral care of the Church'.[4] However when he reflected on the witness of ASDC to the wider community he speculated on the possibility that just as 'catechumens' have become an identifiable group again, so 'penitents' might become the same. Here, he thought, ASDC could provide an example for the whole community.

It is a delicate question and the analogy cannot be taken to its logical conclusion because in the case of the invalidly married the penitent is not permitted to make satisfaction and rejoin the eucharistic community.[5]

At that same conference there was a powerful presentation on the subject by Dr Kieran Moriarty, a consultant physician and gastroenterologist, who spoke from his experience of marriage and personal breakdown. He remarried with the blessing of the Church, but what he said reflected his concern for so many fellow ASDC members who are not free.

Many of us have endured, do endure, and will always have to endure, pain and suffering of such severity, that it requires no description to anyone who experiences it, and yet could not possibly be adequately described to anyone who has not. There is one reason, and one reason only, why we suffer as we do, namely because we believed in, we hoped in, and above all, we cherished, both the concept, and the very essence, of the absolute sanctity and indissolubility of marriage and family life ...

Of course, it may not be a sin to remarry or it may be forgivable. It may be possible to prove the nullity of the first marriage or the Internal Forum Solution may be sought. If neither of these is applicable, however, a remarried Catholic is forbidden to receive the Sacraments of Penance and Holy Eucharist for the rest of their life, with the exception of the Sacrament of the Sick.[6]

In 1972, Cardinal Joseph Ratzinger, who has since become the Head of the Sacred Congregation for the Doctrine of the Faith in Rome, wrote 'the concession of communion to a remarried couple cannot depend on an act that would be either immoral (i.e. terminating the marriage) or factually impossible (i.e. for the couple to be permanently celibate)'.[7]

The physical impossibility and undesirability of lifelong celibacy for a normal, healthy, loving couple was also clearly recognized by Pope Gregory II when he said: 'Magnorum est' – which translates – 'it is beyond the ordinary strength of a married couple to be permanently celibate'.[8] Sadly, in the past, Pope John Paul II has favoured the so-called 'brother and sister solution' and has not been able to accept Pope Gregory's pronouncement, which is of course known to be true by all who fully understand the feelings, biology and lifeforce of a normal, healthy, loving, marital relationship.

Consider, please, those sacred words which we say just before we decide whether we shall receive the Holy Eucharist: 'Lord, I am not worthy to receive you, but only say the word, and I shall be healed.' We communicate, not because we are worthy, but because we are not worthy ...

In truth, many know that divorced and remarried Catholics are just as worthy or unworthy as any other Catholics. 'You say the word and I shall be healed.' We must all learn to listen more carefully, for God may well choose that moment to speak to us . . . There can be no more sacred Internal Forum.

For those who cannot receive the Eucharist, please remember Spiritual Communion, the Sacrament of Desire.

[Dr Moriarty furnished me with the text of his address. I have added notes 6, 7, and 8.]

This passage, like the whole address, is carefully worded. Dr Moriarty had obviously gone to a lot of trouble to measure his presentation so that he could reach out to all his audience. He was not recommending that people should ignore the law; he was careful to stay within the ASDC tradition of not being confrontational, but, like Bishop Budd before him, he sought some meaning in a highly charged and often incomprehensible state of affairs.

The Rainbow Groups

Unlike ASDC the Rainbow Groups were not founded by the laity, but were an official ecclesiastical response to the problem of broken marriages in the Archdiocese of Liverpool. Effectively they now fulfil the same purpose as ASDC groups.

The history of the Rainbow Groups dates back to 1982.[9] Like ASDC it was a response to a growing need. With the support of Archbishop Worlock and under the direction of the Department of Pastoral Formation a pilot project was begun at St Monica's, Bootle. The first meeting was on 17 June 1982 and provided 'for people who were divorced and feeling isolated as a result of that experience'.[10] In due course the clergy of the diocese were informed of its progress and encouraged to establish new groups. At the end of 1994 there were fifteen active groups, each with its own chaplain, ten other contact persons and a diocesan co-ordinator.

The original correspondence sent to the clergy about Rainbow is revealing. It contrasted its aims with those of ASDC:

Our understanding of the situation was that a small group, personal approach was more suited to the personal needs of people who have experienced failure in their marriage, rather than the public approach of the Association. (Archdiocese of Liverpool: Department of

Pastoral Formation, 12 January 1983)

The original aims of the organization were as follows:

1. A group run by lay people and priests with the support of the Archdiocese, for the spiritual and practical support of the separated and divorced.
2. To recognize and meet the special needs of separated and divorced Catholics, and to be open also to include the non-Catholic partner of a marriage which has ended. Many such people struggle to bring up their children in the Catholic faith to prevent further upheaval; they need much support and encouragement.
3. The Rainbow Group will try to promote a sense of 'belonging', not as a separate group but as part of the whole Church. United in Christian love it will help people to continue their lives, cope with past hurt and live in their present reality with hope in the future. In order to do this the group will seek to provide, above all, the opportunity for its members to deepen their spiritual lives, and so contribute to the Church as a whole.
4. The Rainbow Group will seek to recognize that some people who have separated or divorced do not wish to join a group. The group will try to provide support and guidance on a one-to-one basis also.
5. The Rainbow Group will draw to itself the best helpers in the community, whether they have suffered marriage breakdown or not. Those with proven counselling skills and ability in spiritual leadership will be asked to contribute to the service offered by the group.
6. The Rainbow Group will establish links with other helping services to encourage the separated and divorced to support one another and offer their services to society at large. (Archdiocese of Liverpool: Department of Pastoral Formation, 1 February 1982)

Although there are many similarities between these aims and those of ASDC, Rainbow Groups are already defined within the ecclesial community and therefore do not have to seek 'converse with the Church'. There is an emphasis too on counselling and leadership: a service provided by the organization for those in need.

In practice there is little to distinguish the two organizations and they have developed a good working relationship. Those initial fears in Liverpool that ASDC might be too public and not sufficiently personal have proved to be unfounded. However one ironic difference between them is that the links with the hierarchical Church, which ASDC so carefully continues to nurture, are considered by some who minister in Rainbow unduly restrictive.

The Beginning Experience

The arrival of BE in England and Wales followed shortly after the birth of the other support groups. In 1983 Mrs Martha Freckleton, seeking support in the wake of the breakdown of her own marriage, followed up an advertisement for BE in a publication from North America, where it already existed.[11]

The response was swift and effective. In the autumn of the following year a training team of sixteen, largely from the United States but including one from Australia, came to England, paying its own way. The Passionists at Minsteracres provided the venue. Forty-one people, mainly from the North-East but also from other parts of Britain, participated and 24 of those returned the following weekend to be trained for the first British BE team.

The movement had begun in Texas in 1974, when Sr Josephine Stewart, who was a professional family counsellor, and Mrs Jo Lamia, who had been divorced, designed a programme to help those grieving the loss of a spouse through death, separation or divorce. The immediate catalyst for this had been a letter of closure [closing the relationship] to her partner, written by Mrs Lamia on a weekend family enrichment programme.

The BE programme was designed for Catholics and has its roots in the Catholic tradition and sacramental life, but it is also ecumenical, and has been open to people of all faiths from its inception.

It had spread quickly in the United States and numbers 125 teams there. In England the Hexham and Newcastle team remains strong, there is a team which serves London and teams have also formed in the dioceses of Arundel and Brighton, Leeds, Liverpool and Portsmouth. New teams have emerged in the Northampton and Plymouth dioceses and another in Kent.

Unlike ASDC and Rainbow, BE is a very intensive experience based on the principles of bereavement therapy.[12] Increasingly members of the other support groups are attending BE weekends and there are a number who remain involved with both BE and their original group. Others move to one of the other support groups after attending a BE weekend.

It should be noted that while BE is not mutually exclusive of the other two, it does demand a different kind of commitment. ASDC and Rainbow could be described as open-ended organizations, available to those who feel the need and find such group support helpful: they are organizations to which one may freely come and go. By contrast BE is a much more structured organization, believing that intervention is necessary to initiate a process of healing and restoration.

BE has helped to heal, strengthen and support thousands of people in different parts of the world. Perhaps because of the intensity of the ministry at a BE weekend, I became more conscious with this group than with any other that for some people the experience of marital breakdown can be the catalyst for a spiritual growth that they could not have anticipated.[13]

As with all growth it is usually long and painful and that is why BE has stages to mark the progress of its ministry. Nevertheless it is the confronting of the problem at the initial weekend which makes such healing and growth possible. And not only does it provide the setting for individual growth, but it also offers the community an opportunity to grow. For me, the most compelling moment of the weekend came at the service of reconciliation, when clergy from the different denominations publicly apologized for any hurt their Churches had caused. This simple demonstration of gospel humility created the atmosphere in which people were able to begin the process of forgiving and being forgiven.

Findings from the group meetings and interviews

Relating within the groups

From the very early days of the research it became clear that, given the opportunity, many people wanted to tell their stories again. Once an interview or group meeting warmed up much time could be spent on recalling the pain of lives that had become intolerably stressful in hopelessly unhappy marriages. They wanted me to know just how hard it had been. They wanted to be sure that I had understood and that I would faithfully report this truth to their bishops.

As Catholics they are not immune to the dreadful sense of failure and loss that comes from marital breakdown. As one ASDC member put it, 'I think sometimes the Catholic Church doesn't realize we are human as well as Catholic'. Indeed for many their faith only compounded their pain, for divorce was something they did not believe could or would happen to Catholics. An older man, whose family had grown up and who had done a lot of reading and reflecting since the breakdown of his marriage put it this way:

> When I got married ... there was love, honour, obey ... you know, you thought marriages were going to last for ever. You didn't question anything; everything was there: hell was there, heaven was there, the Church was there, ... I took the wife and kids to church every Sunday. If somebody said: 'he's divorced' ... ugh ... All of a sudden you are divorced ... I find I question everything now. (ASDC member)

It is clear then that separated and divorced Catholics need to be listened to, they need to know that someone cares for them and on a number of occasions I watched in admiration as groups tended to their suffering members. Over and over again I have heard people say that the group was their salvation, precisely because they were accepted unconditionally. A few examples will serve to illustrate this point:

> 'ASDC was a life-saver for me.'
> 'This is now home for me and these people are my family.' (Rainbow member)
> 'Being in ASDC ... helped me tremendously. It actually was the first part of anything in the way of the Catholic Church which recognized me and my family. Nobody else in the Catholic Church gave us any recognition as a family.'
> 'Absolutely marvellous.' (Five Rainbow members commenting on a BE weekend)

A trained counsellor, also a member of ASDC, spoke powerfully about the gospel value of this basic human ministry:

> I also found marriage breakdown covers so much really – I mean it covers loss of home, loss of children, health problems, alcoholism, homelessness – so all the people that are there in the Gospel are at an ASDC meeting ... They have usually been bounced off everywhere

else ... We're the ones who don't turn anyone away.

Such loving acceptance leads to honesty, which in turn enables people to discern the truth about themselves, and it is this truth which can set them free. Here they experience at first hand the power of the gospel of love, where people take Jesus at his word and do not judge, where people are given all the time they need to come to terms with themselves and their situations. People's spiritual lives really do grow very deeply in this situation of care and nurture.

People suffering the tragedy of marriage breakdown do not need to be reminded of what a social evil divorce is: they need to experience at first hand the warmth of a community which believes in the unconditional love of God, who can make all things new. And the irony is that many of those who took part in the research admitted that, prior to their marriages breaking down, they had failed to grasp this and had themselves looked down upon separated and divorced people. One ASDC member said:

> Before I was divorced I thought my marriage was very sound and would go on for ever. And I had a bigoted view towards divorced people. So I was one of the non-practising Catholic laity who would ... practise distancing from divorced people.

Most experienced a deeply ingrained prejudice against divorce in the Catholic community and, although the climate is changing, it is important to remember that when ASDC was founded in 1981 it was regarded by many with deep suspicion. It takes many years to remove such prejudices and broaden the horizons of a whole community.

Prior to the 1980s there was no recognized pastoral ministry for the separated and divorced within the Church community in Britain. The same was true for most other parts of the world. Individual priests and people may have been sympathetic and supportive, but in general it was a condition in which Catholics were not expected to find themselves. If they did, then it was regarded as unfortunate; there might be the possibility of an annulment, but otherwise they were expected to make the best of it.[14]

Today, with the rapid advances in modern psychology, we know that people are likely to be profoundly disturbed by the shock of marital breakdown and may need a great deal of counselling and support. While it would be wrong to apportion unreasonable blame to the Church author-ities for not having provided a network of support in the past, today there can be no excuse for continuing to ignore the problem or wish it would disappear.

There is evidence that if people do not find support in the Church community they will be forced to seek it elsewhere.[15] Indeed it has been argued by a number of commentators that the reason some people rush into second and third unsuccessful marriages is because they are searching for the solace which they have failed to find in their extended families and local communities. My own research does not offer any specific evidence one way or the other on that question, but it did uncover some important information regarding membership of the support groups in relation to their own objectives.

In ASDC in particular I found a real sensitiveness regarding the public perception of their society. Any suggestion that groups are like 'singles' clubs', providing a kind of dating service under the umbrella of the Church, causes deep offence. In the other two associations, perhaps because of their nature (Rainbow with its official diocesan status, and BE with its definite rehabilitation programme) I did not find the same sensi-tiveness to this problem.

It is a measure of the maturity that the groups have achieved that when occasionally new partnerships are formed within their ranks, they seem able to rejoice with the couple and support them. Linked to that I found that all three organizations possess a realism which acknowledges that they are not seeking life members: indeed the sooner people feel able to move on, the more successfully the associations consider they have done their work.

There was a great deal of discussion about those who do not seek support from one or other of the groups. They can be placed into three categories. Firstly, those who give up on the Church altogether as a result of the breakdown of their marriages, either because they are convinced that they have put themselves beyond the pale, or because they lose faith in a Church which cannot accommodate them. Secondly, those who have decided that the Church is out of touch and who make up their own minds.[16] Thirdly, those who, for a variety of reasons, are not attracted to a group. This last category cannot be overlooked. Most groups reported people coming just once. Often such people offered no explanation for not returning, so one can only surmise that they did not find the group helpful or more positively that they received what they wanted from that one meeting. Others actually indicated that they were not ready to share with the group.

A number of ASDC groups provide a service of private support through their chairperson or secretary, but this is not structured and works on an *ad hoc* basis. The Rainbow Groups, because they are dependent on the diocesan pastoral formation team and trained counsellors, necessarily have this back-up service in a more structured way. The work of their co-ordinator Sheila O'Neill in ensuring that information is disseminated and contacts followed up is clearly invaluable.

I conclude this section with a word of caution regarding the work of BE. Those who have entered deeply into the psychology of their situations and have grown through the painful processes of self-analysis may consider that this is the only way truly to recover from the trauma of marital breakdown. Understandably they will wish to promote the work of BE. However, the key to the process is freedom: a salvific freedom which is caught up in the mystery of Christ's death and resurrection. As with the faith, it cannot be forced or imposed. Modern psychology has uncovered many personality types and many stages of growth. The BE programme is intense and care should be taken that those who enter it are psychologically ready to cope with it. For some it will never be a wise option.

Relating to the wider Church

People's relationships with the group are built around the freedom which they have to share their own experiences, and therefore to be themselves. For many their experiences have much to do with the Church.

In the first place, those who come to such groups tend to be the ones who want to do the right thing by the Church; usually their religion means a great deal to them, and the pain of their marital breakdown is increased by the fact that it so deeply affects their relationship with the Church.

Secondly, there remains a remarkable level of ignorance about what the Church officially teaches on many issues. A surprising number of people still thought that civil divorce in itself excommunicated them;[17] at the other extreme there were one or two who actually thought that the Church had come round to accepting divorce.[18] It is a measure of how much work has to be done in clarifying and communicating the

Church's teaching that two such diametrically opposed perceptions can co-exist.

Between those extremes lie the mass of people. Among them there is nothing but confusion about what the Church now teaches and how their situations can be resolved. A recent convert at an ASDC meeting in Rochdale, who was immensely grateful for all the love and support she had received both from the group and the wider community of the Church, asked:

> I'm leading this life of celibacy. I don't know where I stand with the Church. Am I going to wreck my religion if I get involved with sexual relations?

And this is the third point: the majority of people seeking pastoral support from the Church are primarily concerned with where they now stand and how their situations can be resolved. They are not particularly interested in the niceties of theological or canonical argument: they want to know how they can rebuild their lives and remain in good standing with the Church.

We have seen that to provide the forum in which separated and divorced Catholics can address their problems successfully, the support groups must begin from a wholly non-judgemental position. While the hierarchical Church is beginning to acknowledge and even applaud this development, such acceptance will take much longer to become part and parcel of the ordinary life of the Church. Many do feel a deep sense of rejection. A typically sad comment was the following:

> You feel very isolated and you feel very much that you're something to be very wary of, certainly by the Church itself. I can't say that so much of the parishioners. But then again it is very difficult: people don't reach out to you, and you haven't got the energy, or the courage or the enthusiasm to search it out for yourself; so you are left very much on an island. The Church is there and there's an amazing amount of work to do and it is just not being touched. (Rainbow member)

Even where developments were taking place in the local church and new ministries opening up to the laity, it did not necessarily follow that the divorced would be found a place. An ASDC member in the North-West commented:

> The parish is run more or less completely by lay people. Where does somebody in a marriage breakdown situation fit in to that? I felt really pushed away by the situation in my own parish which is supposed to be a developed one. There was no lay support or support from our parish priest. It may be that it hasn't evolved enough and maybe the priest intends that we will have a group of our own.

Many members of the support groups are honest enough to admit that they are possibly oversensitive, but that is often true of people in vulnerable situations, and it does not excuse a lack of sensitivity towards them on the part of the wider Church community. Here I must stress what was a constant complaint against the clergy and the bishops: the ease with which, in their homilies and pastoral letters, they couple divorce with what they regard as the other social evils of our time, such as abortion, child abuse and violent crime, without any qualification or explanation. The Pope himself acknowledges that some divorced people are 'unjustly abandoned' (FC 84). But even when that is not the case many are making heroic efforts to keep going and to stay within the family of the Church. For that to go unrecognized can be deeply hurtful. Here is the way one interviewee expressed it:

> Being a member of ASDC and being trained as a counsellor – predominantly to help with divorced, divorced and remarried couples within the Catholic Church – I think the most hurtful point is the non-recognition; the non-recognition of them, the non-recognition of their families. And why it's most hurtful is they know it could be changed overnight if the real good-will was there from the bishops … It comes up over and over again at meetings and national assemblies … why can't bishops, when they come for Confirmation, pay recognition to this, acknowledge divorced people in the congregation; … pay recognition to the fathers who haven't been living with the children and have supported their children through Catholic education; pay recognition to the couples who are there together on Confirmation day. People and families in our position are always being told what we've failed at, but never what we've succeeded at.

Lack of sensitivity is one thing, suffering the hostility and prejudice of their fellow Catholics is another. Many members of the support groups reported that they had been ostracized, some even by their priests. A number reported that they had suffered verbal abuse from fellow parishioners and I was told of other occasions when posters in the church porches were either taken away, vandalized or smeared with graffiti. To one ASDC poster was added 'Try Harder'.

At the fundamental level of how the teaching Church can uphold the ideal and at the same time offer effective pastoral care, there were some excellent discussions in the groups. In Guildford there was a keenly contested exchange, occasioned by a woman who thought that time would force the Church to change its position. She began by arguing that history itself offered us different models of marriage, and she continued:

> People have said to me: 'any minute now the Catholic Church will recognize divorce', and I think they're right. I think they're going to have to. And unfortunately it is going to be forced on them from the bottom – you know, like a lot of things in the Church … and they will appear … to have done it too late.

This argument is employed by many people who believe that, just as the sea can erode the coastline, so the forces of change will have their way no matter what obstacles authority or society may try to erect to stop them. Since a key element of the Church's teaching and pastoral policy is built around the conviction that it must attempt to stem the rising tide of divorce, this aspect of the debate is of some significance.[19]

The above argument did not go unchallenged in the group. She was immediately asked: 'What does that do to the institution – to the ideal?' Likewise when someone else said that in 20 years' time it would be absolutely normal to have second relationships, others immediately asked: 'Does that make it right?' In other words there was a strong defence of the ideal and a recognition that the Church could 'get itself into a terrible tangle' by simply supporting every relationship that people wished to enter.

The teaching Church is rightly suspicious of the *ad hominem* argument which claims that change will be forced upon it because of the social conditions in which it finds itself.

Lest we lose sight of the argument, I wish to reaffirm at this juncture that this study is not seeking to argue that the dissolution of marriage and the possibility of remarriage should be made easier in the Catholic Church because of the high incidence of marital breakdown in society today. What is being argued is that the high incidence of marital breakdown is forcing the Church to reconsider its ministry in this field.

Just as the *ad hominem* argument above does not hold, neither does the one which insists that publicly the Church must maintain an uncompromising stand against divorce lest it lose its credibility in the eyes of society. The danger with such a position is the double standard. One position is taken in public, another in private. With the avid attention of the media to anything controversial the danger of unwelcome exposure adds a new dimension to the problem of scandal.

The subtle temptation for the Catholic Church to take pride in its public image is especially prevalent in Britain today. In the autumn of 1993 the government introduced a policy of 'Back to Basics', which foundered on a series of scandals affecting senior members of the government itself. By contrast the Catholic Church has often been presented as one institution which knows what it believes and where it stands.

However, there is more to the argument than just the public image of the Church. For believers the Church is the Body of Christ, offering salvation to all the world. That salvation is achieved not by all the world conforming to the rules, but by individuals conforming themselves to Christ. The survival of the nation was an Old Testament understanding of salvation. While not denying the social dimension of the Christian notion of salvation, in Christ we know that every individual is called to personal salvation. No one can be sacrificed for a vision which is concerned *primarily* with the good order of our earthly society. In the Synoptic Gospels this point is made by emphasizing Jesus' struggle with the Pharisees and scribes. They are portrayed as being preoccupied with a kind of servile conformity while their hearts were far from God (Matthew 15:1–9).

A remarkable element of this research has been meeting people who can tell the story of their conversion, the broadening of their horizons, the deepening of their spiritual awareness in the midst of their painful journey through marital breakdown. They are not calling for a lowering of moral standards to accommodate them, but asking that they may be able to live the Gospel to the full. They live with the tension of the situation and do not presume to suggest there are glib or easy answers. One such story, told in some detail, was that of a BE member. I am presenting it in detail because I believe it illustrates powerfully the conversion process and represents the heartfelt cry of so many others who may not have been able to articulate their stories so clearly.[20]

> I found myself in a terrible dilemma. When I made my marriage vows they were for life, and then I found myself in a destructive situation. My wife had got involved in an affair ...
>
> For one thing I was determined not to pick up the first stone and throw it. I didn't see myself as the innocent party. My problem was I wanted to do the right thing. Just to put that in perspective a little bit: several years before that I had spent several years in a monastery as a monk. I left because I had got to the stage where I had to come to a decision to take final vows or not, and I decided there was some doubt. I met my future wife a year or two after leaving. She had spent six years in a convent as a nun.
>
> My marriage vows are as sacred to me as my religious vows had been ... As a child ... I somehow felt that God would love me if I kept the rules and that if I broke them he would punish me. And that was at variance with what I felt at gut level with a loving God ... There is a disparity between what the Church is saying ... and this idea of a loving God who wants me to grow as a person ...
>
> The loving thing in this situation was to let Margaret go, which was the first thing I did ... But then I went through a period when I thought: 'The Church disapproves of me: God somehow must disapprove of what I have done.' And I tortured myself through probably the best part of a year to eighteen months ...
>
> In the interval I had joined BE and I realized that I had gone through my grief and I had to let go of it ... In the end the only way I could work my way through it was to start to say I would take responsibility for my own actions.
>
> I will always believe in God. And to me the way through it was to concentrate on my perception of God ... So I clutched to a God point of view rather than a Church point of view. I felt somehow the Church, by its insistence on rules and regulations in the early stage, had placed an insupportable burden, which I couldn't carry and which I didn't want to carry. So I eventually divorced Margaret because I thought it was the loving thing to do ...
>
> I know that I feel a whole person now. I am quite happy to tackle the next stage when it comes along. And if I did get involved in a relationship I would have to look at this question of whether I want an

annulment or whether I would just disregard the annulment and say: 'Do I need an annulment in the first place?' Somehow to me it seems almost a double standard in the Church, almost hypocrisy. You can't have a divorce because marriage is indissoluble, but somehow or other we will bend the rules and get you a divorce through the back door, through annulment ... I realize it is not quite as simple as that but I honestly feel I had a valid marriage and that somehow for somebody to turn round and say to me, years later on, 'your marriage was null and void', would almost devastate me ... I would find it easier to live with the fact that I have come to terms with what happened about my marriage.

I have come to terms with my relationship with God. I am accepting responsibility for my life as it is now, and if I thought I could grow in a loving relationship, then I would have no qualms about entering into one. In fact I have made it almost a criterion for judging whether I trust God enough ...

I have known Christians who have been in situations where they have got divorced and wanted to remarry and they have tortured themselves. Somehow I feel it is not quite right. Why should people find themselves in this situation where they are tortured? I solve it for myself, I think, but I don't quite know how to solve it for anybody else.[21]

Drawing a clear distinction between God and religion, Christ and the Church, was a common attitude. This, it seems, has been the only way many have been able to survive: to know that Christ loves them and accepts them, no matter what the Church decides about their situations.

The desire to reach out and help others was evident in the final section of the above testimony. Often it is simply a willingness to stand beside people in their pain, but I also noted a growing desire in all the support groups to challenge perceived injustices. This was well illustrated in the concern over the position of divorced Catholics teaching in Catholic schools. One celebrated case, widely reported in the press, drew a fair amount of comment, and as a matter of justice a clause in the standard contract for Catholic teachers was called into question.[22]

Relating to the clergy

During every discussion and interview with the laity much time was spent reviewing people's experiences with their clergy. It would be true to say that each story of rejection was balanced by another, in which understanding, compassion and support were recalled with gratitude. Stories ranged from the priest who 'has never officiated at a mixed marriage and doesn't intend to start now' to priests who 'just turn a blind eye' or 'tell you to follow your conscience'.

Traditionally Catholics in England and Wales have lived in awe of their priests. An ASDC member, received into the Church in 1955, said: 'I was received into a Church that led me to believe that priests were the be all and end all. I was in absolute awe of this Church.' Another asked: 'Do you think the priests actually know how much the people rely on them?'

There were many positive testimonies. Here is a sample of comments from all over the country:

> 'Catholic priests: they're wonderful.' (ASDC member)
> My priest 'gave me a hundred per cent'. (ASDC member)
> 'My priest has been very helpful.' (ASDC member)
> The priest originally approached was 'very supportive and caring'. (Rainbow member)
> 'I never had a problem with the clergy. The curate was very good.' (Rainbow member)

There were negative comments too:

> 'I used to feel very bitter because he [the priest] ignored me.' (ASDC member)
> 'No priest came near at first.' (Rainbow member)
> 'I would have expected the priest to come and see me . . . when I really needed help.' (ASDC member)

Many spoke of being disappointed with their priests rather than angry. A common complaint was that the priests were insensitive and, being ill at ease, felt duty bound to reiterate the Church's teaching. This was graphically described by one ASDC member:

The only person I thought I could talk to was my priest and all he could say to me was: 'oh, my dear, you can't get married again' – I could have thumped him. It was the last thing I wanted to hear.

Another example of a priest's insensitivity was the following:

'That's what happens when you marry a non-Catholic.' (ASDC member)

By far the majority of respondents felt that the real problem was that so many priests had received wholly inadequate training in this area. At a number of meetings time was spent discussing this aspect of the question. Many expressed sympathy for the clergy, but recalled a lack of professionalism:

'I know he [the priest] doesn't know what to do.' (ASDC member)
'I haven't found a priest who is able to offer me counselling of any description.' (Rainbow member)
'I think priests should be trained in marriage break-up. I can remember eight years ago talking to a group of priests and they didn't have a clue because they weren't trained.[23] All they knew was there was such a thing as annulment.' (ASDC member)

At the Rochdale ASDC meeting the local chaplain was present – a priest ordained in 1987 – and he described how only four of his class of 16 opted for a course in counselling skills. What was disturbing about this was that the course had to be made voluntary because of the objections of those who did not wish to face the personal self-examination which all such counselling courses demand. Undoubtedly this is a matter to which the bishops must give serious attention.

Some people seemed to think that the priest should be able to respond to every situation and were aggrieved if the priest referred them to another agency:

'I was disappointed that the priest wouldn't counsel us and that we were pushed away to CMAC.' (ASDC member)
'I think priests do need training. When I was having my problems with my son, he [the priest] could only suggest we went to the Citizens' Advice Bureau. My son was an altar-boy.' (ASDC member)

The majority did not feel that every priest could be equipped or available for counselling in every situation. What they did consider important was that all their priests should be well informed on what help is available and be ready to refer people to the respective counselling agencies or support groups. Thus one man, who repeatedly stated that he was optimistic, said:

> It seems quite good to me if we can get to a stage where a priest holds his hands up and says: 'I'm not very good in this area at helping divorced and separated people, but I know somebody who is.' (ASDC member)

There was considerable dissatisfaction at the number of priests who remained un-cooperative with the support groups. Again members were generally willing to make allowances and understood that the priests should not shoulder all the blame:

> 'Some priests won't have ASDC posters in churches, not because they are uncharitable, but because they are frightened of upsetting other parishioners.' (ASDC member)

There were happier stories of priests who were very co-operative with the support groups, promoted them and introduced people to them. The Rainbow Groups have an advantage here because each has an appointed chaplain and, being part of the diocesan pastoral programme, the groups are less likely to be held in suspicion. Nevertheless people in Rainbow still reported some disturbing experiences with the parochial clergy. One member described how she received wonderful support from her parish priest, only to feel sadly let down by his successor. Fortunately the Rainbow chaplain then proved very supportive.

This same interviewee introduced another important matter; namely the difficulty that many priests experience with women who are in deep distress. Often the priests are embarrassed and nervous about sending out the wrong signals. We have noted that it would be unrealistic to expect every priest to be a trained marriage counsellor, but the provision of coun selling as part of a comprehensive ministry in this field is the first of two special needs I will now consider. The other is the care of the children of broken marriages.

Special needs and looking to the future

We have seen that the origin of each of the associations was a response to a pastoral need. They were formed to provide a ministry which at the time the Church community was not providing.

My assessment is that this is an opportune time for seeking to promote the work of the support groups and providing networks of communication through which their ministries may become more available to those who need them. While their memberships continue to increase, they still represent a tiny proportion of those within the Catholic community who suffer from marital difficulties or whose marriages break down.

ASDC is essentially a group support ministry. This is sometimes supplemented by one-to-one support when experienced members recognize that this is appropriate. Such ministries are usually the result of the secretary or chairperson responding to enquiries from potential new members and realizing that they need the support of a confidant as well as the therapy of the group. Such care cannot be said to fall under the umbrella of trained counselling.

Rainbow is furnished with a number of trained counsellors, which gives their ministry an added dimension, although the counsellors themselves would be the first to admit that there is far more work than they can cope with, and in practice they have to entrust most of the therapy to the groups, making themselves available to those who especially need their help at any given time.

One of the criticisms of this system from some members of Rainbow is that the counsellors are all happily married people: they would like to see their numbers enhanced by others, graduating from the group, who would have the added advantage of having experienced the pain of marital breakdown.

Likewise members of ASDC raised the question of training counsellors from among their ranks. Many who have experienced the healing ministry of the Church in their groups or in counselling elsewhere believe that they have much to offer not just to the separated and divorced but also to the wider community. One member of ASDC expressed it in this way:

I've just got this strong belief that ASDC as a group and people within it would be a great source of talent to the Church in strengthening existing Catholic marriages. I think there are a lot of people in ASDC who have a great deal to contribute in the way of counselling, experience and practice ... I think ASDC people have the talent and the ability to have a great deal to give both in pre-marriage counselling, which most of us would now recommend very very strongly, and also in marriage counselling itself.

The BE process is designed to lead people to that stage of growth where they are willing to 'reach out' and help others. Thus BE teams are always looking out for potential new team members to ensure that the work continues.

Ideally if the work of the various groups was better co-ordinated in the dioceses and deaneries, the different ministries could complement one another much more successfully than at present. Not everyone whose marriage breaks down will need counselling, or the intensive group therapy of BE or even the support of ASDC or Rainbow. However it is clear that many more could benefit from these ministries if they knew they existed or how to get in touch with them.

Catholic Marriage Care could play a part in helping to bring this co-ordinated vision to fruition. Their approach is becoming more and more professional, as evidenced by the fact that they have a stringent selection process for new counsellors, and their training programme since 1993 has had accreditation from Leeds University.

Inevitably I heard stories from people who had not found their counsellors particularly helpful and from others who misguidedly thought that their role was only to save marriages from breakdown or insist on unqualified adherence to the teaching of the Church on all moral issues. However as always the bad experiences were tempered by the good ones, and there were those who spoke with gratitude about the help they had received.

There will remain the problem that some consider it an admission of failure even to approach a counsellor or a support group, and it was noticeable that the women usually outnumbered the men by at least two to one at the meetings.[24] Nevertheless the Church is always called to bring the healing of Christ to those who are abandoned or marginalized. During the past decade the support groups have shown the way in ministering to the separated and divorced. I believe now is an opportune time for the administrative Church publicly to acknowledge that fact and seek to ensure that these ministries are affirmed and developed.

In recent years a great deal of good literature has come on to the market, providing self-help for those traumatized by separation and divorce.[25] By making these available some of the support groups provide an invaluable extra service.

Another matter of considerable importance is the care of the children. Many groups take practical steps to ensure that the children are looked after when members attend meetings or special functions. For example, when I attended the Tenth Anniversary Celebration of Rainbow at Upholland College, I was impressed with the way the children of all ages were entertained throughout the day. Then they took a central part in the celebration of the Mass which brought the day to an end.

But the groups themselves can only do so much. Repeatedly I heard calls for the Church community to be re-educated. The National Chairperson of ASDC, Joan Hall, spoke of her distress at receiving no support when in another forum she raised the question of what schools and parishes are doing to help the children.

There are the practical problems that many events are run in groups and while everyone is encouraged to take part, often no thought is given to the single parent with no car and two or three children. One young mother who wanted to be involved in a parish renewal programme spoke of her isolation at not being able to become involved. Likewise people spoke of the difficulty of attending meetings for sacramental programmes.

It was also pointed out that often the children's personal needs may be forgotten: they too will be grieving the loss of someone who is not dead. One ASDC member spoke passionately about this.

Unless something is done about the children, they take the guilt. They will take it with them for life unless they get some kind of counselling. If you look at any of the research, that's why patterns of behaviour repeat themselves. I think we need to take that on board as a church.

A Rainbow counsellor who is a teacher and has made the care of the children her special concern spent a long time on this subject in a personal interview. She pointed out that often the parents will insist that the break-up of the marriage was for the children's good and therefore 'tend to deny there are any problems arising from it'. She spoke of the need to educate teachers and indeed school communities to become sensitive in dealing with all those who are marginalized through separation or divorce. It is so easy to stereotype even little children. An obvious example of unwitting discrimination is to choose children only from apparently happy united families to take the lead roles on special church occasions.

A poignant story concerned a child whose mother had remarried. Shortly afterwards, on meeting the priest at the church, they had been made welcome, but the mother was reminded that she could no longer receive Holy Communion. The child's response had been: 'I don't want to go if they don't want her', and subsequently both had stopped going to church altogether.

Three key issues produced a great deal of data from the support groups. They are the *annulment process*, the use of the *internal forum* and *scandal*. Since a great deal of data was also forthcoming from other sources on each of these subjects, I have chosen to avoid repetition by assembling the data and dealing with each subject in its most appropriate setting. Thus, the annulment process will be considered in Chapter 7 on the work of the diocesan tribunals; the internal forum, which by its nature involves the clergy, in Chapter 5; and scandal, which is integrally linked with the use of the internal forum, also in Chapter 5.

Summary

This chapter has presented the results of a quite comprehensive consultation with a section of the laity. From these certain important conclusions may be drawn.

Firstly, in a very real sense, this group of people, a marginalized and often spiritually abandoned group, is now evangelizing the wider Church by its example of pastoral care and ministry.

Secondly and by the same token, this group of people is exposing the hopelessly inadequate provision of pastoral care within the official administrative organs of the Catholic Church.

Thirdly and most significantly, this part of the research has demonstrated that the *sensus fidelium* as expressed within this same group is in harmony with the Church's fundamental belief in the sanctity and permanence of marriage, but has enormous problems with the discipline which has evolved as the means of protecting that belief.

Notes

1 Cecilia Hull, 'Crucified by marriage breakdown', *Catholic Herald* (19 April 1991), p. 10.
2 These aims are published in a printed leaflet.
3 Reporting the National Conference at Wolverhampton, 2 May 1992, *The Universe* (10 May 1992) began its report as follows: '"We are no radical group making demands for this and that – we just want to be understood," was a strong message from the conference. "Be open, inform."' (p. 4)
4 'Commending members for their witness, he said, "You take a non-judgemental attitude to people's failure. That doesn't mean you have no values and no vision but that you are prepared to accept people where they are"': *The Universe* (10 May 1992), p. 4.
5 The tradition of the early Church is clear: the community can dismiss those who are recalcitrant (see 1 Corinthians 5:1–13; Titus 3:9–11). However, there is a clear distinction between those who are excommunicated and those who are punished by the community and are to be forgiven. Indeed on one occasion Paul is concerned that if the community does not 'forgive and console', the man in question 'may be overwhelmed by excessive sorrow' (2 Corinthians 2:7).
6 I feel this should be clarified by pointing out that the significant factor here is that in danger of death a person may be given absolution and admitted to the Eucharist as well as receive the Sacrament of the Sick (Canon 1352.1).
7 Dr Moriarty is quoting here from Ladislas Örsy SJ, *Marriage in Canon Law: Texts and Comments; Reflections and Questions* (Leominster: Fowler Wright, 1988), p. 292. The reference to Joseph Ratzinger is 'Zur Frage nach der Unauflösigkeit der Ehe' in *Ehe und Ehescheidung* (Munich: Kösel, 1972), p. 55.
8 This is a reference to Gregory II's reply to Boniface regarding a husband's situation if the wife can no longer have intercourse because of some permanent disability (letter of 22 November 726). Gregory writes:

> It would be good if he could remain as he is and live a life of continence. But this requires great virtue. So if he cannot live chastely, it is better that he remarry. But let him not cease to support her [his first and incapacitated wife].

The Latin formulation of this concession is: 'sed quia hoc magnorum est, ille qui se non poterit continere, nubat magis': see Mackin, *Divorce and Remarriage* (New York: Paulist Press, 1984), p. 235.
9 The name 'Rainbow' was carefully chosen. A memo from the organization explains:

> The Rainbow is ... a sign of God's mercy and forgiveness. 'I set my bow in the clouds and it shall be a sign of the Covenant between me and the earth' (Genesis 9.13) ... It is a symbol of peace after a storm, a sign of God's faithfulness and promise for the future.

10 Report of the first few months of the first Rainbow Group from the Marriage and Family Life Committee (Archdiocese of Liverpool, Department of Pastoral Formation), 12 January 1983.
11 I am indebted for the information in this section to Mrs Martha Freckleton (interviewed on 18 November 1990) and Fr Luke Magee CP, the national chaplain of BE (interviewed on 21 November 1991).

12   In his notes Fr Luke Magee explains the key elements of both the psychology and the theology of BE:

Psychology

The psychology of BE is 'passing through', i.e. passing through the stages of grief (denial, anger, bargaining, depression and acceptance) and then moving to the sixth stage, which is 'reaching out' beyond one's own grief to caring for others.

The crisis event can be a great threat to one's integrity and wholeness and can lead to almost total loss of self-esteem. The stages have to be passed through, not passed over or buried. Time of itself will not heal. There is no way around grief, only a way through. If feelings of anger, bitterness or hatred are buried and not dealt with, grief will remain unsolved. Unresolved grief produces a vulnerable person; grief resolved is life-giving. A person can remain trapped in one of the stages of grief and remain in a state of deadness. There is a need to rediscover affectional, relational and ultimate meaning.

BE provides the environment for passing through the stages of grief. The basic underlying principle is the belief that those who have suffered the significant loss of a spouse can, through the shared pain of others, find the capacity to heal and be healed.

Theology

The theology is rooted in the Passion, Death and Resurrection of Jesus who passes through death to a new mode of being. Through his Spirit he continues that death resurrection in us. 'If the Spirit of God who raised Jesus from the dead, lives in you, then he who raised Christ from the dead, will also give life to your mortal bodies by the presence of his Spirit in you' (Romans 8:11).

Jesus went through his passion and death. We cannot 'pray away' our distress, ask God to perform some kind of magic; that would be to miss the life-giving effect of resurrection. His death resurrection takes place in us as the human beings that we are. Sometimes a person may express the feeling of being trapped in a marriage; the resurrection experience may be the opportunity offered to bring to wholeness those parts of their lives buried or diminished by the marriage.

13   Rosemary Haughton analyses this subject of growth from the perspective of a new consciousness in women.

We simply cannot go on pretending that we can put back together the pieces of a theology of marriage which has been shattered by experience. For many women, the moment of conversion, the true metanoia, has come when they reach the decision to seek a divorce. This is not necessarily because the husband is abusive, but often because he has been cast, willy-nilly, in a role which he cannot break out of, and which makes it impossible for the relationship to be honest – and therefore impossible for the woman to live with integrity. Such discovery is very painful, and even involves that loss of family, money, and approval of which the Gospel speaks. To compare the decision to seek a divorce to the choice of discipleship may seem shocking – but that can be what it really is: the choice of life over death, spiritual freedom over bondage. ('Marriage in women's new consciousness' in *Commitment to Partnership: Explorations of the Theology of Marriage*, ed. William P. Roberts (New York: Paulist Press, 1987), pp. 149–50)

14   Some might argue that the Church tribunals were offering a very powerful

ministry and that many received great strength and healing from the annulment process. I do not dispute this and we will see evidence for it when we assess the work of the tribunals in Chapter 7, but I do contend that ministry in this forum is accidental, a by-product of the process rather than its *raison d'être*.

15   Many priests and people confirmed this from their experience.

16   Since my research was confined to the situations in which we actually find pastoral care in the Church, I can offer only anecdotal evidence to support the fact that there appears to be a growing number of people in this category: namely those who continue to practise the Faith without any qualms of conscience, convinced that the Church's teaching is out of touch with reality and with what they perceive to be God's will for them. One priest in particular was strongly convinced that the situation is comparable to the birth control question. In other words large percentages of people are making up their own minds on the subject without reference to the Church authorities. By any statistical assessment the number of Catholics receiving pastoral care is a minute proportion of the number of Catholics whose marriages have failed. Furthermore, with so few of the younger divorced people attending the support groups, one is led to conclude that the next generation may well be establishing a different agenda for future discussion of the subject. It is worth recalling that as far back as 1979 Hornsby-Smith calculated that two out of three Catholics thought that divorce should be permitted. If we translate those statistics into practice then it is possible that many Catholics have made up their own minds.

17   The Church in Britain has never imposed a formal excommunication on divorce, but even in relatively recent times couples who separated were required to obtain the permission of the local ordinary. One elderly ASDC member recalled having to go through this procedure in the 1960s, and she was asked to promise that she would not marry again. While the law is no longer invoked in this way, the 1983 Code of Canon Law infers that a decree of the ordinary should be the norm unless 'there is danger in delay' (Canon 1153).

18   Here we are confronting misconceptions created by confused media coverage. One interviewee commented that she thought divorce was now accepted because she had read of so many prominent Catholics who had been divorced and who continued to practise the faith.

19   Continuing the tidal metaphor, I have heard many priests and people argue that if the Church relaxes its position the floodgates will open. This must depend on one's perspective. In many ways the floodgates have already opened and there is no indication that the present pastoral position is successfully stemming the tide either within the Church or in society at large. In those circumstances there is the real danger that any modifications the Church makes to its pastoral policy will be interpreted as capitulating to social pressure rather than a genuine response in faith to the needs of the faithful. That is why I believe it is of paramount importance that the Church takes positive initiatives to support the spiritual needs of families and individuals at the level of the local community, and pays less attention to defending its beliefs against a sometimes hostile and often godless society.

20   Lonergan's theology of 'horizons' coupled with the spirituality which is built around the concept of developmental growth are explored in Walter Conn, *Christian Conversion: A Developmental Interpretation of Autonomy and Surrender* (New York: Paulist Press, 1986).

21   The text is taken verbatim from the tape. The participant gave full permission for

his story to be used in the hope that it may be a help to others. The name of his wife has been changed.

22 The case of Mr Hans Formella, deputy headteacher of St Osmund's Primary School, Barnes, was the case in question. He was a divorced and remarried Catholic, but not in good standing with the Church, though he was described as an active Catholic (see *Independent*, 17 December 1990, p. 5). His possible appointment as headteacher was thwarted by the Church authorities who replaced four of their appointed governors. The relevant clause referred to is Clause 4 (iii) of *The Contract of Employment with a Headteacher or Teacher in a Roman Catholic Aided School*:

> The Teacher Hereby Agrees to have regard to the Roman Catholic character of the School and not to do anything in any way detrimental or prejudicial to the interest of the same.

23 In fact it was a group of seminarians.

24 This problem is not peculiar to Catholics. In general men find it more difficult to speak about their failures and seek advice at the personal level. John Abulafia has written on this subject in *Men and Divorce: Coping, Learning, Starting Afresh* (London: Fontana Paperbacks, 1990).

25 Two examples are: Paula Ripple FSPA, *The Pain and the Possibility: Divorce and Separation Among Catholics: An Affirming and Healing Guide for the Divorced and Separated, Their Parents and Relatives, Neighbors and Friends* (Notre Dame, IN: Ave Maria, 1978); James J. Young CSP, *Divorcing, Believing, Belonging* (New York: Paulist Press, 1984).

5

The opinions of the clergy

The pastoral structure of the Church is centred on the bishop as the pastor, and his team of priests. In that theological vision all pastoral care in the Church receives its authenticity, for it is administered in unity with the bishop. This was the explicit teaching of Vatican II, whose horizons embraced all pastoral care including a variety of ministries among the faithful, who also share in the one priesthood of Christ (LG 18–38).

To imagine that such a vision is widely understood would be to misrepresent the reality of people's experience at this present time. For many, educated with much narrower horizons, the Church is still almost entirely identified with the hierarchy and their clergy.

We have seen in Chapter 4 how vitally important for so many people the reactions and responses of the clergy have been and this is no accident. The priest is integrally caught up in the process of marriage from the very beginning. It is to the priest that a couple will go to arrange the marriage, to be prepared for their marriage and to have it validly solemnized.[1] Should the marriage fail and there is question of an annulment, it is probable that they will approach the priest for advice and information. If an annulment is petitioned for, then priests may be involved at every stage of the tribunal process and in making the judgement.[2] When people find themselves unable to receive the Eucharist they may well seek the advice of the clergy either directly, or indirectly through friends and relatives.

At the same time the horizons are broadening in all these areas and the laity are beginning to take up new ministries in the marriage field. For example, in some parishes the whole marriage preparation programme has been delegated to teams of lay people or Catholic Marriage Care, and many diocesan tribunals now employ lay people in key roles, including judges.

However, such developments are achieved usually when the clergy are part of the initiative and enable the laity to take responsibility. I would go so far as to say that the broader exercise of pastoral care flourishes only when the clergy enable it to do so, and that a balanced and harmonious development of ministries continues to depend upon the good will and co-operation of the clergy.

The clergy are at the sharp end of the pastoral question because they are called upon to interpret the theology and the law for God's people in practical day-to-day living, not in the rarefied atmosphere of intellectual debate. The uncertainty and anxiety that they repeatedly expressed to me suggest that there is something gravely wrong with the present situation.

I have gone out of my way to seek out the full range of clergy opinion. My primary source for data collection was provided by group meetings, but data are also included from the writings of the clergy and their opinions expressed in the media. I will record the substance of that data before analysing their pastoral implications, especially in regard to the use of the internal forum. Then I will point to some of the conclusions I drew and how I put these to the test at two large gatherings of clergy in Nottingham and Westminster and with an individual priest, who was willing to represent the opinions of the more conservative younger group of clergy.

Very few of the clergy were found to hold extreme positions. The overwhelming weight of opinion is pooled in an uneasy centre, where the hope is that some way forward will be found. In a television documentary Mgr Peter Smith, then Rector of Wonersh and now Bishop of East Anglia, gave expression to this opinion.

I think pastorally, as a priest, that one of the big difficulties is this question of people who have been married: whose marriages have broken down. They have remarried, in inverted commas, and they cannot or do not feel they are fully part of the church. They cannot participate in the Eucharist and Penance as they would wish. I would love that to be resolved, but, I mean, I think I should also make it clear it is not a thing which is going to be easily resolved or very quickly. But I think we ought, we need to put, as a church, more effort into that, to try and see the theological, disciplinary implications of it, and see to what extent we can help people. In the meantime I think we have got to be very sensitive to those who are in those sort of situations; and to really convince them, as I say, they are not rejected by the church; they are part of the church; and it may be for them that this is part of their Calvary, their carrying of the cross; that there is a blockage at the moment.[3]

During the programme Mgr Smith had sought to explain the Church's present discipline, but, like so many of the clergy I have interviewed, faced with the anomalies and injustices of the system, had to admit that it is unsatisfactory and inadequate in the face of the present pressing pastoral needs.

Julie's fictional case history, used to focus the group meetings with the clergy, is to be found in Appendix 2 (see p. 186).

The story was designed to include as many complex theological, pastoral and legal problems as possible. Julie's situation incorporates *pastoral* problems associated with the reception of the sacraments, faith commitment, ecumenism and the implications of her situation for the wider communities of church and school; *moral* problems associated with conversion, invincible ignorance, justice in her present situation and possible scandal, as well as the *moral* dilemmas associated with the nature of sin, freedom of conscience and the whole area of the internal forum; *dogmatic* problems relating to the definitions of the sacraments of marriage, the Eucharist and reconciliation; *legal* problems arising from canonically irregular marriages: in her case the one involving the Catholic partner being easily resolved because of lack of canonical form, but ironically the one involving the non-Catholic partner requiring an annulment, even though it had not been a Christian celebration.

Thus the case history provided the clergy with a framework for their discussions and the context in which to share their personal experiences.

I was very impressed with the quality of the clergy discussions. In this section I aim to provide a clear picture of what they said and where the weight of opinion lay. As in the group sessions with the support groups, the discussions ranged across a whole gamut of issues and inevitably different issues became the focus for different groups. However, as far as possible I ensured that every discussion embraced the key questions within the four categories: pastoral, moral, dogmatic and legal.

Legalism and personalism

By the very nature of the subject as a whole, discussion of one aspect regularly overlapped into others. However, I believe the complexity of these discussions can be reduced to the simple analysis of the difference between the horizons of those with a legalist outlook and those with a personalist one. To illustrate this we can compare the initial contributions of three priests. One priest, twelve years ordained, and representing the personalist view, said:

> I think this is a very typical case. Since arriving as a new parish priest I want people to feel welcome. In fact having visited the whole of the parish nearly, I would say that 90 per cent of the Catholics don't feel welcome in our inner city parish and I think the reason they don't feel welcome is that they are in situations like Julie … Like Julie they probably got married at an age when they did not know what marriage was and they are in a second relationship, and everything in terms of canon law is hopeless. I have come to believe that the only way we are going to make our people feel part of our community is to give them something to do at the Eucharist and if you say you cannot come to Communion, I think that is a very big thing.

By contrast the following was the contribution of a priest, thirteen years ordained, and approaching the case with a more legalist mind-set:

> I think my first response actually would be to say that there is a problem. And that we ought to investigate the possibility of trying to put it right. I mean if it was all so disastrous as they make out there is every chance that it could be put right. And I think you owe them that to begin with. Now it may create further problems later on but I think from our own point of view, I always feel personally that you have got to start from some sort of basic principle. I would want to know a little bit more about both those previous marriages and the possibility of them being annulled. I mean in her case there is no problem: if she's a Catholic – it's lack of form. It's quite possible that her husband could get his first marriage annulled as well. I think it is just too easy to assume that there is another way round this without actually first directing one's attention to the Church law as it stands. Now that might just be postponing the problem in one sense and it means that obviously you have got to provide a different form of pastoral support until such time as you get an answer, 'yes' or 'no' from the tribunal.

Of course it would be wrong and absurdly simplistic to try and classify all the clergy and place them into two clearly distinct camps, the personalist and the legalist. All but a few notable exceptions were torn between the two, well illustrated by this third example, a priest, 23 years ordained.

My first reaction to the case is that, at the beginning, Julie is somebody who wants to do the right things and seems to love God, and at the end of it she is a problem. And she has been made a problem not because she has changed – she is still exactly the same – but she has been made a problem in my mind-set because there are all sorts of laws that I am not all that happy about. So you end up just wishing Julie would go away and talk to somebody else, which is terribly unfair because you have contradicted the basic gospel principle: you have condemned her. You are almost in danger of writing her off as a hopeless case for no good reason other than that it is going to be an awful bother to get this sorted out.

The kind of pastoral care offered by the clergy depends very much on the fundamental mind-set of the priest in a given situation. If he comes from a legalist position, it does not mean that he does not have compassion for the person or wish to minister God's love to the person, but it does mean he begins with the law as the will of God for that person. He will be seeking ways in which that person can be enabled to fulfil the law and fit into the system. However, if his fundamental position is that of personalism, then he begins, not with the law, but with the person and seeks to discern how far he can lead that person towards the ideal expressed in the law. Inevitably the position of the priest will convey itself to the person from the very beginning and I think that many of the difficulties expressed by the laity in Chapter 4 can be attributed to the fact that the vast majority of the clergy have been trained into a legal mind-set. Thus when people like Julie come to them, they cannot help but convey the message: 'You are a problem.'

At the same time, as the theological perspective moves towards personalism, more and more clergy are adapting their pastoral policy and everyone admits that the climate today is totally different from that of a few years ago. It is not surprising then that the clergy are experiencing a great deal of tension during this transitional period. You will see that tension articulated throughout this chapter, and I believe it is a reflection of the tension which is inherent in the Church's teaching. In *Familiaris Consortio* we are all urged to welcome divorced people into the assembly of the Church (FC 84). This is a perfect example of the new theology of personalism and comparable statements will not be found in papal documents or theological treatises prior to Vatican II. However, the legal outlook of the old moral theology comes to the fore in the same article of the Apostolic Exhortation when we are told that the law of not admitting to eucharistic Communion those in second irregular unions stands. The welcome extended to the divorced immediately becomes a qualified welcome.

The centrality of the Eucharist

All the discussions looked closely at the official ban on the reception of the Eucharist for those in irregular marriages (FC 84). It became clear that there are diverse pastoral practices in operation.

Undoubtedly the most extreme position on the liberal wing was taken by a parish priest who declared that he is willing to conduct marriage ceremonies for those in irregular unions. He declared unequivocally:

> I remarry people in the church who are divorced and give them a service. I give Communion to people I know to be in invalid marriages. That is my practice, which I am perfectly up front about. I don't think there is any great problem about my pastoral practice. I am perfectly clear about what I do and why I do it.

He went on to say that he would also receive people into the Church in spite of the fact that they are in invalid unions, adding 'whatever an invalid union is'. He explained that the services he holds when remarrying divorced people are always in private, and he made a very clear distinction between the public and private fora.

> The Church has two roles. A prophetic role to preach the Gospel, and it is perfectly clear that the Gospel in relation to marriage is one man, one woman for life. But the Church always has a pastoral approach to these matters ... It is clear to me that it is a consistent part of the Catholic Church's teaching that whilst at the level of principle we say one thing, at the level of practice it is totally Christian and charitable and Christ-like to do something different. But you mustn't muddle up those two fora.

He employed the basic criterion that people must be 'in good faith and good conscience'. If a nullity was possible he would encourage them to petition for one, but if for whatever reason they did not deem it possible, he would work the situation out with the couple. He argued: 'because it's a bond between two people, and not a magic thing: if the bond goes, the marriage goes and therefore the person is free'. He said he always made it clear that these marriage services had no legal standing, that the couples could not claim to be married in the eyes of the Catholic Church, but they could claim to be married in God's eyes. He added: 'I regard it as an opportunity to help them grow morally, to make some decisions which they probably hadn't made before.'

At the other end of the spectrum, a few of the clergy held rigidly to all the prescriptions of the law, considering any deviation as a betrayal of Christ and the Church. Thus, one priest immediately attributed bad faith to Julie:

> She would probably want to go to Communion with her children. I presume that is her intention for coming. And I would suggest that she would love to go for that day and you probably wouldn't see her again.

He said he would not agree with pastoral solutions that would allow people in these situations to go to Communion either on a regular basis or even on special occasions such as a First Holy Communion or a funeral. However, he was challenged by others in the group who were willing to apply pastoral clemency on special occasions.

This was an issue that arose in a number of the meetings and was sometimes illustrated by poignant personal experiences. One priest, ordained 24 years, spoke passionately about a pastoral problem he had faced on the very morning of our meeting. Preparing to preside at the funeral of a parishioner he was approached by one of the two sons of the deceased person, who 'desired very, very much' to join his brother at Holy Communion. However he was in the all too familiar situation of being remarried after a divorce. The priest said he had heard of 'numbers of priests' who would advise that in these situations you give people Communion, but he felt constrained by the law and told the son to come for a blessing. He described the man as 'broken-hearted', and the decision clearly troubled the priest because he went on to describe how during the Mass itself he reflected on the double standard he was now applying in this matter. At the funeral were some children from the school who had come to lead the singing and although he knew that half of them would not have been to Mass for weeks, he did not feel constrained to deprive them of Communion, as he would have done some years ago. He concluded:

> The same rules and regulations that are binding me I was able to ignore regarding children – and I think 99 per cent of people would ignore them. But on the other hand, I could not bring myself to ignore the one about the divorcee. And I just felt it is all a sham. And I felt very very uneasy about it myself and I felt I had let that man down, who perhaps will drift further away from the Church now because of the hurt ... I really felt I had let that man down when he needed me most, when he needed Our Lord most of all. And in the same Mass I just could see there has to be a better balance, there has to be a fairness in applying Our Lord's sacraments to people ... There is a tremendous conflict within myself. It is going to become more and more, and I think a lot of good priests will go under with the pressure of it all.

There followed a lengthy discussion about the importance of enabling people to make their own decisions with regard to the sacrament of reconciliation and reception of the Eucharist. This was introduced by a priest who had spent all his priestly life – eighteen years – serving the diocesan marriage tribunal in a part-time capacity. In a remarkably candid comment he acknowledged the value of his work for the tribunal, but admitted that it hardly began to address the greater problem.

> For our diocese we would deal with between high forties, low fifties in cases a year, which is more than we used to do. When I started eighteen years ago we did one in my first year. But if you look at it as an overall scene, it is a pinprick. Of all the Catholic marriages that go wrong in the diocese, I mean fifty is not many in an area of this size. I would say there are many more grounds ... but nevertheless it is all hedged around with rules and regulations. If you don't fit into the pattern it is no use to you really. I would think as a tribunal ourselves ... that we have become more efficient: but it's very hard to be caring. It can be helpful, but it is painfully slow; that's one thing, I think. We have dropped from about five and half, six years to about two and half, three, but it is still an awful lot of time to ask people to wait if they are 37 and wanting to start a family and get married ... The only

thing that makes it worthwhile as a task for me in life is to be able to say I have helped some people officially. But I don't think it is anything more than a loophole to be honest. The crucifixion of the whole thing comes when you have got a weeping person in front of you wanting something that you can't give on that level.

He went on to accept that it is possible to deal with matters on another level by referring such situations back to sympathetic parish priests, but admitted he could not trust many of his fellow priests to be sympathetic. He concluded: 'It is a pain. I don't personally see any way round it until there is some deeper view of church.'

The internal forum – a cause of controversy

Since the internal forum is an exercise of pastoral ministry which necessarily involves the clergy, now is the time to look closely at how the clergy regard this field of pastoral care and the laity's experience of this ministry.

During the course of the research the question of the internal forum received a high profile because of an article in *The Tablet* by Theodore Davey and the response it evoked from Cardinal Joseph Ratzinger.[4] In his letter Cardinal Ratzinger virtually outlawed the use of the internal forum in marriage cases. There is evidence that his comments have been widely noted.[5] However on the evidence of this research, including study days with two large groups of clergy, it is clear that the matter is far from closed.[6]

To obtain a balanced and accurate view of the clergy's understanding of and use of the internal forum is complicated by the fact that we are looking at something which, because it is internal and concerned with conscience, is bound by the rules of confidentiality and privacy and often by the seal of confession.

Disagreements surfaced and conflicting opinions were aired, but we never reached the kind of impasse which this type of discussion can provoke. Indeed one priest commented that it was the first time he had been able to discuss the subject without it breaking down in an acrimonious exchange.[7]

In general the priests who were at ease with the internal forum were those whose horizons have embraced a wider view of the Church, and who were able to live with the tension which its usage brings when faced with the letter of the law. In the tradition of classic moral theology, arguments of casuistry were usually invoked to justify its usage, but occasionally someone would advance a more fundamental, personalist argument, akin to the processes of lateral thinking.[8]

For example, one priest, ordained for almost 40 years and much revered in his diocese as a man whose gentle spirit makes him easily approachable, spelt out that he did not wish to see the laws of the Church abandoned; indeed he argued that only with the law in place do we have a yardstick by which to judge any issue. He pointed out that he does not break the 'No Entry' sign going into the hospital, but the ambulance can. He reminded us that Jesus had come to bring the law to fulfilment and that the law is for liberating people, not keeping them down. 'We are frightened to take responsibility ourselves', he said, 'we should be able to take responsibility and to treat the law with dignity and respect as well.'

Exhorting his fellow priests to have the 'courage to step out in faith' and lead the people, he insisted that this did not mean dispensing with the 'No Entry' signs, but coping with the different situations as Jesus would cope with them. He seemed absolutely confident that what he was doing was at the very heart of the Gospel. When it was clear that the Spirit of God was working in someone's life, then he would act, encouraging the person to make conscientious decisions before God. By the same token, if he was unsure about someone's motivation, he would act with great caution.

The majority of the priests who contributed to this research indicated a willingness to seek pastoral solutions in the internal forum in some circumstances, though the variety of circumstances was considerable and I came across nothing remotely approaching a consistent policy. Most welcomed the fact that I had been commissioned to seek a coherent policy, but while wishing me well, few held out much hope that such an objective could be achieved.

There remains much uncertainty about the meaning and use of the internal forum. Some regard it as a purely canonical process, now legislated for in Canon 130 of the 1983 Code of Canon Law and applicable only when governed by a set of strict criteria. Others regard it as the forum for dealing with people at the level of conscience, where the only criterion is the sincerity of the individual. Again much will depend on the mind-set of the priest concerned.

To ensure that this reflection is based on precise interpretations of language it is important briefly to examine three key concepts: *epikeia*, equity and *oikonomia*.

Epikeia

Traditionally the Aristotelian notion of *epikeia* has been accepted as a corrective in every good legal system, including that of the Church. It arises out of the conviction that while the law seeks to ensure justice, in some circumstances there is no law which is applicable, while in others a strict application of the law would only lead to injustice. Örsy writes:

> Justice for all can be achieved only through the subtle and judicious dialectics of imposing the law in most cases and letting *epieikeia* [*sic*] prevail in some cases.[9]

Canon 209 provided this corrective in the 1917 Code by stating that the Church supplied jurisdiction in the external as well as the internal forum in cases of common error or positive and probable doubt whether of law or of fact. By contrast in the 1983 Code Canon 19 introduces the idea of 'canonical equity', while Canon 130 deals with the exercise of the 'internal forum'.

Equity

Equity cannot be equated simply with *epikeia*, although historically its practice in the courts of the English chancellery can be seen as a comparable effort to ensure justice when the literal observance of the law would have led to injustice.[10] However, *equity* is a concept which is outside the field of law and arises out of the conviction that the law alone cannot resolve some problems and therefore higher principles must be invoked in those cases.

> When, in the concrete life, a case arises that cannot be justly resolved by law, it is right that the community should turn to philosophy or religion and let them prevail over the positive law. When this happens, there is authentic equity.[11]

Oikonomia

This exercise of pastoral ministry is not part of the Western tradition, but is used in the Orthodox Churches, especially the Greek Orthodox. There *oikonomia* is invoked to solve seemingly unsolvable cases. It too is beyond the law, but it is part of a theological tradition which focuses on the mystery of God and his inscrutable ways. Thus the bishop, the *oikonomos* of the house of God, takes these problems before the Lord. 'He searches and seeks how the Lord in His power would heal a wound, would redress an injustice, would bring peace where it is needed.'[12]

The solution is found in the community of faith, where the Lord abides. Christ's redemption is understood to be able to reach into every situation and the bishop, as leader of the community, is able to exercise the Church's power to bind and loose.[13] It is a healing ministry and depends solely on the power, the love and the forgiveness of God.[14]

It is clear that such a ministry cannot be governed by law and therefore it may appear to the logical Western mind to be intangible and unworkable. Certainly there is nothing comparable to it in the history of Western theology or canon law, but my research has shown that there is a growing interest in the *oikonomia* of the Orthodox Churches. I was genuinely surprised at the number of priests and people who raised the question with me. Some members of the support groups have attended talks which have explored potential future developments, raising the possibility of an ecumenical development whereby the Catholic Church might one day incorporate the Orthodox solution, which it was so careful not to condemn at the Council of Trent.[15] That is an issue which I will return to in Chapter 8. For now we can note that *epikeia* and equity are options which are invoked in the legal and pastoral traditions of the Western Church and they have provided the basis on which criteria have been formulated to govern the use of internal forum solutions.

Conflict and hardship cases

It has to be said that during the past 25 years contradictory directives have been issued from official teaching sources. Cardinal Ratzinger's recent opposition to the internal forum is in stark contrast to his explicit directive to the priests in the Archdiocese of Munich-Freising, less than two months after the Synod of Bishops had discussed the marriage question in Rome in 1980. On that occasion, with reference to readmittance to Holy Communion, he encouraged his clergy to deal sympathetically with those in the so-called 'conflict' situations (namely where there was subjective certainty that a former marriage was invalid even though it could not be proved in the external forum of the tribunal).[16]

Conflict cases are commonly contrasted to *hardship* cases, the latter being defined as those in which the validity of a former marriage is not in question.[17] The need for this distinction was a response to the fact that the original attempts to formulate criteria for the application of internal forum solutions concentrated largely on those cases where in spite of subjective moral certainty that a previous marriage was invalid, sufficient evidence could not be produced to support a decision in the external forum.

However, no such distinction was made by the Sacred Congregation for the Doctrine of the Faith (CDF) when it offered a directive on the subject on 11 April 1973.

> In regard to admission of the sacraments, local bishops are asked on the one hand to stress observance of current discipline, and on the other hand to take care that pastors of souls exercise special care to seek out those who are living in an irregular union by applying to the solution of such cases, in addition to other rightful means, the Church's approved practice in the internal forum.[18]

At the request of the bishops of the United States of America this statement was duly clarified by Archbishop Hamer, secretary of the CDF.[19] He gave two conditions, which for a while were treated almost as standard criteria.

> These couples may be allowed to receive the sacraments on two conditions, that they try to live according to the demands of Christian moral principles and that they receive the sacraments in churches in which they are not known so that they will not create any scandal.

The wider use of the internal forum in marriage cases can be traced to the publicity which these statements subsequently received. The directives of the CDF were themselves responses to the growing debate in the Church 20 years ago.[20]

It is a measure of how unsatisfactory the whole situation remains that the confusion persists. The meaning of the phrase 'the Church's approved practice in the internal forum' is as open to debate today as it was in 1973.

This research has underlined the fact that there is no common understanding among the clergy of what is approved and what is not. Every discussion was surrounded by a sense of unease. As one priest succinctly put it: 'The trouble with the internal forum is that it is internal.' When the theological system and the law which arises from it are built around absolutes which depend on one another to form a coherent whole, it is difficult to accommodate a principle which is not so easily definable.

For this reason theologians and canonists have sought to make the internal forum accessible by providing detailed criteria upon which individual cases may be judged. Some of these sets of criteria are limited to conflict cases and would include the fact that the external forum must first have been tried: these criteria tend to define the internal forum solely as a canonical provision (Canon 130) and therefore an extension of the law. Other sets of criteria extend to hardship cases and would arise from a broader interpretation of the internal forum, invoking *epikeia* or equity as procedures governing moral and pastoral theology when the law proves inadequate.

None of these attempts to clarify the pastoral approach has won widespread acceptance. The situation remains unclear. One bishop confidently declared in public that he thought the majority of the English and Welsh hierarchy would accept the use of the internal forum in the conflict case, when a proper discernment process had been undertaken.[21] I have spoken privately to other bishops who would be sympathetic to many hardship cases as well.

Confusion and uncertainty are inevitable in the present situation. Since the CDF sanctioned the use of the internal forum as an approved practice in 1973, the Roman magisterium has gradually retracted, with Cardinal Ratzinger now arguing that 'the magisterium has not sanctioned its use' because of 'the inherent contradiction of resolving something in the internal forum which by nature also pertains to and has such important consequences for the external forum'.[22]

The origin of the change of position in the Roman magisterium is undoubtedly the relevant text in the 1981 Apostolic Exhortation *Familiaris Consortio*. In Article 84 Pope John Paul II, having taken the unprecedented step of calling upon 'pastors and the whole community of the faithful to help the divorced, and with solicitous care to make sure that they do not consider themselves as separated from the Church',[23] proceeded to outlaw any process of readmitting those in irregular marriages to Holy Communion.

> However, the Church reaffirms her practice, which is based upon Sacred Scripture, of not admitting to Eucharistic Communion divorced persons who have remarried. They are unable to be admitted thereto from the fact that their state and condition of life objectively contradict that union of love between Christ and the Church which is signified and effected by the Eucharist. Besides this, there is another special pastoral reason: if these people were admitted to the Eucharist, the faithful would be led into error and confusion regard-

ing the Church's teaching about the indissolubility of marriage. (FC 84)

It has to be said that this paragraph and those which qualify it leave many questions unanswered. The practice is said to be based on Scripture though no reference is given. Two reasons are given for insisting on this discipline.

Firstly he argues, presumably according to a Scholastic metaphysical principle, that the disunity of the irregular marriage state so contradicts the unity effected in the Eucharist that it debars the person from receiving Holy Communion. In the course of my research I have met very few who find this argument persuasive. Indeed quite the contrary: the vast majority were led to wonder how, if that is the case, anyone could be confident of receiving Communion, bearing in mind that all our lives lack integrity to some degree. One interviewee went so far as to ask why this teaching does not apply to the whole Church on account of the scandalous historic divisions within Christianity itself.

The second argument is that of scandal. The difficulty is that scandal is always a relative phenomenon. St Paul acknowledges this in chapter 8 of his first letter to the Corinthians. There the problem concerns the eating of certain meats. The principle Paul enunciates is: 'Take care that this liberty of yours does not somehow become a stumbling block to the weak' (v. 9). It is important to notice that Paul's emphasis is on the weakness of those who take scandal rather than the cause of the scandal.

The risk the Church takes in a delicate area such as this is that the method it employs to try and avert scandal may itself become a scandal. Any lack of integrity within the system will eventually refashion public opinion.

The stigma surrounding divorce has virtually disappeared in Britain today. This was the inevitable consequence of the change in the law and the dramatic increase in the number of divorces granted. For its part, in its official capacity, the Catholic Church, while wishing to maintain a strong public opposition to divorce, has acknowledged the suffering of many who have been trapped in unhappy marriages, and has sought to alleviate the problem of broken marriages by broadening the scope of the annulment process. At the same time it has applauded those who have striven to remove the stigma from divorced men and women, recognizing with the Pope in *Familiaris Consortio* that many may have been 'unjustly abandoned' (FC 84).

What the Church must also accept is that there is a subtle contradiction in its position. Once the stigma is removed, the scandal argument loses its force. My research wholly supports the position, advanced by Theodore Davey, that 'in a curious reverse way it often happens that scandal does arise in a parish where the remarried are forbidden the Eucharist'.[24]

The majority of those who took part in this research considered the present confusion a far greater scandal than the fact that some people might be readmitted to the sacraments through the internal forum.[25] That is not to say that people were not sensitive to the possibility of others being scandalized if they are not re-educated. Indeed in one very fruitful discussion at an ASDC meeting a whole range of opinions was offered. People were genuinely sensitive to the fact that some might easily be scandalized by too liberal an approach. As one person put it: 'People who have stuck to the rules and now see younger people doing what they want can become very bitter.' However, at the same meeting it was noted that even people, highly qualified in their own fields, can be ignorant of what the Church actually teaches in all these sensitive areas, and that if they were educated, scandal would be less of a problem. One person expressed her concern strongly: 'If they knew more about it and were taught more, they might have more compassion.'

As far back as 1970 Morris West and Robert Francis had identified a source of scandal to be the matrimonial laws of the Church. Their book *Scandal in the Assembly*[26] remains a serious challenge to the teaching Church. The book serves as a reminder that scandal may arise from many sources, even the Church's own discipline.

I have come to the conclusion that much can be done when the local pastor and his team of catechists and pastoral workers adopt a policy of understanding and compassion, which ensures that the whole community takes a non-judgemental line. Thus, for example, when a priest is confronted with opposition to the formation of ASDC in his parish, if he takes a gentle but firm line and uses the occasion to instruct his people, such a development will be an occasion of growth for all concerned. Such parishes stand out as places of warmth and welcome.

I have mentioned that theologians have formulated criteria for the use of the internal forum and at the end of this chapter will be found the most recent example of such criteria, offered by three of the German bishops to their priests and people. A common factor in all these sets of criteria is that a true discernment can take place only when the second marriage has been in existence for some time. A real difficulty is that this position has nothing to say to those who, recovering from the trauma of marital break-down, are wondering about future relationships. Such situations arose repeatedly during the course of the research.

This problem must be faced. It is often correctly stated that divorce in itself does not debar someone from the Eucharist, and the support groups do an excellent job in dissuading people from thinking otherwise. However, when people are recovering from the trauma of their broken marriages and beginning to wonder whether they dare form a new relationship, they often ask where they stand. If, for whatever reason, the annulment process is not an option, then they are not slow to see the anomaly of a position which offers them a solution only in the distant future, when they have proved themselves. Indeed these situations stand in marked contrast to those of people who are able to obtain an annulment so that they can have another church wedding, but who have little or no attachment to the church community and no intention of practising their faith.

My criticism of the guideline is not in regard to it as part of a valid discernment process for those for whom it was formulated, namely those who have regularly attended Mass for many years and who have not been going to Holy Communion, but as a criterion for the use of the internal forum in every situation.

Of course it must be understood that many theologians and canonists tread warily, using language sparingly and offering carefully constructed safeguards to placate the Church authorities. When the internal forum was being explored as a way forward for those who could not find redress through the tribunals the concept was regarded by most as quite revolutionary. Thus the criteria needed to offset the inevitable anxiety that would surface among those who took a stricter stand.

Father Sean O'Riordan CSsR wrote tactfully on the subject in an article in *Alpha* in 1989.

The 'pastoral solution', wisely and discreetly utilised, has a centuries-long history behind it. (I was interested to see it being discreetly used in the diocese of Rome itself when I first started working there 30 years ago.)

The Roman authorities have, in fact, no objection to its prudent use but are opposed to giving it publicity in the life and pastoral practice of the Church in case the belief of the 'simple faithful' might thereby be weakened.[27]

This is entirely in keeping with a tradition of prudent pastoral care in the internal forum of the confessional, where the Church has always respected the rights of individuals to confidentiality and where the seal of secrecy is absolutely binding. But it does not answer the problem that I have confronted in the research, namely how to respond when the internal forum solution is no longer so exceptional and people are wanting to know whether it is applicable in their situations.

Ironically it is articles such as Father O'Riordan's in popular journals – albeit in this case in Ireland – which have helped to spread the message. Likewise as some members of the support groups in England and Wales have benefited from the ministry of their priests in the internal forum, so others have sought similar relief and interest has grown. Rome may be trying to retract a position to which previously it had given guarded approval, but my experience of the situation is that events are overtaking the Church.

Whatever debates may be taking place at the theoretical level, this research reveals that the internal forum is a pastoral option now freely discussed in the support groups. It is a topic for guest speakers at group meetings and for workshops at national conferences. It was referred to at some support group meetings as if it were a perfectly normal and well-regulated process.

People occasionally spoke of the resolution of their problems in the internal forum. Generally it was clear that a genuine process of discernment had taken place and I never gained the impression that there was a cavalier attitude abroad where priests were taking the law into their own hands. For example one ASDC couple spoke movingly about how they had been together for seventeen years without receiving the sacraments. 'Then we heard about the internal forum in this very room.' A visiting priest had addressed the group on the subject and later ministered to this couple. He told them that the fact it was so long was the evidence he needed and if it had been only five years he might not have felt free to act. In turn they considered it was right that it should have taken that length of time. 'We might not have been ready had we heard about it right away.'

I am not suggesting that the evidence of the research points to the fact that the use of the internal forum is now normal pastoral practice; indeed I found some groups and individuals who had never heard of it. The point I am making is that it is becoming more commonly known and discussed and therefore less exceptional.

The irony is that the more pastors seek to bring pastoral relief and introduce people to the available options the more they compromise the very solutions they are advocating. If Sean O'Riordan is correct and it is the publicity which creates the anxiety in Rome, then this truly is a no-win situation.

The danger for the Church is that it lays itself open to the charge of dishonesty if it is willing to support a secret code of practice provided it remains secret.[28] I am not questioning the Church's right to exercise a ministry in the internal forum which is private and confidential – such a ministry is vital for the moral and spiritual welfare of God's people and is at the heart of the sacrament of reconciliation. However, I am asking the question: Does not the new pastoral situation, which this research has identified as the sheer number of broken marriages, require some new initiative on the part of the Church to eradicate the confusion now surrounding the available pastoral options?

Too many questions remain unanswered and too many people's lives are at stake for the present confusion to go unchallenged. The internal forum as a means of resolving irregular marriage situations can no longer be regarded as the discreet ministry described by Sean O'Riordan – it has already received too much publicity. Nor can the solution be to prohibit its use. Where would that leave all those who have received internal forum solutions?

An example of the problem of people who have been guided by their priests in the internal forum subsequently being placed in bad faith arose early in 1993. Bishop John Jukes (Auxiliary in Southwark) spoke out against the use of the internal forum on a BBC *Heart of the Matter* documentary (see p. 139, note 5). He said:

> I regard those priests as wrong and mistaken. There's a kind of setting up of credit, you know – put enough credits together and therefore you become entitled to receive the blessed Eucharist. I think that advice is dangerous. It's certainly against the teaching of the Church, but it's dangerous as well. In my experience the couple may follow that advice for a while but then eventually their good judgement and good sense starts [*sic*] to intervene. They start to see a dichotomy, a separation between what they're doing and what they start to see as the objective reality about God's will for the people who are married and those who are not married. That's the problem about this internal forum solution.[29]

As a result of this comment I was informed by an ASDC organizer that some of her members, who had been counselled in the internal forum, had been thrown into a state of turmoil.

It could be argued that their turmoil confirmed the point Bishop Jukes was making, namely that deep down in their consciences people remain uneasy. It could also be argued that the consciences of most Catholics have been so conditioned to depend on authority that they are incapable of making conscientious decisions in the internal forum. In the first instance they depend on the authority of the priest who guides them, but when someone in a more authoritative office sows a seed of doubt, they are unable to retain their peace of mind.

The other television documentary illustrated the difficulty Catholics have with regard to authority.[30] In that programme Fr Joe Mills in Glasgow was seen compassionately seeking to resolve Mary's irregular marriage situation. She was hopelessly ignorant of the possibility of any solution to her problem. Fr Joe initiated the annulment process for her and in the mean time tried to bring her pastoral relief through the internal forum. She was unable to grasp fully what he was seeking to do, and when interviewed she said that he had given her 'a special dispensation' to go to Holy Communion.[31] This he insists he did not do, but it is what she understood him to have done as he tried to minister to her in the internal forum.[32]

In the end Mary found herself in the quite paradoxical position of thinking that Fr Joe was 'the greatest thing in the world' for enabling her to go to Communion (transcript, p. 26) while at the same time believing that until she obtained the annulment, she was still 'breaking one of the commandments' (transcript, p. 27). Would it not be more accurate to describe this as a problem of education rather than conscience?

Testing my findings

The roots of the problems relating to the internal forum and the pastoral care of the separated, divorced and divorced and remarried in general are to be found in the long and complicated theological history of marriage in the Catholic Church, outlined in Chapter 2. I have come to the conclusion that some of the key pastoral decisions in that history have created a complicated web of law which fails to address the situations confronting us today. Indeed quite the opposite, the web has become a net which traps the Church and prevents it from acting.

As this conviction became firmer I was grateful to have the opportunity of testing it with two large groups of clergy. One was a study day open to all the Nottingham clergy, the other a presentation to the Westminster Senate. Both occasions were attended by over 50 of the clergy and I was encouraged by them to pursue the study with determination. I had drawn attention to the sense of frustration which I had sensed among the clergy throughout the research and asked whether this was an accurate reflection of their mood. While a number in both groups were cautious about how the matter should be addressed, all agreed that there are some serious anomalies in the present system, and I was left in no doubt that they do experience a great deal of frustration. A letter from the then secretary to the Westminster Senate of Priests, himself a canon lawyer, expressed the appreciation of the clergy.

Thank you so much for your very valuable contribution at the Senate of Priests. The value of what you said was very much appreciated by the priests who were present. It seems to have been very well received indeed and I heard many positive comments on your contributions on both days.

In their group sessions the clergy were generally unquestioning over the distinction the Church makes between sacramental and natural marriage and the special nature of the consummated sacramental bond as wholly indissoluble. Their questioning was centred on the difficulty of establishing how and when this absolutely indissoluble bond is created rather than on the nature of the bond itself.

Nevertheless when I raised the underlying theological question about the nature of the bond at the study sessions with the Nottingham and Westminster clergy I found a willingness to consider any developments which might enable them to act with greater pastoral flexibility.

While it is true that the older generation of clergy are familiar with the Scholastic categories which explain the definition of the bond in canon law, that same knowledge cannot be presumed among the younger clergy.

This was impressed on me when I interviewed a young priest who is a defender of the bond for his diocesan tribunal. I had asked him for the interview because he had a reputation for being a committed priest and for having a rapport with young people. I was confident that he would express the views of a younger group of clergy who are expressing anxiety about liberal trends in theology and wish to see more discipline in the life of the

Church in general. Knowing that I considered this was a group which had not been adequately represented in the clergy gatherings, he kindly agreed to the interview.

He had hoped to assemble a small group of like-minded clergy but in the event none was able to join him. The interview surprised me. I had expected someone who would take a rigid stand on Church teaching and hold to the letter of the law. In fact I met a very sympathetic priest, conscious of the limitations of the system and willing to act occasionally in the internal forum. However, he was deeply concerned to uphold the ideal of the permanence of marriage and spent some time explaining how he approached the subject in his marriage preparation talks.

I explained that none of this was in dispute and introduced a discussion on the bond, its history and the ontological principles which now determine its definition in canon law. He responded by explaining that he had never studied Scholastic metaphysics and wondered whether I was not exaggerating its importance in my analysis.

For me this was a telling moment. Here was a young priest, extremely well educated in Rome and Oxford, working for his tribunal as a defender of the bond, who seemed content to define the bond in general terms as the principle of permanence rather than in ontological terms as a reality. I estimate that most of the clergy would be content with such a definition.

The initiative of three German bishops

Although my social research was confined to the experiences of the Church in England and Wales, it is important to remember that this is an issue which affects the universal Church and especially the developed regions of Europe, North America and Australasia.[33]

Other Episcopal Conferences have given the subject a considerable amount of thought. For example in the autumn of 1992 the German bishops spent a week in Würzburg discussing the whole matter under the direction of Fr Bernard Häring. The following autumn three of the bishops wrote a joint pastoral letter for their dioceses, offering quite definite direction in the field of pastoral care. Regarding the admission of people in irregular marriages to the Eucharist they were concerned that while people's conscientious judgements must always be respected, they should not just make up their own minds, but should enter into a discernment process with a priest. They reasoned that the Eucharist is always an official act of the Church and they insisted that they did not wish to give general permissions or exclusions. The criteria they considered indispensable for this use of the internal forum were as follows:

- When there is serious failure involved in the collapse of the first marriage, responsibility for it must be acknowledged and repented.
- It must be convincingly established that a return to the first partner is really impossible and that with the best will the first marriage cannot be restored.
- Restitution must be made for wrongs committed and injuries done insofar as this is possible.
- In the first place this restitution includes fulfillment [*sic*] of obligations to the wife and children of the first marriage (cf. Code of Canon Law, Canon 1071, 1.3).
- Whether or not a partner broke his or her first marriage under great public attention and possibly even scandal should be taken into consideration.
- The second marital partnership must have proved itself over a long period of time to represent a decisive and also publicly recognizable will to live permanently together and also according to the demands of marriage as a moral reality.
- Whether or not fidelity to the second relationship has become a moral obligation with regard to the spouse and children should be examined.
- It ought to be sufficiently clear – though certainly not to any greater extent than with other Christians – that the partners seek truly to live according to the Christian faith and with true motives, i.e., moved by genuinely religious desires, to participate in the sacramental life of the church. The same holds true in the children's upbringing.[34]

The three German bishops had presented their guidelines as an interpretation of *Familiaris Consortio* (84) which calls upon pastors 'to exercise careful discernment of situations'. One year later Cardinal Ratzinger and Archbishop Bovone for the CDF countered by insisting that *Familiaris Consortio* does not allow of such an interpretation. Effectively they condemned the use of the internal forum in all situations barring those in which people would be willing to abstain from sexual relations, arguing that because marriage 'is essentially a public reality' only the public resolution of a situation in the external forum is admissible.[35]

In the weeks following the publication of the CDF letter reports from around Europe suggested a level of unease among a number of hierarchies. Bishop Lehmann, a co-author of the German initiative, was reported to have considered this 'a harsh answer',[36] and a number of the German bishops spoke out in support of their three colleagues.[37] While both the Swiss and Austrian bishops' conferences were said to support the Vatican position, the priests' council of Innsbruck, presided over by their bishop, issued a statement saying they could not accept it. They argued: 'In showing such high regard for the internal forum, we feel confirmed by church tradition and Catholic moral theology.'[38] The Belgian bishops reaffirmed the importance of the individual conscience as final in this as in any other case.[39]

I will return to this whole matter in my final analysis in Chapter 8. For now I simply point to yet another remarkable anomaly as a result of the CDF letter. Pastoral ministry in the *internal forum* for the vast majority of priests and people is associated solely with the problem of marital breakdown. Now it is the one area in which it is being offically outlawed.

Summary

The consultation with the clergy complemented the findings from the consultation with the laity in some significant ways. Although the clergy came in for considerable criticism from the laity, it became clear that many are well aware of the inadequacies, anomalies and injustices of the present discipline, though they often feel constrained by it. They recognize that in many instances they have failed their people and they yearn for someone to release them from the trap in which they feel caught.

As with the laity they demonstrated a belief in the sanctity and permanence of marriage, confirming what I believe is the *sensus fidelium* in this matter. However, the majority had serious misgivings about the official discipline which so limits their pastoral effectiveness.

It seemed to me that few of the clergy had given serious consideration to the underlying theological problem of the definition of the bond which I have isolated as the key to the problem. Nevertheless when they were invited to reflect on this question I found them not only sympathetic, but positively encouraging.

Notes

1 See Canons 1063–1072, which deal with the duties of the bishop and the priest in relation to the preparation for marriage.

2 See Canons 1400–1707, which deal with ecclesiastical courts and the process of marriage annulment.

3 *Catholics and Sex*, transcript of Programme 3 on *Divorce* (London: Compulsive Viewing Limited, 1992), p. 30. Transmitted on Channel Four, 7 December 1992.

4 See Theodore Davey, 'The internal forum' in *The Tablet* (27 July 1991), pp. 905–6; letter from Cardinal Joseph Ratzinger, *The Tablet* (26 October 1991), pp. 1310–11.

5 See *Twice Married, Twice Blessed?*, BBC, *Heart of the Matter* series, transmitted 17 January 1993 (transcript of the programme). Joan Bakewell, the presenter, had introduced the topic as follows:

> The use of the internal forum had been growing on the quiet ever since Vatican II, the liberalising years for Catholic doctrine, but now the Vatican in Rome is hardening its position against. Cardinal Ratzinger, Prefect of the Congregation for the Doctrine of the Faith, the man who masterminds papal doctrine, has now denounced abuses of the internal forum. The impact of his statement completely reversed the practice of priests like Father Michael Clifton, who had previously, on his own authority, readmitted remarried couples to communion. (p. 14)

Mgr Peter Smith had also referred to this letter in programme 3 of *Catholics and Sex*. He said:

> Well I think there is such a thing as the internal forum solution, although Cardinal Ratzinger recently had something to say about that, and doesn't seem very keen on it. (Transcript of the programme, p. 21)

6 The days in question were a study day with 60 priests at Nottingham Cathedral on 22 October 1992, and sessions with the Westminster Senate of Priests at London Colney on 23–24 November 1992.

7 Comment of priest at the end of a group meeting with his fellow clergy:

> Speaking personally I think it has been the most instructive discussion on this subject ... ·Whenever this discussion has been held in the past it has always ended up with people getting rather hot-headed and hot under the collar.

8 Edward de Bono developed the concept of 'lateral thinking' in a number of publications during the 1960s and 1970s, including *The Use of Lateral Thinking: Break the Stranglehold of Logical Thinking* (Harmondsworth: Penguin, 1971) and *Lateral Thinking: A Textbook of Creativity* (Harmondsworth: Penguin, 1970). He continues to explore the value of freeing our thinking from the strictures of traditional logic. In a recent publication, *I Am Right – You Are Wrong: From This to the New Renaissance: From Rock Logic to Water Logic* (London: Penguin, 1991), de Bono argues that the brain is a self-organizing information system, whose potential is stifled when it is controlled by the rigid categories and absolutes of the traditional logic of Western thinking. He acknowledges the contribution that such logic has

made to progress and development and notes the influence of the Church on Western thinking, but he challenges the idea that argument and the adversarial system of debating an idea is always the best way to reach the truth (see pp. 204–10). He offers this telling comment on the defects of argumentation:

> There is the adversarial posture and the role-playing (so destructive for example in divorce proceedings). There is polarization and a win/lose substitution for exploration. Almost the entire time is taken up on attack and defence rather than on the creative construction of alternatives. Win/lose implies staying within the starting positions while creative design involves designing new positions that can offer real values to both sides. (p. 207)

I have introduced this concept of lateral thinking because although no one actually offered it as the basis of their thinking, it provides a category for explaining what in practice they are doing or are seeking to do in their efforts to find ways out of seemingly intractable pastoral problems.

9 'Introduction' in CCL-USA, p. 42.
10 CCL-USA, p. 42.
11 CCL-USA, p. 43.
12 Örsy, CCL-USA, p. 44.
13 It is important to note that it is only the bishop or a synod of bishops who exercise this ministry. See Örsy, CCL-USA, p. 44.
14 See Humphrey O'Leary CSsR, '*Oikonomia*: a more excellent way?', *Newsletter: Canon Law Society of Australia and New Zealand* (Spring 1992), pp. 33–42.
15 See DS 1807.
16 See James H. Provost, 'Intolerable marriage situations: a second decade', *The Jurist*, 50 (1990), pp. 586–7.
17 James H. Provost in 'Intolerable marriage situations revisited', *The Jurist*, 40 (1980), pp. 141–96, deals with the distinctions in detail.
18 See Ralph Tapia, 'Divorce and remarriage in the Roman Catholic Church today', *Thought* (September 1982), p. 185, cited by Fr Barry Brunsman, *New Hope for Divorced Catholics* (San Francisco: Harper, 1989), pp. 79–80.
19 See Theodore Davey, 'The internal forum', *The Tablet* (27 July 1991), pp. 905–6.
20 Provost contributed articles on 'Intolerable marriage situations' to *The Jurist* in 1980 and 1990, but the series began with an article by Ladislas Örsy, 'Intolerable marriage situations: conflict between external and internal forum', *The Jurist*, 30 (1970), pp. 1–14. This issue also carried the following accompanying articles:
Peter Huizing SJ, 'Law, conscience, and marriage', pp. 15–20.
Bernard Häring, 'Internal forum solutions to insoluble marriage cases', pp. 21–30.
Anthony Kosnik, 'The pastoral care of those involved in canonically invalid marriages', pp. 31–44.
Leo C. Farley and Warren T. Reich ST, 'Toward "An immediate internal forum solution" for deserted couples in canonically insoluble marriage cases', pp. 45–7.
Richard A. McCormick SJ followed the debate in 'Notes on moral theology', *Theological Studies* (1971–82).
21 Comment of an area bishop to his clergy during a study day led by Fr Theodore Davey CP: London Colney, 12 February 1991.
22 Cardinal Ratzinger, *The Tablet* (26 October 1991), p. 1311.
23 From the context it is clear that the Pope is referring not just to the divorced, but to the irregularly remarried divorced.

24 See Theodore Davey, *The Tablet* (10 August 1991), p. 906.

25 Apart from all the planned interviews, I have discussed the research with hundreds of other people in the course of the past six years. In general people expressed the hope that something will be done to alleviate the suffering of those who are unable to receive Holy Communion because of the present discipline. Among the most vociferous in calling for a way forward was the new army of religious sisters now working in parishes.

26 Morris West and Robert Francis, *Scandal in the Assembly: A Bill of Complaints and a Proposal for Reform on the Matrimonial Laws and Tribunals of the Roman Catholic Church* (London: Pan/Heinemann, 1970).

27 Sean O'Riordan CSsR, *Alpha* (23 November 1989), p. 10. (This journal, published in Dublin, has since ceased publication.)

28 Sean O'Riordan alludes to this point though he does not deal with it. In the article quoted he wrote:

> Critics of this 'two-tiered' approach of Rome to this and other complex problems of today – notably American critics such as Fr Charles E. Curran – characterise it as 'dishonest' (stating one thing in principle and doing something quite different in practice).

29 Transcript of *Twice Married, Twice Blessed?*, p. 13.

30 *Catholics and Sex*, Programme 3, *Divorce*, transmitted on 7 December 1992.

31 Transcript of *Catholics and Sex*, Programme 3, *Divorce*, p. 25.

32 Fr Mills explained the situation to me during a telephone interview, 16 August 1993.

33 Archbishop Worlock, commenting on his disappointment that the 1980 Synod did not respond more positively, said:

> The turn-down at the Synod, following our National Pastoral Congress, was far more overwhelming than I had expected, and was a clear indication that our problems and solutions were not shared by the universal Church, or at least the non-European majority. (Letter to the Committee in response to the draft report for the 1994 Low Week Meeting of the Bishops' Conference, 25 January 1994)

There is no doubt that the energy expended on these problems is different in the underdeveloped parts of the world, but they do have their problems. The superior of the Redemptorist mission in Tafara, Zimbabwe, told me that his attempt to effect an internal forum solution failed because local custom would not permit it. He had tried to resolve the problem for a couple for whom the bridal price would not be paid for many years. The community had no problem about the couple living together, but there was no question of them receiving Holy Communion until all the contracts had been fulfilled and the wedding ceremony had taken place.

In the focus group meeting with the clergy in Birmingham, one priest had recently returned from the foreign missions and was bewildered at the tenor of the discussion, especially when the problem of cohabitation was raised. He pointed out that where he had been working the girls had to prove that they were fertile before there was any question of a wedding.

34 Oskar Saier, Karl Lehmann and Walter Kasper, *Zur seelsorglichen Begleitung von Menschen aus zerbrochenen Ehen, Geschiedenen und Wiederverheirateten Geschiedenen* (Freiburg i.Br., Mainz and Rottenburg-Stuttgart: 10 July 1993),

p. 29. The translation is taken from *Origins* (Washington, DC: CNS (Catholic News Service)), vol. 23, no. 38 (1994), pp. 670–6 (p. 674).

35 Congregation for the Doctrine of the Faith, *Letter to the Bishops of the Catholic Church Concerning the Reception of Holy Communion by Divorced and Remarried Members of the Faithful* (Vatican: Libreria Editrice Vaticana, 1994), p. 7.

36 *The Tablet* (22 October 1994), p. 1360.

37 *The Tablet* (29 October 1994), p. 1388.

38 *The Tablet* (29 October 1994), pp. 1388–9.

39 *The Tablet* (19 November 1994), p. 1485.

6

Irregular marriage situations and RCIA

Candidates in the RCIA process who have been divorced and remarried pose a special problem. In 1991 the subcommittee of the Bishops' Conference for RCIA asked me if it would be possible to investigate the question within the context of RCIA separately. In the autumn of 1992 our agreed plan was put into effect and priests and their RCIA teams were interviewed in ten parishes across the country.

Prior to the interviews, anecdotal evidence and the opinion of the subcommittee suggested that on average between 25 and 50 per cent of enquirers are in irregular marriage situations according to Catholic canon law. I had anticipated that this was one of the few statistics that I would be able to confirm, but in the event it was not. None of the parishes reported figures approaching those percentages as a norm.

In general the numbers of enquirers and candidates were small. Apart from one parish which averaged 35 people received per year over ten years, only two parishes were averaging ten candidates per year and the other seven ranged from three to seven. These figures included people from other Christian communities as well as non-Christian backgrounds.

Although the percentages were not as high as expected, all the parishes reported the experience of people in irregular marriages, usually at least one or two per year. Thus they were able to contribute to the debate. Indeed both priests and people spoke animatedly on the question, the few cases they had encountered having left deep impressions on them.

Some priests and teams had established definite criteria for dealing with situations as they arose, but most had not, which meant that my questions, prepared in sequence and interdependent on each other, were often inappropriate. Therefore I was often forced to adjust this part of the interview, leaving them free to relate their own experiences. Where necessary I introduced hypothetical cases to test their opinions on experiences not yet encountered.

The problems surrounding broken marriages in the RCIA process and the available solutions are exactly the same as those affecting Catholics in general. It is the circumstances which are different.

In the first place there is an anomaly, which applies to all situations in which those concerned are not Catholics, that while Canon 1 in the 1983 Code states that 'the canons of this Code concern only the Latin Church', the canons on marriage become retroactive for people seeking reception into the Church. Of course this has been true for people seeking reception prior to the introduction of RCIA. What RCIA has done is highlight the problem in a new way, because it has brought it more sharply into focus for the wider community.

There is a feeling of embarrassment among many priests and people, when having reached out to others in a missionary spirit and offered them an initial welcome to the community of faith, they find themselves forced to temper that welcome and make it conditional on the Catholic resolution of a marriage problem long since resolved in every other way. And of course the problem becomes accentuated the more successful RCIA proves to be.

Is it unreasonable to ask whether St Paul's resolution of the problems he encountered with the early converts in Corinth (1 Corinthians 7:10–16) should set a precedent which could enlighten our examination of the present problem? The circumstances he encountered were confined to converts from non-Christian backgrounds and his solution 'in favour of the faith' formed the basis upon which the later theological distinction between natural and sacramental marriage was made. It is this later theological development which is the root cause of our inability to act with ease today, yet the reason for Paul's decision was that Christians are called 'to peace' (v. 15).

Enquirers and eventual candidates for RCIA come for a variety of reasons and from a variety of backgrounds. Few enquirers are likely to have much knowledge of Catholic jurisprudence or the canon law governing divorce and remarriage.

The second case history in Chapter 3 pointed to the fact that it can save later embarrassment if the facts regarding an individual's marital status are established in the early stages of the RCIA process. Many of the parishes interviewed had come to this conclusion, some as a result of bitter experiences. Others still left it to chance and trusted that the matter would arise because of the openness of the group.

Where steps were taken to establish the facts, it was usually in a personal interview with the clergy, during which the subject would be delicately broached. Two had an initial questionnaire which included details on marital status. Almost all expressed a feeling of unease, but considered it preferable to the later embarrassment.

In one parish the whole problem was causing deep distress. There was a flourishing RCIA process and had been for many years, yet two members of the team were unable to receive the sacraments. One was a Catholic in an irregular marriage, the other someone who, having taken part in the process, had become fully active in subsequent years – indeed had been responsible for seven others being received into the Church – yet had been unable to be received into full communion herself. The priest confessed that it 'broke his heart' and that for fear of leading anyone else into this situation he had actively dissuaded a number of enquirers from the very beginning.

The pastoral options

The annulment process

Once a problem came to light the usual policy of the clergy was gently to investigate whether it could be resolved in the external forum by the tribunal. One priest mentioned that he immediately 'phoned a pal of his at the tribunal'.

The general impression I received from the whole of the research was that these cases would be looked upon by the tribunals with special sympathy because of 'the circumstances'. It seems to me that this is right because it is acknowledging, albeit subconsciously, the importance of the community of faith. However the problem remains that the only official solution is one designed to preserve the integrity of a theological system that makes distinctions which have no bearing on the experiences or the understanding of those concerned. In these circumstances it is highly unlikely that the scandal argument will be relevant; quite the opposite, those involved in RCIA tend to be scandalized that the Church has not evolved an effective way of dealing with the problem.

The remaining argument is the metaphysical one which draws distinctions between the unity of the Eucharist and the disunity of the irregular marriage situation (FC 84), which in turn leads us back to the theology of the ontological bond.

The internal forum

All the clergy interviewed in this part of the research declared themselves willing to test the external forum first; opinions varied as to how far they would pursue this if they came to the conclusion that it was pastorally undesirable. It is fair to say that when in doubt, most were prepared to err on the side of freedom and seek some pastoral solution outside the law.

There was one exception to this rule and in that parish the priest considered it his duty not only to inform enquirers immediately if there were complications, but also to warn them of the impasse to which this could lead. In that parish alone did they report that some had dropped out of the RCIA process because of irregular marriage problems. During the previous six years he had been able to resolve three situations in the external forum, including one involving the Petrine privilege, while three people had left the process because of their circumstances. I should add that during the conversation surprisingly the priest did not rule out the possibility of using internal forum solutions in his ordinary pastoral ministry.

It was particularly interesting to hear how bishops and tribunals sometimes connive to resolve problems. One priest described how he sought an annulment but the petitioner could not provide witnesses. It was the vicar general of the diocese who eventually told him 'to deal with it'. Another priest described how his vicar general always insisted that 'rules must never get in the way'. I was told of a story which had dragged on unresolved for over two years. When messages on the tribunal answerphone remained unanswered and the bishop was consulted, he suggested that the messages were probably left unanswered 'for a reason'. The person was duly received that Easter. I was told that some bishops suggest that on these delicate issues it is better not to ask for permissions which cannot be given, the inference being that prudent use of the internal forum is quite in order.

An interesting example of Catholic casuistry was provided by a team leader who described how she now resolves the whole problem. Firstly she reminded me that in the early days of RCIA forms had to be completed and forwarded to the vicar general and any irregularities were likely to be challenged. However under the present dispensation candidates are accepted by the bishop at the Rite of Election, prior to any form-filling exercise. She argued that she had no business raising difficulties if a candidate had already been elected by the bishop. Another example of sidestepping the problem was given by those who fill in the forms, but simply write 'Married'.

One priest, who had taught Moral Theology at the seminary many years ago, was able to make a complete distinction between the internal and external fora. He insisted that the magisterium must continue to make a public stand on the ideal, leaving the clergy free to deal with individual cases of conscience. He was genuinely concerned that this research might unearth information which would lead the bishops to make unhelpful statements. He wondered whether he was becoming cynical, but thought it better to leave well alone.

Reception into the Church without the sacraments
On the question of the reception of divorced and remarried non-Catholics into full communion with the Catholic Church the CDF did issue the following directives to the Scandinavian bishops in 1976:

1. As concerns baptized non-Catholics, whose present marriage cannot be ecclesiastically regular because of the previous marriage of one of the two parties, such persons can be received into the Catholic Church, but not admitted to the sacraments. A dissolution of the previous marriage 'in favour of the faith' is possible only for the non-baptized.
2. With regard to the admission to the sacraments of the previously divorced and remarried, the Congregation requests that you not introduce any innovation. In case you propose theological arguments for a change of practice, the Congregation is gladly ready to investigate them.

At this point it is worth noting the interesting anomaly that according to the 'Rite of Reception' the candidate celebrates the sacrament of reconciliation before the profession of faith and the celebration of the 'Rite', and thus receives one of its sacraments before being a member of the Church. In my second case history in Chapter 3 I have already demonstrated how this arrangement can create most difficult pastoral situations.

The advice given by the CDF to the Scandinavian bishops and article 84 of *Familiaris Consortio* contain *non sequiturs*: in what way is someone who is debarred from the Eucharist truly in communion with the Church? Misunderstandings and the injustices which arise from such confused teaching already abound. The magisterium must face these questions and offer a response to the faithful: they have a right to know that these questions are being seriously considered and just solutions sought.

It cannot be right to argue that the private forum of conscience is always available but that publicly the Church must hold the line. The private forum of conscience is not available to many who never hear anything but the public pronouncements or who, in 'shopping around', do not find the right priest.

As part of the RCIA research I asked everyone to give an opinion on the directive given to the Scandinavian bishops. With the exception of one priest and one team member, my interviewees heard these directives in amazement. None immediately noted the development of pastoral practice, which provided for the admission of candidates in irregular marriages. All focused on the inherent contradiction of receiving people into communion and depriving them of Holy Communion.

It is a testimony to the successful catechesis through this century that the faithful are now so eucharistically centred. Either our eucharistic theology is wrong or our theology of marriage is wrong, but it is not enough to tell people to make 'spiritual communions' or that God has other ways of looking after them.

Looking to the future

I inquired as to whether it was the expectation of those involved in RCIA that the problem of the pastoral care of the invalidly married in this context would be the catalyst which would force the magisterium to reconsider pastoral care to Catholics in broken marriage situations. I was surprised to find that few had given it much consideration and generally they did not anticipate any major developments as a result of pressure from this quarter.

For myself I do believe that it may provide the context in which a serious re-examination of the teaching can take place. If the numbers involved in RCIA continue to increase – in the Archdiocese of Westminster 600 people were presented for election in Lent 1994 – pressure will inevitably mount on the teaching Church to seek a solution, possibly within an extension of the grounds 'in favour of the faith'. Furthermore there is the whole question of the so-called *Roman Option*, resulting from the decision of the Church of England to ordain women to the priesthood. If whole congregations decide to seek admission into the Catholic Church it is certain that among their number will be those who have been able to communicate in the Anglican Church, but who would be barred from receiving Holy Communion in the Catholic Church.

Familiaris Consortio refers to the 'supernatural sense of faith', explained in *Lumen Gentium* (LG 12), and insists that it 'does not consist solely or necessarily in the consensus of the faithful' (FC 5). However, when priests and people are virtually unanimous in their concern, their voice must be heard.

The work of RCIA is being hailed by the Church as a work of the Spirit, a process which responds to the needs of today's world and speaks a language which people understand. Participants learn to tell their stories and see those stories as part of God's story – God's redeeming love for the world, revealed in Jesus Christ. There is something wholly contradictory in the suggestion that there may be certain situations which cannot be reached by that redeeming love. And that contradiction is accentuated when the theological language of the ontological bond is presented as the explanation.

Summary

The findings of this chapter reinforce those of Chapters 4 and 5. What makes these data significant is the context in which they were gathered. Here the ecumenical dimension was highlighted, re-emphasizing the *non-sequiturs* of the present Roman position.

7

The tribunals

In my thesis I provided detailed information on the working of the tribunals in England and Wales. For the purposes of this book it will be sufficient to summarize my findings and concentrate more on the experiences of the faithful who have encountered the system. It will be clear from much of what I have already written that I have serious theological problems with the annulment process. However, that does not mean that I do not acknowledge the enormous amount of pastoral relief which this system has brought to many people.

I have argued that pastoral problems evoke pastoral solutions. In the mounting workload of the tribunals we have a classic example of that principle being put into effect. The Church in England and Wales has responded energetically, seeking to improve the efficiency of its tribunals.

While it is to the Church's credit that the process of annulling marriages has been made available to many more people in response to the crisis of marital breakdown, the fact that at the end of the twentieth century Church courts exist almost solely for this purpose reveals something of how the law and the theology of marriage have become inextricably bound together.

It is well documented that the Church has been adjudicating on marriage questions throughout its history. We have noted the origin of the Pauline privilege in Chapter 7 of Paul's first letter to the Corinthians. In that same letter Paul had already told the community to ban someone who was living with his own stepmother (5:1–13). The development of doctrine on marriage and the local and universal decrees that accompanied this development can be traced in detail through Mackin's trilogy of books on 'Marriage in the Catholic Church'.[1]

In this matter as in every other the Church has had periods of strictness and leniency. By the twelfth century 'marriage cases were generally heard according to the regular judicial process', but while his predecessors expressed concern that the ordinary judicial processes were not always being observed, 'Pope Clement V, in his decretal *Dispendiosam*, explicitly permitted marriage cases to be heard by a kind of summary process, a process that would be carried out, as he said "simpliciter et de plano, ac sine strepitu iudicii et figura" (simply and easily and without the pomp and circumstance of a judicial proceeding)'.[2] The Council of Trent insisted on the judicial process and the local ordinary alone was empowered to hear the cases.[3]

Laws may be enacted and decrees issued but abuses will still occur. By the middle of the eighteenth century Pope Benedict XIV was so concerned about the situation that he issued a constitution *Dei miseratione* (3 November 1741). It was this document which prepared the way for the modern process by introducing the role of 'defender of the bond' and requiring an appeal against every first instance case. Laurence Wrenn describes the situation which led Pope Benedict to act.

> Oftentimes the respondent would not appear at the trial at all, so there would be no one to defend the marriage (there was, in those days, no one designated as a defender of the bond). Sometimes both parties would appear, but either the respondent would be in collusion with the petitioner, or he or she would simply not be interested in appealing higher – the marriage would then be declared null after a single hearing (there was, in those days, no mandatory appeal). As a result, according to Benedict, men and women alike were having their first, second, and even third marriages declared null and were, with the blessing of the Church, blithely entering still another.[4]

Whatever abuses may have occurred in earlier centuries, in this century the Church took firm control. The 1917 Code of Canon Law determined that all marriage cases were to be heard by three judges, 'every contrary custom being disapproved and all contrary privileges revoked' (Canon 1576).[5] In fact the 33 canons on marriage cases (Canons 1960–1992) proved so forbidding that in the following years very few marriage cases were dealt with at the local level. The Holy See attempted to improve matters by issuing a new Instruction, *Provida mater* (15 August 1936), but its 240 articles served only to compound the problem.[6]

It is not surprising that the common perception of annulments immediately prior to Vatican II was that they were granted in Rome and that they were very rare.

Post Vatican II – tribunals respond to the new situation

For our purposes the most important factor in understanding the present situation is that in the wake of Vatican II some local churches did begin to act. The North American Church led the way. As early as 1968 the Canon Law Society of America had produced a set of norms, which the National Conference of Bishops in the United States of America proposed to Rome for approval. 'The principal features of the *American Procedural Norms* were the recognition of the petitioner's residence as a source of competence, trial by a single judge, discretionary publication by the judge, and discretionary appeal by the defender.'[7] Rome approved and they became effective on a trial basis from 1 July 1970, remaining in place until the promulgation of the 1983 Code of Canon Law.

These provisions motivated the Church in the United States to seek efficiency in processing a vast number of cases. To this day the majority of all annulments is still granted in the United States of America.

The overall increase in the number of annulments granted worldwide became quite staggering. Fr Barry Brunsman in his book *New Hope for Divorced Catholics* states that 'even as late as 1968 there were only 338 annulments granted. The numbers swelled to 52,000 by 1983, a 15,000 per cent increase in just fifteen years.'[8]

During the same period in Britain the workload of the tribunals also dramatically increased. In 1968 just twelve of those 338 annulments were granted in Great Britain. In 1970 the number had risen to 45, and steadily increased throughout the following two decades.[9]

Unfortunately all the advantages of the American system, most notably the special interim arrangement which permitted an annulment to be granted at a first instance hearing if the defender of the bond chose not to appeal, were not available in other parts of the world. However the Holy See did respond to the rapidly developing situation and issued a *motu proprio*, *Causas Matrimoniales*, on 27 March 1971, which modified the prescriptions of the 1917 Code.[10]

By 1980 the diocesan tribunals of England and Wales were issuing nearly 500 decrees of nullity per year, and by 1990 over 1,000 per year. The last published figures are for 1993: 1,087 first instance cases given affirmative judgements, 1,219 second instance cases ratified and decrees of nullity issued.

The attraction of a more efficient annulment system seems to have appealed to the English-speaking world in a way which has not been repeated elsewhere. The Canon Law Society of Great Britain and Ireland presented a comparative study of the 1986 figures for the world. They show that the six English-speaking countries, Australia, Canada, Great Britain, Ireland, New Zealand and the United States of America, account for over 90 per cent of all the annulments granted.[11]

While it would be naive to suppose that absolute uniformity could be obtained, it would surely be to everyone's advantage if the process could be standardized across the dioceses of England and Wales and a regular forum of communication established. In the thesis I was cautious in interpreting the data, but they do reveal that some parts of the country are served better than others, a fact strongly supported by the evidence of the meetings and interviews of this research.

Contrasting experiences

In general the clergy and laity who work for the tribunals expressed gratitude for being able to bring pastoral relief to many people. Some are largely unquestioning about the adequacy of the system and seek only to ensure that their tribunals are run as efficiently as possible. Others work equally hard to achieve those ends, but are less convinced that the system is satisfactory.

For example at a group meeting with the clergy one priest expressed frustration with his tribunal but continues to work for it because it is all that is available. It was significant that his fellow priests expressed their gratitude to him for providing for them an approachable and compassionate link with the system.

I think it is important to make some distinctions regarding the nature of the arguments presented. Those who defend the tribunal system tend to appeal to the authority of the Church and the fundamental need to preserve the ideal. One priest, clearly feeling himself under pressure from the group and in the minority, argued that he took courage from saints like John Fisher and Thomas More, who were willing to stand up and be counted.

The love of the martyr is our ideal for married people as well as for celibates and single people. There is a social pressure on all of us at present to compromise on that kind of quality loving.

He feared that the emphasis now is primarily on a search for human happiness and neglects the true purpose of life. He also spoke of the faith tradition in England, 'where we have esteemed those who were willing to pay the price out of commitment to Jesus in love'. In conclusion he thought that 'a lot of us are under pressure to say that two and two make five because if we say that it will make you happy'.

At the root of the argument presented by this priest was a concern that the debate was being held out of context, outside the ultimate meaning of Christianity and the faithful and obedient following of Christ.

Although they were always a minority, a sizeable number of priests and people staunchly defended the Church's official discipline, and there were some lively exchanges at a number of group meetings. Analysing these discussions I noted that the defence of the system was often related to a wider concern about the lowering of moral standards in general and the danger of constantly conceding ground to liberal views which are judged to accelerate a decline in behavioural standards.

By contrast those who held a contrary position were also concerned that they could not raise the debate in context. They considered the Church's official position to be highly disputable. They were at pains to insist that they were not disputing the ideal of marital fidelity nor the sanctity of the marriage bond. Their concern was that the system of dealing with marriage breakdown in the Catholic Church was failing to bring justice to many people's situations and is a contradiction of other fundamental gospel precepts. Their anxiety was that it is impossible to discuss the foundations upon which the discipline is based without being accused of a type of betrayal.

This is a problem which is not peculiar to the discussion of marriage, but tends to inhibit free discussion about many issues in the Church. Thus while one priest said: 'Once we break ranks, I do think that diminishes faith in the Church as the true Church and confuses people's thinking as to who is right, who has authority', others argued that the only way to effect change is to break ranks.

The voice of moderation, of the middle way, was also heard. One religious priest, a teacher of canon law, who had served the tribunal over many years, spoke of the importance of owning the past. He pointed out that the tribunal process can effect 'tremendous healing', given the right personnel, but equally that the 'civil servant approach' can cause a lot of harm. In the same vein another priest spoke of canon law as 'a tool and a servant' but not equivalent to the will of God.

There is no doubt that some people have benefited greatly at the hands of sympathetic auditors and an efficient system, using the time and opportunity to grow in understanding and heal the wounds of the past. For them the annulment process was a good experience of a pastorally caring Church. One ASDC member commented that she 'found annulment a healing process: like the twelve steps'.[12]

Among the support groups naturally there is great interest in the annulment process because for many it may provide an official solution. Thus when priests from the tribunals are invited to speak about the annulment process and their talks are advertised, invariably there is a larger attendance than usual. As one Rainbow member explained: 'There must be a great need. We have had as many as fifteen in the group. That night we had forty or fifty people.'

Further evidence of the interest in the annulment process was the fact that a number of people indicated that they were familiar with books such as Ralph Brown's *Marriage Annulment in the Catholic Church*, Geoffrey Robinson's *Marriage, Divorce and Nullity: A Guide to the Annulment Process in the Catholic Church* and Joseph P. Zwack's *Annulment: Your Chance to Remarry Within the Catholic Church*.[13] Some local support groups make such books available for their members.

This increased awareness has a cutting edge. As people become more familiar with the process and its value, they also become more familiar with its drawbacks and its anomalies. This was particularly well illustrated for me by the story of Susan Lawrence.

Susan's interest in the nullity process and what decided her to study canon law was misinformation from a priest regarding her own canonical status after the breakdown of her marriage. She sought a second opinion and discovered that hers was a straightforward case of 'lack of canonical form'. In due course she trained as an auditor in her diocese and continued to attend canon law classes.

While Susan found her work as an auditor rewarding, she became increasingly concerned that the basic ignorance of the majority of those who petitioned the tribunals created unnecessary complications for all concerned. She became convinced that people would benefit from a legal advice service and after consulting a number of clergy friends decided to provide one.[14] Her contention is that petitioners and witnesses have a right to know how the system works and that furnished with a proper understanding of the process they would be able to supply better depositions, which would be to their advantage and to the advantage of the tribunals.

Surrounding the annulment process is a kind of mystique, which conveys the impression to those outside that here is a process beyond the comprehension of most and best left in the hands of those who are competent.[15] Petitioners, respondents and witnesses are expected to provide evidence by answering the questions asked, but are not expected to understand the value of their evidence, nor be party to the analysis of that evidence and the way judgements are reached.

The conclusion I have reached is that this is counter-productive. If the annulment process is to serve its purpose and preserve the integrity of the marriage bond, it is surely important that all those who are involved, and especially those who are seeking annulments, should understand the nature and workings of the process.

Monsignor Pompedda argues that only experienced judges are qualified to decide marriage cases (see note 15). By concentrating on the complexity of many of the cases he explains why the Church is cautious in these matters, requiring 'two concordant decisions be handed down by competent tribunals in order for the judgement to be definitive and executive; cases of marital nullity must be judged by collegial tribunals consisting of three judges' (p. 4).

That is one side of the story but it is not convincing when tested against the case of someone like Peter Desmond. He was a cradle Catholic. A year after finishing university he married at the age of 23. Less than four years later he was separated and subsequently divorced. In September 1983, twenty months after his wife left him, she petitioned Portsmouth Tribunal for an annulment. A negative decision was given in March 1985. His wife lost interest, but Peter pursued the case and after further evidence was presented, it was given an affirmative judgement on appeal to Southwark in September 1986. Rome insisted on taking the third hearing. A long delay ensued, largely explained by the ill-health of the priest in Portsmouth who was handling the correspondence. This was not resolved until January 1990 when Southwark took up the case again. In the summer of 1993 Rome finally gave a negative judgement.

Apart from the question of natural justice (a young man is made to wait ten years for a decision) it is not easy to explain the anomalies of the system. Mr Desmond might reasonably ask why he should be expected to believe that the judgement of the judges in Rome is more reliable than those in Southwark. After all, if the case with the extra evidence had been heard in Southwark in the first instance, it is not unreasonable to presume that it would have been granted in the ordinary course of events by the

Appeal Tribunal at the second instance.

Furthermore on the question of the need for a large number of competent judges giving their opinions, we have already noted that in United States of America between 1970 and 1983 a case did not have to go before a second set of judges if passed at the first instance. And even more remarkable is the fact that an Episcopal Conference can permit individual diocesan bishops to entrust cases to a single judge. Having previously granted specific dispensations for this practice in both the Arundel and Brighton and East Anglia Dioceses, the Bishops' Conference of England and Wales at the Low Week Meeting 1994 issued a general permission to all the dioceses 'to establish a single judge tribunal according to the provisions of Canon 1425 n.4' (resolution 6).

This further demonstrates a desire that the tribunals in England and Wales should seek ways of managing their workloads as efficiently as possible. However it does suggest that, as with advice offered by individual priests, how one's case is dealt with will depend very much on which diocesan tribunal one approaches.

The research revealed that the majority of people, including those who are grateful for having received annulments from the Church, see the process as little other than the Church's way of resolving the problem of broken marriages. The state grants divorces, the Church annulments. Thus while people may learn something of *how* the annulment process works, few gave any indication that they understood *why* the Church operates this system.

While for some the annulment process was an important part of their growth and healing, for too many others it has been a harrowing experience, characterized by insensitive handling at every level, including intrusions into the most private and personal aspects of their lives, forcing them to revive painful memories from which they were desperately trying to recover. For example, for some women to have been questioned by celibate males about the intimate details of their sexual lives served only to intensify their pain and sadness. There are those who could take no more and who opted out of the process, others who are deeply embittered because their petitions failed, and others who, hearing what it entails, cannot bring themselves even to begin the process.

There is a growing number of people who will not petition for an annulment because they do not wish to establish that their marriages never existed. Even when they have been told that the length of the marriage and the fact that they have a family are not insuperable obstacles if it can be established that there was something defective in the original consent, they remain adamant that they do not wish to dispose of that period of their lives in such a way. Closely linked with this is an anxiety about the status of the children after an annulment. In spite of all the reassurances to the contrary, many people consider that the logical consequence of an annulment is the illegitimacy of the children. Sometimes it is the children themselves who have brought pressure to bear on their parents not to proceed.

This category of divorced people, who for a variety of psychological reasons will not approach a tribunal, may have grounds for an annulment which can never be put to the test.

Some people described in detail their encounters with their local priests or with tribunal personnel. One man explained that he insisted that his case be presented to the tribunal although his priest had told him he had 'no chance'. Seventeen days later a priest at the tribunal phoned to remind him that on his wedding day he had said 'for better or worse', adding 'well this is it: for worse'. When the petitioner remarked that this seemed a little uncharitable he was advised to apply to another tribunal.

A woman told of how her daughter reluctantly agreed to co-operate as a witness. The daughter was unhappy because she did not wish to criticize her father and also because she could not understand how the Church could say that her parents had never really been married. The mother went on to say that 'although it was a washout, we all did our best; we did have some good times, so how can you say it has never been a marriage over 29 years?'

Contrasting annulment and divorce

A good number of people made comparisons between the divorce process and the annulment process, which is especially significant in view of the continuing debate in Britain about the divorce laws. This comment from an ASDC member was typical of the apprehension felt by many:

> There's no real reason why I want an annulment. From what I have gathered it gets very personal and I've already gone through a separation and divorce and I'm not sure if I want to go through the personal part of my marriage with anybody, because I didn't have to do that in my divorce: we've just both agreed to get a divorce, no arguments, no nothing.

The Divorce Reform Act of 1969 radically changed the nature of divorce in Britain in that it became possible for a couple to be granted a decree of divorce after two years' separation if they mutually consented to the fact that their marriage had irretrievably broken down. By 1975 this was the ground for 30 per cent of divorces granted to husbands and 24 per cent granted to wives.[16] The figures have remained largely unchanged in the intervening years. Divorce no longer had to be a process between adversaries.

New legal prescriptions are introducing a mediation process for couples with marriage difficulties. This has two objectives: firstly to try and save as many marriages as possible; secondly to try and ensure the least amount of acrimony and dispute should a marriage have irretrievably broken down.

Such a development in thinking is of particular importance for the Church, whose annulment process can often be quite adversarial. Although tribunals are not engaged in trying to apportion blame, the very nature of a process which seeks data to support the theory that there was something defective in the consent of the couple at the time of the marriage inevitably includes the examination of the couple's behaviour patterns both before and after the wedding. The outcome can be quite acrimonious, especially in view of the prescriptions of Canon 1598, which insist on the right of individuals to be informed of the contents of their partners' depositions, albeit that judges do retain some discretion in this matter.

At the same time Church pronouncements on the breakdown of marriage, while restrained and tempered by comparison with the past, often make distinctions between those who should be regarded as victims of their situations and those who should be held responsible for them. *Familiaris Consortio* itself uses such language.

> There is in fact a difference between those who have sincerely tried to save their first marriage and have been unjustly abandoned, and those who through their own grave fault have destroyed a canonically valid marriage. (FC 84)

Such an approach stands in marked contrast to the attitudes of many of those interviewed during the research. There is a definite movement away from seeking to determine the guilty party towards a mutual acceptance of failure. I sensed that many people were concerned to live in peace, seeking to remain friends with their former partners for their own peace of mind and for the sake of their children. Any process which might threaten that harmony was held in suspicion. Such an attitude mirrors that sought by parts of the new civil legislation in Britain. It is a fundamentally Christian position and should influence the ongoing debate over the efficacy of the annulment process.

When marital breakdown was rare it was possible for both the State and the Church to maintain a strong public position opposed to divorce, while at the same time resolving the problems of the few. The State granted a limited number of divorces on restricted grounds, the Church ministered to a small number through the tribunals. Once the equation changed and the numbers reached today's proportions, that dual approach is no longer feasible. People compare the relaxation in the divorce laws and the associated increase in divorces with the broadening of the grounds for annulment and the corresponding increase in the number of decrees granted. In both cases the question is whether the legal changes were responding to the demands of the new situation or whether they created it.

The first objective of this research has been to analyse the situation as it stands. The clock cannot be turned back. If people are entitled to annulments, then in justice they should be granted them and granted them speedily. It cannot be right to suggest that the number of annulments should be curtailed solely to prevent the possible cause of scandal to others. To deny justice to one group of people for the sake of what is perceived as the greater good of the rest is a moral contradiction.

I would suggest that the atmosphere has changed to such an extent that a new problem now confronts us: namely that when a Catholic marriage breaks down there is an automatic presumption on the part of many that it must have been invalid and therefore will be open to a declaration of nullity.

This expectation is the consequence not only of the increased number of annulments now being granted, but also of the grounds on which they are being granted. It is an examination of this aspect of the question to which we must now turn.

The new grounds for annulling marriages

Much attention is now given to Canon 1095 of the 1983 Code, which has extended the whole notion of those who 'are incapable of contracting marriage' for psychological reasons. In his commentary on this Canon Thomas Doyle writes:

Until the mid-twentieth century, ecclesiastical jurisprudence recognized the invalidating effect of mental illness only when it precluded the possibility of a responsible human act at the time of consent. Traditionally, the ground of nullity was known as *amentia* or insanity.[17]

He goes on to consider the development of understanding which has taken place and which is now enshrined in parts 2 and 3 of the Canon, *lack of due discretion* and the *incapacity to assume the obligations of marriage.* Writing about the latter he states:

The development of jurisprudence in this area expanded with scientific advances in understanding the nature and effects of the personality disorders ... Since the sixties, an abundant jurisprudence has developed concerning the effect of the personality disorders on the ability to assume and fulfill [*sic*] marital obligations. (p. 777)

In Chapter 5 of *Marriage Annulment in the Catholic Church* Ralph Brown deals with the psychological grounds in detail (pp. 87–107). A comparison between this, the text of his third edition (1990), and the text of the 1977 edition (pp. 44–54) shows that, because of the developments that had taken place after Vatican II, the concepts enshrined in the 1983 Code of Canon Law were already firmly in place prior to its publication. Although, unlike English Law, Church Law is not established by precedent, nevertheless tribunals all over the world keep a close eye on the decisions of the Roman Rota as a guide to what is acceptable in current jurisprudential practice.[18] In fact it was some important decisions in the early 1970s which provided the springboard for the dramatic increase in the number of annulments granted.[19]

In surveying all the diocesan tribunals of England and Wales I sought information on this matter and discovered that almost all of the 22 dioceses reckon that the majority of their annulments are granted on psychological grounds: ten estimated 90 per cent or more.

This new knowledge, relating to the interpretation of the psychological factors governing the validity of consent, radically extended the field of work in which the tribunals operated. As one judge, who had been working in the tribunals since the 1930s, said to me: 'I now grant annulments on grounds that could never have been imagined twenty or thirty years ago.' It could be argued that what happened was a natural development of a system already in place, but by the same token it could also be argued that a wholly new system has evolved which bears little resemblance to what preceded it.

Jean Bernhard analyses this development of what is coined 'psychiatrization' of jurisprudence and asks whether this is the appropriate forum for dealing with such matters.[20] He contrasts 'the shift from a procedure leading to a "declaration of nullity" to a procedure "annulling" marriage' (p. 113), the former justified in the perspective of marriage seen as a contract, the latter a way of dealing with the broader vision of marriage as a community of life and love. He points out:

> When Christians come to our courts they are usually not looking for a judicial decision about the validity of their consent from the beginning. Rather, they seek a human and evangelical evaluation of their conjugal life, of the legitimacy of their break-up, and even of their second marriage. (p. 110)

He quotes Fr Hayoit, the *Officialis* of Tournai:

> When we are dealing with a problem that is specifically juridical, it is normal to follow purely juridical criteria, but is such really the case in our matrimonial nullity proceedings? The marriage bond and the matrimonial experience both go far beyond their undeniably juridical aspects. The fault of the juridical process consists in reducing to purely juridical facts these realities, problems and situations which do not depend, at least exclusively, on the juridical. (p. 110)[21]

I think these are vitally important considerations. Clearly tribunals will continue to play a part in the life of the Church, judging disciplinary matters. Among these will be situations in which the validity of marriages will be in question and judgements can be made. The question now before us is whether the tribunals are the correct forum for dealing with the broader issues, arising from a new theology of marriage and our increased awareness of the psychological nature of human relationships.

My reading of the situation is that there is a limit to how effective the tribunals can be in this continually developing field. There are many grey areas and however well organized the tribunals become, it is hard to envisage the situation in which they are competent to deal with all the problems of marital breakdown encountered in the community of the Church.

Bernhard concludes his discussion of the question by presenting the hypothesis: 'would a stronger form of insertion of the couple into the Christian community allow us to consider what we call a "declaration of nullity" in a new light?' (p. 114). He argues for a new consciousness on the part of the couple and the wider community which would recognize mutual commitments which if not fulfilled could lead to a 'declaration of nullity'. He suggests that we would be dealing 'with the non-integration of the marriage commitment considered as a "pilgrim" form of consent, rather than as a momentary consent given at the time of the celebration of the wedding' (p. 115).

We are dealing with people's lives, which are in process, whose spirituality is that of a pilgrim people, growing in the love of God and each other. Yet our system for dealing with difficulties in the most precious and sensitive of those human relationships is based on a theology which is static and immoveable.

Summary

It will always be possible for marriages to be rendered invalid by certain impediments, and provision should be made by both the State and the Church for such marriages to be declared null and void. However, as has been amply demonstrated by the data in this study, when this is the prime avenue of investigation into broken marriages, many people are left bereft of pastoral help.

I have isolated the cause of this unhappy situation as a static theology, which defines the bond of Christian marriage as an ontological sacramental reality: the theology which still underpins the discipline of the Church. When the theology of marriage concentrated heavily on the notion of contract, to make a legal declaration that a marriage was null and void because the bond had never been formed was logical. Such a static theological position does not sit so easily with Vatican II's understanding of marriage as a covenant, caught up in God's unfolding revelation of love: a love in which the couple mature and grow together.

Conclusions from all the empirical data

Chapters 3 to 7 have presented detailed accounts of my research in the Catholic Church among people who have experienced separation, divorce and remarriage, among the support groups and the clergy, among RCIA teams and the tribunals. I began by addressing certain key issues, which I was aware of from my own pastoral experience. These could be summarized under the two headings: *perceptions* about divorce among Catholics; and the *experiences* of Catholics in dealing with divorce in the Church. Two articles in the *Catechism of the Catholic Church* provide us with convenient texts with which to contrast these two factors. Article 1614 expresses the common perception of Catholics that divorce is wrong and forbidden. It states:

> In his preaching Jesus unequivocally taught the original meaning of the union of man and woman as the Creator willed it from the beginning: permission given by Moses to divorce one's wife was a concession to the hardness of hearts. The matrimonial union of man and woman is indissoluble: God himself has determined it: 'what therefore God has joined together, let no man put asunder.'

By contrast article 1640 explains the position the Catholic Church seeks to maintain in practice.

> Thus *the marriage bond* has been established by God himself in such a way that a marriage concluded and consummated between baptized persons can never be dissolved. This bond, which results from the free human act of the spouses and their consummation of the marriage, is a reality, henceforth irrevocable, and gives rise to a covenant guaranteed by God's fidelity. The Church does not have the power to contravene this disposition of divine wisdom.

Here we are comparing not just nuances of language but differences of emphasis and interpretation, which considerably affect what people experience. The differences sum up the tension I consistently encountered during the research.

I was not surprised to find that there remains a general perception that divorce is forbidden by the Catholic Church and therefore Catholics entering this state instinctively feel alienated and rejected. That instinctive feeling is often reinforced by the reaction of fellow Catholics, priests and people alike.

At the same time there is also a general perception that sometimes it is possible to 'sort out' the problem and that there are 'ways round' it if you can get in touch with the right people.

All this I tried to examine in detail through my interviews and group sessions. As the research progressed it became clearer and clearer that my original instincts were correct and that the processes employed by the Catholic Church, namely the heavy dependence on annulments in the external forum, were little understood by priests and people alike. For some there was a ready acceptance that if this is what the Church has decreed it must be the correct way to proceed, but for many others there was a growing mistrust of the system, which was often born of a direct involvement in it. The anomalies, inconsistencies and injustices of the present pastoral situation have been highlighted repeatedly in this study and I will offer my conclusions on these in Chapter 8. What also emerged from the social research, and what I was less prepared for, was the discovery that long before addressing the technicalities of a person's situation, there is need for a ministry which can reach out and embrace the person in distress. It was clear that such a ministry had been hampered by the suspicion which surrounds the very word 'divorce' in Catholic circles. The support groups which sprang up in the early 1980s addressed that problem directly and provided a ministry which had been sorely lacking. I noted this fact and in my report to the Bishops' Conference I urged that these ministries be encouraged and supported.

To that report and to how I envisage a theological solution which is both systematically and pastorally sound we must now proceed.

Notes

1 Theodore Mackin *What Is Marriage?* (1992), *Divorce and Remarriage* (1984), and *The Marital Sacrament* (1989; all New York: Paulist Press).
2 Laurence G. Wrenn, 'Matrimonial procedures' in CCL-USA, p. 1009.
3 Council of Trent, Session XXIV, chapter 20. See Wrenn, CCL-USA, p. 1009.
4 CCL-USA, p. 1009.
5 See Stanislaus Woywod, *A Practical Commentary on the Code of Canon Law* (London: Herder, 1926), II, p. 206.
6 See Wrenn, CCL-USA, p. 1010.
7 See Wrenn, CCL-USA, p. 1010. The full text of these procedural norms is printed in the first edition of Ralph Brown, *Marriage Annulment in the Catholic Church: A Practical Guide* (Leigh-on-Sea: Kevin Mayhew, 1977), pp. 111-16.
8 Barry Brunsman, *New Hope for Divorced Catholics* (San Francisco: Harper & Row, 1989), p. 61.
9 See *Canon Law Society of Great Britain Newsletter*, No. 8 (March 1971), Appendix 1. (Further references to the newsletters, which subsequently included Ireland, will be in the abbreviated form: CLSN plus volume, year and page numbers.)

10 For the text of *Causas Matrimoniales*, see Brown, pp. 107–11.

11 CLSN 80 (1989), p. 32.

12 This refers to the process followed by Alcoholics Anonymous and other such '12-Step' groups.

13 Brown, *Marriage Annulment* (3rd edn; Rattlesden: Kevin Mayhew, 1990); Geoffrey Robinson, *Marriage, Divorce and Nullity* (3rd edn; London: Geoffrey Chapman, 1985); Joseph P. Zwack, *Annulment* (New York: Harper & Row, 1983)

14 Susan Lawrence has outlined the service she offers in a short handout. In this she makes some important observations:

> Many people would like to find out more about the Catholic teaching on marriage, divorce and annulment but are discouraged from doing so, often for the following reasons:
> **Fear** of having to confide their problems to the clergy.
> **Fear** of being harshly judged and rejected by those to whom they turn for help.
> **Guilt** that their marriage has failed.
> **Guilt** arising from the belief that the Church has turned its back on them.
> **Ignorance** of the Church's teaching on what makes a valid marriage.
> **Ignorance** of the grounds on which marriage may be declared null.

15 In an article in *L'Osservatore Romano* Mgr Mario F. Pompedda insisted that 'subjective opinion' should not prevail over 'objective truth'. He argued that judgements about the validity of marriages must be left to those competent to judge:

> We can immediately and easily demonstrate the complexity of a judgement regarding the nullity of a marriage: in addition to cases which concern the substantial form of the celebration or the existence of impediments that are easy to recognize and prove, there are all the cases which concern the presence, integrity and sufficiency of consent, in which a judgement is very complex, so much so that some cases also require the help of an expert. In this context, it is very difficult to understand how anyone could give priority to a subjective conviction and neglect the judgement made in the external forum by experienced judges, a judgement which is well-considered, competent and enlightened by the proofs offered by experts. ('Noted Rotal auditor explains the canonical status of Catholics who are divorced and remarried', *L'Osservatore Romano* English edn (16 September 1992), pp. 4–5)

16 See Lawrence Stone, *Road to Divorce* (Oxford: OUP, 1990), pp. 440–1.

17 'Marriage' in CCL-USA, p. 775. Ralph Brown points out that the Latin term *amentia* does not translate easily and 'does not mean insanity as such, although a person suffering from insanity (not a clinical term) would be regarded as *amens* or suffering from amentia. It is a condition in which either temporarily or permanently the person does not enjoy the use of reason': Brown, *Marriage Annulment* (3rd edn), p. 88.

18 See Brown, *Marriage Annulment* (3rd edn), pp. 20–1.

19 For examples of such cases see Doyle, CCL-USA, pp. 775–8.

20 Jean Bernhard, 'The evolution of matrimonial jurisprudence', trans. G. Morrisey OMI and James H. Provost, *The Jurist*, 41 (1981), pp. 105–16.

21 P. Hayoit, 'Valeur et limites du jugement prudentiel lors d'un constat de nullité de mariage', *Revue de Droit canonique*, 30 (1980), p. 135.

8

The theological future

Writing about the sociology of Roman Catholic theology Gregory Baum defended the thesis 'that until now contemporary Catholic theology, despite its pluralistic form, is characterized by a strong pastoral orientation'.[1] He claimed that this approach had been fashioned by Vatican II, noting that 'the opposition to the imposed Thomistic orthodoxy in the years prior to Vatican II was usually inspired by pastoral concerns' (p. 131). Referring to the tension theologians experience with the magisterium he concluded:

> They realize that if they defend themselves against the magisterium in purely academic terms they will not be heard, but if they can show that their thought is pastorally significant and actually corresponds to the Christian life of the community, then – they trust – they will be able to keep their theological approach alive in the Church. (p. 132)

Pastoral concerns have dictated the course of this theological enterprise and it is my hope that for that reason this issue will continue to remain very much alive. I was very conscious of the three objectives agreed with the Committee for Marriage and Family Life of the Bishops' Conference:

(a) To get in touch with the experience of Catholics in the breakdown of marriage and family, and discover how the Church in England and Wales responds in such situations.
(b) To discover to what degree those in canonically irregular marriages consider themselves to be members of the Church, and what steps the

Church takes to integrate such people into itself, with particular reference to sacramental practice.

(c) To suggest a coherent pastoral policy based on a sound theology of sacrament and Church.

I am satisfied that in response to the first two objectives in my report to the bishops I was able to present a clear and detailed presentation of the situation in England and Wales and offer a series of practical pastoral recommendations concerned with developing the ministry of the support groups, re-educating clergy and laity alike and ensuring the efficient running of the tribunals. However I found it much more difficult to respond to the third objective because it became clear that the discipline of the Church was not underpinned by a sound theology of sacrament and Church. I am confident that in focusing on the ontological bond I have isolated the reason for this and in this chapter I offer a way forward.

I have argued from the beginning that the theological history of this question together with the data from the social research led me to the firm conviction that the Catholic Church in its efforts to defend the principle of the sanctity and permanence of marriage has succeeded only in defending a medieval metaphysical concept: *the absolutely indissoluble consummated ontological bond*. In my opinion this imposes dangerous limits on the Church's pastoral effectiveness.

Facing the theological impasse

My conclusion was that I could not formulate a coherent pastoral policy because the present *discipline* of the Church is not based on 'a sound theology of sacrament and Church'. That is not to say that a sound theology of sacrament and Church is not available. The theology of Vatican II and the insights which continue to flow from it provide the Church with a sound base for addressing the present pastoral problems surrounding marriage. It is my contention that the discipline codified in the law does not reflect that theological development.

This is clearly illustrated by the remarkable assertion in Canon 1055.2 that 'a valid marriage contract cannot exist between baptised persons without its being by that very fact a sacrament'. It is true that the historical struggles between Church and State explain the context from which such a formulation arose, but today we must assert categorically that this is an erroneous teaching, for it fails to take account of the fact that faith is a precondition for any sacramental action. This legislation in company with that which so carefully defines the nature of the bond of marriage and how that bond is established are the result of that theological tradition which was preoccupied with determining the matter and form of each sacrament and the precise moment at which sacramental grace was imparted.

Today's theology has expanded our thinking to encompass a broader view of sacrament and the sacramental life of the Church. Karl Rahner was at the forefront of this theological development both before and after the Vatican Council. The genius of his work is that his doctrine of the 'supernatural existential' succeeded in bridging the gap between the Scholastics and the present day. In terms acceptable to Scholasticism he saw the primary meaning of grace as 'God's presence to and indwelling within the human person'.[2] What he did not accept was that an absolute division could be drawn between the natural and supernatural: extrinsecism. He takes the position that because God wills the salvation of all people and the whole of creation, the supernatural order of grace cannot be regarded simply as being imposed on the purely natural by an external decree of God.

> For an ontology which grasps the truth that man's concrete quiddity depends utterly on God, is not his binding disposition *eo ipso* not just a juridical decree of God but precisely what man *is*, hence not just an imperative proceeding from God but man's most inward depths? If God gives creation and man above all a supernatural end and this end is first '*in intentione*', then man (and the world) *is* by that very fact always and everywhere inwardly other in structure than he would be if he did not have this end, and hence other as well before he has reached this end partially (the grace which justifies) or wholly (the beatific vision).[3]

The implications of this teaching in regard to our understanding of sacramental marriage are immense, for it poses a huge question mark against a theology which makes an absolute distinction between natural and sacramental bonds. It points rather to the earlier Augustinian tradition, which saw a sacramentality in marriage *per se*.

To understand the sacramental theology of Rahner and his contemporaries it is necessary to begin by studying the whole notion of sacrament. Bernard Cooke states that 'less than a half-century ago, the universal Catholic approach to describing Christian sacraments was to think of them as "channels of grace", liturgical situations the faithful came to in order to be sanctified'.[4] Today we would not attempt to explain the relevance of each of the seven sacraments until we had examined the meaning of sacrament as symbol: the symbolic expression of God's presence among his people. Rahner insists that when we speak of symbol in this context we are speaking of something real. Herbert Vorgrimler notes that Rahner's 'favourite example is the human body: the human being is only "real" in the fundamental symbol of his/her body; the human spirit "expresses" and realizes itself in its bodiliness. External bodiliness "means" the human spirit acting within it.'[5]

Vorgrimler goes on to explain that 'if all human reality is symbolic reality, this is certainly true of the relationship God has willed to establish with human beings, and that decisively shapes human reality from beginning to end. If God desires to be present to human beings, God's presence must create a symbolic expression for itself in order that it can be "real" for human beings, since the complete disparity between God and the human makes an unmediated presence and communication of God impossible' (p. 10). Rooted in the Judaeo-Christian tradition is the conviction that God has communicated with his people in various ways until in the end he sent his Son (Hebrews 1:1–3). Thus Jesus is seen as the *Primordial Sacrament* of God, his whole life and his death making God present among his people: 'he has made known to us the mystery of his will, according to his good pleasure that he set forth in Christ, as a plan for the fullness of time, to gather up all things in him, things in heaven and things on earth' (Ephesians 1:9–10).

If Christ is the Primordial Sacrament, then the Church may be defined as the *Fundamental Sacrament*, for the Church is the community of believers in which Christ is made present in every succeeding age. Repeatedly the Pauline epistles speak of this community as the body of Christ (e.g. 1 Corinthians 12:12–30; Ephesians 4:12), all the members united with the head (e.g. Colossians 1:18; Ephesians 5:21–33). There is an obvious parallel here with Rahner's favourite example of the human body as the means whereby the human spirit expresses itself: the mystical body of Christ, the Church, is seen as the means whereby the Spirit of God is made visible in the world. And in Ephesians 5, marriage is used as the ultimate example of how this is achieved.

In this richer and more expansive understanding of the sacramental life of the Church the seven sacraments are understood as the occasions when we consciously encounter Christ and celebrate his real sacramental presence. We have seen that the Scholastics had difficulty in determining the matter and form of the sacrament of marriage (pp. 49–50), but in this vision of things marriage can come to the fore as the most natural sacrament of God's loving saving presence. Bernard Cooke offers this comment:

> Explanation of the individual sacraments traditionally starts with baptism. Apparently it is the first sacrament Christians are exposed to, and the one all the others rest upon ... However, as we attempt to place the sacraments in a more human context, there is at least the possibility that we should begin with another starting-point. Perhaps the most basic sacrament of God's saving presence to human life is the sacrament of human love and friendship. After all, even the young infant who is baptized after only a few days of life has already been subjected to the influence of parental love (or its lack), which in the case of Christian parents is really the influence of the sacrament of Christian marriage.[6]

One thing is certain and it is that we can no longer discuss the sacraments as isolated channels of grace. They can be understood only in that broader understanding of Christ as the sacrament of God and the Church as the sacrament of Christ. *Lumen Gentium* presents this vision of the sacramental life in examining the *mystery* of the Church:

> All those, who in faith look toward Jesus, the author of salvation and the principle of unity and peace, God has gathered together and has established as the Church, that it may be for each and everyone the visible sacrament of this saving unity. (LG 9)

In this vision it would be absurd to isolate the *sacrament* of marriage as an event which can take place outside the life of the faith community, and even be effected without the knowledge of the ministers and recipients.[7]

The theology of Vatican II concentrated on marriage as a covenant:

> Christ our Lord has abundantly blessed this love, which is rich in its various features, coming as it does from the spring of divine love and modelled on Christ's own union with the Church. Just as of old God encountered his people with a covenant of love and fidelity, so our Saviour, the spouse of the Church, now encounters Christian spouses through the sacrament of marriage. (GS 48)

This focus enriches our understanding far beyond the static notion of marriage as a contract, which had so dominated previous theological thinking. Yet in spite of two references to *covenant* in the 1983 Code (Canons 1055.1 and 1063.4) this is not the theology which informs the canon law of Marriage. Contracts can be legislated for but not covenants. Contracts by their very nature have conditions, but the covenant of marriage is called to reflect the unconditional love of Christ for his Church. To that extent it can indeed be argued that marriage is the most natural sacramental setting for Christ's saving work of reconciliation. And this leads us back to the whole notion of the sacramental life of the Church, not as individuals *receiving* sacraments, but as the community of believers *being* the sacrament of the risen Christ.[8]

This richer theology of sacrament draws the Catholic tradition much closer to that of the Orthodox *mysterion* and offers hope that a fruitful dialogue may take place with the Eastern tradition. The traditions of East and West are united in a profound belief in the sanctity and permanence of marriage and its sacramental nature, but in the East it is inconceivable that a sacramental marriage could be celebrated without any public celebration within the community of faith. Likewise for those who experience the breakdown of their marriages, ministry in the Orthodox Churches is not restricted by a mass of legal prescriptions, but is the fruit of communities seeking to heal and forgive. We must now ask how that pastoral tradition might influence the future thinking of the Catholic Church.

The Orthodox tradition

In reporting my findings from the empirical research I noted the widespread interest among priests and people in the Orthodox approach to marital breakdown and briefly looked at the ministry of *oikonomia* in the Eastern tradition (pp. 125–6).

It has become common for modern Western theologians and canonists to turn to this Eastern tradition of *oikonomia* as a potential solution when confronting the legal complexities of their own tradition.[9] I believe this is a laudable development, and in view of the renewed urgency that Rome is showing in its quest for unity with the Orthodox Churches, may yet prove to be a vital factor in forcing a theological reappraisal of the present Western discipline. In due course I will comment on the recent papal documents, *Orientale Lumen* and *Ut Unum Sint*,[10] but firstly we must examine the Eastern tradition regarding divorce and remarriage more closely.

J. H. Erickson warns: 'The position of the Eastern Orthodox churches on divorce and remarriage is frequently referred to in Western discussions of the subject, but less often is it correctly understood.'[11] He contends that 'seldom have such discussions taken into consideration the very different historical circumstances in which Eastern law and practice developed' (p. 39). He further argues that 'as a result, the deepest and most characteristic insights of the Eastern Orthodox have been inadequately explored, while at the same time weaknesses and limitations have been either ignored or misconstrued' (p. 39).

The fact is that the Eastern Churches in common with all the Christian churches have struggled with the tensions which we have been exploring throughout this thesis. And today they too face the new complications of trying to remain faithful to those traditions in the midst of a largely secular society. Thus, towards the end of his chapter Erickson begins to list anomalies in the Orthodox tradition, similar to some of those which I have enumerated in the Western tradition. For example he asks:

> How ... are the marriages of persons who in fact are non-religious agnostics to be regarded, even though these may have been blessed by an Orthodox priest in the Orthodox Church according to the Orthodox Rite of Matrimony? (p. 49)

He notes that widely divergent practices exist and confesses that this shows 'how confused the Orthodox understanding of marriage has become' (p. 49).

Scanning the literature, it is interesting to note that while Western writers invariably connect the Orthodox ministry to the divorced and remarried with *oikonomia*, their own theologians often deal with the same questions without explicit reference to it.[12] Thus Alexander Schmemann[13] compares the Eastern and Western traditions by examining the different interpretations of *indissolubility*. He begins by explaining that in the East 'this doctrine has not been given a "juridical" formulation'; it 'serves as a guiding principle rather than explicit legislation' (p. 98). He goes on to explain how the more liberal pastoral approach to remarriage in the East is not a denial of its belief in indissolubility:

> The whole point therefore is that this is not a 'compromise' but the very antinomy of the Church's life in this world. The marriage *is* indissoluble, yet it *is* being dissolved all the time by sin and ignorance,

passion and selfishness, lack of faith and lack of love. Yes, the Church acknowledges the divorce, but she *does not divorce*. (p. 104)

It is also important to remember that there is a very penitential aspect to the whole process, something which is reflected in the texts of the services for second marriages.[14] This penitential aspect would have to be carefully handled if introduced in the West. When Bishop Budd included a reference to the ancient order of *penitents* in his address to the 1992 ASDC national conference (see p. 88), I recall that many of the delegates, who already regarded themselves as the injured party, did not receive his words with enthusiasm. However, as we have seen it would be naive to imagine that in pastoral practice the Orthodox Churches do not experience similar disciplinary tensions when faced with similar problems in today's moral climate. To complete my social research and to examine more closely the actual process of *oikonomia*, I arranged a meeting with His Eminence Archbishop Gregorios of Thyateira and Great Britain.[15]

This meeting was richly rewarding. Archbishop Gregorios received me graciously and responded to all my questions with gentleness and patience. It was clear that he could not understand how the Roman Catholic discipline had developed in the way it has with an emphasis on legal prescriptions and the process of annulment. Once we began to talk about *oikonomia* he became very animated and it became clear that my questions about how it worked hardly made sense to him. He was, as it were, imbued with the spirit of *oikonomia* so that it was not so much something which he processed but something which he lived. To begin with he spoke about it in the context of the whole of Christian life and the work of salvation:

This is the understanding of the Christian Church about life and about God and about salvation ... God became man using his *oikonomia*. Otherwise it is beyond our understanding and conception.

He linked it with the scandal of the cross (1 Corinthians 1:22–25) and insisted that we miss the point if we do not see that 'God became man for you and for me and for everything'. He went on to say that 'absolution of sin is the *oikonomia* of God' and he concluded that therefore 'we forgive everything'.

He explained to me that *oikonomia* is not something which he holds but which is present in the life of the Church for the good of the whole community. Yes, he is the *oikonomos*, but much of the work is delegated to his fellow bishops and priests and together they try to ensure the good order of the community. It was clear that he trusted them implicitly because they were imbued with the same spirit. This all helps to explain why in the literature the resolution of marriage cases and the ministry of *oikonomia* are not always expressly linked. Örsy's explanation that only a bishop or a synod of bishops may exercise this ministry may be theoretically true,[16] but from what I could gather, in pastoral practice it is far from the reality. There is a court which deals with the cases of marital breakdown and this court is supervised by a trustworthy cleric. The Archbishop told me that sometimes people choose to consult him personally and sometimes he is consulted by the court, but the majority of cases are handled without his being involved.

It is possible for the Orthodox Churches to refuse to countenance a divorce, but I understood that this would usually be reserved for extreme cases where people refused to ensure just settlements in regard to former partners or the children.

Having said all this it should not be imagined that no effort is made to seek reconciliation. Archbishop Gregorios reminded me that is always the first priority, but once it becomes clear that the relationship has died, then a ministry of compassion and forgiveness is invoked. In the article already cited, Schmemann explains that in the East 'the Church neither grants nor acknowledges divorce, but to the lonely and abandoned it sorrowfully grants the right to take another spouse' (p. 106).[17] This may well be the theological theory, but in practice it is clear that the Church speaks about ecclesiastical divorces. The following note is taken from the *Official Year Book 1995 of the Greek Orthodox Archdiocese of Thyateira and Great Britain*:

For Divorces:
An ecclesiastical divorce may be granted after a civil decree has been issued. However, the parish priest must make every effort to reconcile the couple and avert a divorce.
Should the priest fail to bring about a reconciliation, the party seeking the ecclesiastical divorce should address a petition to the Ecclesiastical Court of the Archdiocese stating the grounds for such an action. The petition must be accompanied by:
a) the Degree [*sic*] Absolute of the civil divorce;
b) a copy/certificate of the ecclesiastical marriage which is to be dissolved; and

c) the set fees of the Ecclesiastical Court (being £150.00)
* Statistical Note: For the years 1989–1993 and up to July 1994 there
were a total of 529 applications for Divorce. Most of the applicants
were under thirty-five years of age. The reasons given were lack of co-
operation and extra-marital affairs.[18]

In both *Orientale Lumen* and *Ut Unum Sint* Pope John Paul II
expresses a deep desire for Christian unity, and seems to suggest that he
sees it as a realizable goal with the East. In *Orientale Lumen* he reminds us
that 'we have almost everything in common' (3), yet reflects how 'we are
painfully aware that we cannot yet share the same Eucharist' (28).
However he writes with a sense of real urgency:

The sin of our separation is very serious: I feel the need to increase
our common openness to the Spirit who calls us to conversion. (17)

Every day, I have a growing desire to go over the history of the
Churches, in order to write at last a history of our unity. (18)

In neither of these documents, any more than in the Decree on
Ecumenism of Vatican II, is the specific question of divorce and remar-
riage discussed, but there are references to the ancient and complementary
traditions and the need to be familiar with them, as well as the fact that the
Orthodox Churches possess true sacraments.[19] In a telling passage in
Orientale Lumen Pope John Paul II issues this warning:

If Tradition puts us in continuity with the past, eschatological expectation opens us to God's future. Each Church must struggle against
the temptation to make an absolute of what it does. (8)

It seems to me that the outcome of any dialogue between the Catholic
and Orthodox traditions on the pastoral care of the divorced must lead to a
serious reappraisal of the absolutist Catholic position on the ontological
bond. It is simply inconceivable that the East will abandon its ancient
ministry, based on its salvific understanding of *oikonomia*. Thus
Schmemann writes:

The ontological status of that first marriage is simply never made a
matter of question. To ask the question supposes a static view of

reality. Within the dynamic action attributed to the Holy Spirit by Orthodox theology, marriage can exist only when people actually live a marriage ... The real problem is not the abstract, Aristotelian essence that might remain, but what is to be done in pastoral terms with the existing situation. (p. 111)

I am convinced that there is now an inexorable movement towards change in the Catholic Church. We have seen that its renewed theology of marriage is born of a sacramental theology now more closely akin to the *mysterion* of the Eastern tradition. I am also convinced that the pastoral ministry of the East, inspired by *oikonomia*, is in practice the kind of ministry which the vast majority of those who took part in my research are yearning for, and furthermore I submit that this is a genuine expression of the *sensus fidelium*.

The *sensus fidelium*

It might be stretching a point to suggest that John Henry Newman foresaw the debate over divorce and remarriage in our time when he wrote *On Consulting the Faithful in Matters of Doctrine* in 1859, but it is not unreasonable to conclude that the principles upon which he structured his argument are applicable to this debate. Newman's prime concern was with the education of the laity and their proper relationship with the clergy and the hierarchy, and that underlying issue is very close to the present debate. It is true that the examples he used were strictly about doctrinal matters, notably the dogma of the Immaculate Conception and the Arian controversy over the Nicaean Creed in the fourth century, and some might argue that the divorce question is primarily a moral question, a matter of discipline. Here I would disagree. I believe one of the great mistakes that has been made in this controversy is the ready acceptance of a strict doctrinal position, thus reducing the argument to one of obedience to Church discipline.

In the recent debate between the German bishops and the Sacred Congregation the doctrinal questions were not addressed; the argument was conducted at the level of disciplinary norms in the pastoral arena and was reduced to a trial of strength between the Roman magisterium and the local churches (see pp. 136–8). Newman would certainly have felt strongly about this, for he had to live through that period of Church history when the centralizing power of the papacy as defined by the First Vatican

Council left an imbalance which was corrected only by the decrees of Vatican II. Modern commentators, seeing how Newman's vision was realized in those decrees, now speak of Vatican II as Newman's council.[20]

Newman offered criteria for establishing the *sensus fidelium*:

> Its *consensus* is to be regarded: 1. as a testimony to the fact of the apostolical dogma; 2. as a sort of instinct ..., deep in the bosom of the mystical body of Christ; 3. as a direction of the Holy Ghost; 4. as an answer to its prayer; 5. as jealousy of error, which it at once feels as a scandal.[21]

I contend that the data from the empirical research of this study satisfy these criteria and in particular I draw attention to the second and the fifth. While I do not claim that my research attempted to test Catholic opinion in general, I do claim that it offers a valid analysis of the opinions of those who are immediately concerned with the divorce–remarriage problem and who are steadily educating themselves in the finer points of the argument. The overwhelming weight of evidence from them – bishops, priests and people – is that their *instincts* tell them that something is seriously wrong with the present teaching and that more than that it is a *scandal*. Furthermore I am satisfied that their judgement reflects the opinion of the wider community because while I have not systematically researched its opinion, I have had ample opportunity to test my findings in the course of my ordinary pastoral work over this period. The fundamental arguments presented in this study have not been challenged. Indeed it is surely significant that the only voices raised in opposition are those which appeal directly to authority – the authority of the present Roman magisterium.

I am now convinced that the instincts of the faithful are very close to the tradition of the Orthodox Churches. They do not wish to deny the fundamental doctrinal teaching that marriage is a naturally sacred and lifelong union and is indeed a sacrament in the Christian community, but they fail to see how this belief is supported by the present discipline of the Catholic Church. Their instincts tell them that the saving presence of Jesus must be able to reach into every situation, especially those which cry out to him because they are part of the very brokenness he came to redeem. They see this as the most fundamental gospel imperative and I am sure they are right.

If there is one thing which perplexes these people more than anything else, it is that the Church can make judgements about their situations without necessarily taking into consideration their intentions. We have seen that this arises because of the way the present legislation defines the ontological sacramental bond.

Final thoughts on the bond and indissolubility

This study has argued that the Catholic Church in the field of divorce and remarriage has trapped itself in a web of law, which ironically was woven as a result of its attempts to address the pastoral problems surrounding these questions at different times in history. As pastoral solutions became enshrined in legal prescriptions and those prescriptions were informed by an interpretation of Scholastic metaphysics which defined the sacramental bond of marriage as an entity independent of a couple's relationship, the outcome was inevitably the situation which obtains today. This leans heavily on establishing whether or not a sacramentally, consummated and therefore absolutely indissoluble bond exists.

For the most part the debate within the Catholic Church has avoided directly challenging this doctrinal position which underpins its discipline. I am convinced that substantial progress will be made only when that position is dismantled.

I would like to illustrate this by drawing attention to the work of Kevin Kelly. In his book *Divorce and Second Marriage: Facing the Challenge*,[22] he moved the debate forward. I fully endorse his excellent work of integrating the covenantal theology of marriage, developed at Vatican II, into the disciplinary tradition. Again I fully agree with his concentration on a personalist theology of marriage as a lived state in process and not a static contract entered into at a given moment in time. He uses this perspective to redefine *indissolubility*, arguing that 'when a couple marry, they give their pledge that they will form an indissoluble union of persons through their love for each other. The indissolubility of their marriage is *a task to be undertaken*' (p. 28).

I have no quarrel with the argumentation of this section of his book, but I wonder about the wisdom of trying to redefine indissolubility. The difficulty faced in such an exercise is that you are still working under considerable constraint. The starting point is that the absolutely indissoluble, sacramental, consummated bond, as defined in canon law, does exist, even though it may be impossible to establish its existence for certain until couples have completed their married lives.

I contend that there is no need to redefine the bond or indissolubility.

All that is required is to draw attention to the contradictory statements presented in official Church teaching and draw the necessary conclusions. These contradictory positions are now succinctly presented in articles 1614 and 1640 of the Catechism. 1614 teaches that 'the matrimonial union of man and woman is indissoluble'; only in 1640 does it qualify this statement by explaining that *'the marriage bond* has been established by God himself in such a way that a marriage concluded and consummated between baptized persons can never be dissolved'. We know from our study that the 'way' in which the Church arrived at this position is by no means straightforward, nor is it at all clear that God 'has established' things in this way. Therefore to invest this statement with the authority of an unchallengeable doctrinal position is to do violence to the tradition.

A vivid illustration of the depths to which the argument can descend when trying to define words like 'indissolubility' is to be found in an article in *New Blackfriars*, by Germain Grisez, John Finnis and William E. May.[23] It is presented as an open letter to Archbishop Saier, Bishop Lehmann and Bishop Kasper and not only does it give 'indissolubility' a metaphysical connotation, but also a physical one. The authors argue that valid, sacramental and consummated marriage 'simply cannot fail, nor can the partners themselves or anyone else on earth destroy it, for marriage is without exception indissoluble in earthly society, just as sand is without exception indissoluble in water' (p. 327). It seems preposterous that such an argument can be advanced in a serious publication, but it does demonstrate the degree of fundamentalism which still exists among some proponents of a traditional position. Throughout their article the authors are also at pains to point out that the German bishops' pastoral proposals are a departure from the unbroken tradition of the Catholic Church since before the Reformation.

Of course they are correct in tracing the developments back to before the Reformation because it was then that the Scholastic metaphysics began to influence all our thinking about sacraments. They are wrong in suggesting that the tradition was unbroken. We have seen how the codification of the law in the 1917 Code and its subsequent representation in the 1983 Code only added to the anomalies and injustices already inherent in the system.

Some practical suggestions

I contend that the present legislation on marriage and the breakdown of marriage is not informed by the theology of Vatican II. Therefore an urgent review of the present canonical position is required. We have seen that the abrogation of impossible canonical prescriptions is not unprecedented (see p. 62), and so to begin with I lend my voice to those who call for the abrogation, or at least the revision, of Canons 1055.2 and 1108.[24] While such a move would not solve all the problems I believe it would release a lot of energy particularly in the ecumenical sphere. Canon 1055.2 is the canon which identifies the faithful with the baptized, and Canon 1108 makes canonical form a matter of *validity* for Catholics. Together they create many of the anomalies, inconsistencies and injustices which arise around the question of intention. It is in this area that so many people are left dumbfounded at the Church's reasoning over individual cases, and many examples have been given in this study. It is here above all that the inadequacy of the theology underpinning the Church's discipline is exposed and the vast majority of those involved in pastoral practice know this from personal and often bitter experience.

For the time being though life must go on, and priests and people continue to seek ways of dealing with the pastoral situation. The tribunal system of granting annulments will continue for the time being, and hopefully be run as efficiently as possible. In the longer term I hope that its function will be more like that of the Orthodox courts, described earlier in this chapter. Until then there will be many cases which, for a variety of reasons, will fall outside the competence of the tribunals.

The three German bishops reaffirmed the practice of the internal forum, but were challenged by the Sacred Congregation for the Doctrine of the Faith. I have heard it argued that the Sacred Congregation could not have pronounced otherwise and that the German bishops were mistaken in trying to discuss in public something which of its essence is private. I disagree. It seems to me that a huge problem has developed in this field because of ignorance among both priests and people of some of the most fundamental moral principles. Thus many people never gain access to ministry in the internal forum.

In the last analysis conscience must always be the deciding factor for every individual in any given situation. This is a fundamental moral principle which the Church proclaims and safeguards. Priests and people must be educated not just to know this in theory, but to live it in practice.

Notes

1   Gregory Baum, 'The sociology of Roman Catholic theology' in *Sociology and Theology: Alliance and Conflict*, ed. David Martin, John Orme Mills and W. S. F. Pickering (New York: St Martin's Press, 1980), pp. 120–35 (p. 130).

2   Roger Haight SJ, *The Experience and Language of Grace* (New York: Paulist Press, 1979), p. 123.

3   Karl Rahner SJ, *Theological Investigations* (2nd edn; London: Darton, Longman and Todd, 1965), vol. 1, pp. 302–3.

4   Bernard Cooke, *Sacraments and Sacramentality* (revised edn; Mystic, CT: Twenty-Third Publications, 1994), p. 73.

5   Herbert Vorgrimler, *Sacramental Theology*, trans. Linda M. Maloney (Collegeville, MN: Liturgical Press, 1992), p. 10.

6   Cooke, *Sacraments and Sacramentality*, p. 80.

7   For example when two non-Catholic but baptized people marry in a register office.

8   Bernard Cooke suggests that 'we have scarcely begun to think … about ourselves as Christian communities "doing" sacraments rather than simply "receiving" sacraments': *Sacraments and Sacramentality*, p. 76.

9   For example see Bernard Häring, *No Way Out?* (Slough: St Paul Publications, 1989), pp. 39–52; Ladislas Örsy, 'In search of the meaning of Oikonomia: report on a convention', *Theological Studies*, 43 (1982), pp. 312–19.

10 *Orientale Lumen*, Apostolic Letter of Pope John Paul II to mark the centenary of *Orientalium Dignitas* of Pope Leo XIII (London: Catholic Truth Society, 1995).
    Ut Unum Sint, Encyclical Letter of Pope John Paul II on Commitment to Ecumenism (London: Catholic Truth Society, 1995).

11 J. H. Erikson, 'Orthodox perspectives on divorce and remarriage' in *The Challenge of Our Past: Studies in Orthodox Canon Law* (New York: St Vladimir's Seminary Press, 1990), ch. 3, pp. 39–51 (p. 39).

12 John Harwood, the librarian at the Missionary Institute, London, prepared bibliographies on both subjects at the request of members of staff. This analysis is based on a selection of those writings.

13 Alexander Schmemann, 'The indissolubility of marriage: the theological tradition of the East' in *The Bond of Marriage: An Ecumenical and Interdisciplinary Study*, ed. William W. Bassett (Notre Dame: University of Notre Dame Press, 1968), pp. 97–116.

14 The order of Second Marriage may be found in the *Service Book of Holy Orthodox-Catholic Apostolic Church*, ed. I. F. Hapgood (Englewood, NJ: Antiochan Orthodox Archdiocese, 1975), pp. 291–308.

15 Meeting at Archbishop Gregorios' residence, 5 Craven Hill, London, on 17 October 1995.

16 See Ladislas Örsy, *Theology and Canon Law* (Collegeville, MN: Liturgical Press, 1992), p. 74.

17 In point of fact the Catholic tradition in relation to the dissolution of the bond is not dissimilar. In Pauline and Petrine privilege cases and in non-consummation cases, the Church does not declare the original bonds dissolved, but accepts that the new situations – a new marriage bond or the solemn vows of religion – cause the dissolutions.

18 *Official Year Book 1995 of the Greek Orthodox Archdiocese of Thyateira and Great Britain* (London: Thyateira House, 1995), p. 331.

19 *Orientale Lumen* 1, 5 and 8; *Ut Unum Sint* 50.

20   See *The Tablet*, Editorial (21 October 1995), p. 1331.
21   John Henry Newman, *On Consulting the Faithful in Matters of Doctrine,* ed. John Coulson (London: Collins, 1986), p. 73.
22   Kevin Kelly, *Divorce and Second Marriage: Facing the Challenge* (London: Collins, 1982).
23   Germain Grisez, John Finnis and William E. May, 'Indissolubility, divorce and Holy Communion', *New Blackfriars* (June 1994), pp. 321–30.
24   See Ladislas Örsy, *Marriage in Canon Law* (Leominster: Fowler Wright, 1988), p. 55, note 8.

9

Defending the bond
or the indefensible?

It is four years since this book was first published and I have been intrigued by the reaction, and at times lack of reaction, to what it contains. I am grateful for a series of positive reviews. Cathy Molloy wrote at length in the *INTAMS Review* (International Academy for Marital Spirituality) and concluded: 'Timothy Buckley has served us well with this book.[1] Theodore Davey in *The Tablet* concluded: 'This is a very valuable book, not simply because of the large number of questions it raises but because it is chiefly the result of talking to a very large number of involved people. It gives evidence of a caring Church, but one apparently impotent in the face of widespread marital distress.[2] The Anglican Bishop John Dennis (Cambridge), who wrote appreciatively of 'an illuminating and helpful book', noted my attempt to write sympathetically about the issues. Having recommended the 'Theological History' to 'anyone who wonders at the way in which the Roman Catholic Church finds itself able to distinguish between various types of marriage', he commented:

> Without defending this theology in any way, Buckley's explanations of its history and development are helpful and contribute towards a sympathetic understanding of the dilemmas and difficulties it causes.[3]

He finished his review by noting my concern that dialogue with the Orthodox tradition over the principle of *oikonomia* should be pursued with a will, and added this personal comment:

> Whether such change could be forthcoming is not for someone outside the system to judge, but this is an interesting and informative study,

which leaves this reader with great sympathy for everyone involved as well as a strong desire to see that change brought about.

In *Priests and People* Kevin T. Kelly wrote a full article by way of review.[4] Again I am grateful for his very positive analysis of my work. He described the book as 'extremely important and highly significant.' He was particularly positive about the fact that I had listened to so many people's experiences, and because it was an exercise that had been initiated by the bishops, he concluded:

> Though this book is valuable in its own right, as a symbol of our bishops' desire to listen to the painful experience of those who have been through the trauma of marriage breakdown its value can hardly be measured.[5]

However, unlike Bishop Dennis, Kelly was not convinced that focusing on the Orthodox practice of *oikonomia* was particularly helpful. He is convinced that the bishops have it in their power to resolve the problem and that if the Latin tradition applied the principles of *epikeia* and canonical equity we would have no need to seek for solutions from the East. He argued that *oikonomia*'s importance 'is more at the level of making us aware that there is room for much more flexibility in our position without our being unfaithful to or compromising our gospel-based teaching'. Furthermore, he stressed that, in his opinion, while I had emphasized the inadequacy of our theology of marriage, I had failed to draw sufficient attention to the problems which arise as a result of our failure to implement the teachings of Vatican II with regard to the local church and its relation 'to Rome and to the wider communion of churches'. In particular he would like to have seen this taken up in my treatment of the initiative of the three German bishops (cf. pp. 136–8 above).

I have noted this criticism and understand Kevin Kelly's point of view because I greatly value the work he himself has undertaken in this field. Indeed in the expanded edition of his book, *Divorce and Second Marriage: Facing the Challenge*, he goes to the trouble of giving the texts of the debate occasioned by the German bishops and his own commentary on them.[6] Nevertheless, I stand by my judgement on this matter. It is true that in responding to the challenge to try and present a 'coherent argument, based on a sound theology of church and sacrament,' I concentrated on the inadequacy of the sacramental theology of marriage, particularly the way in which the notion of the bond is defined. I am still convinced that only when this dogmatic problem is addressed will a wholly satisfactory way forward be found in the Catholic Church. Of course, Kelly is right in drawing attention to the inadequacy of our theology of church and the need to persuade the bishops to fulfil their special pastoral role within their territories. But I believe there is a limit to what we can expect them to achieve in the present circumstances. Certainly, after the CDF challenged their conclusions, the German bishops of the Upper Rhine pursued the matter with Rome very determinedly and it is clear that they are intent on keeping the debate alive. Nevertheless, they felt constrained to inform their people of the disagreement with Rome. They conceded 'the fact that as a result of the congregation's letter certain statements in our pastoral letter and in the principles are not accepted by the universal Church and therefore cannot be the binding norm of pastoral practice.'[7] They insisted that there was no disagreement with the CDF over doctrinal matters, but only over pastoral practice in relation to decisions of conscience. And here they argued that they were making a careful distinction between 'an official admission' and 'an approach to the table of the Lord'.[8]

I applaud these bishops for their courage and commitment. There has been no comparable stand by a group of the bishops of England and Wales, though in fairness they have continued to express their concern and make representations to the Roman authorities when opportunity has arisen. For example, Cardinal Hume, speaking on behalf of the Conference, addressed the Pope during the *Ad Limina* visit in 1997 in language which clearly suggests that they consider there is much still to be done:

In this work of reconciliation we are continually confronted, as pastors, with the situation of those in an 'irregular union' for whom there is no perceived possibility of canonical regularisation. We must maintain the clear and consistent teaching of the Church concerning marriage. We must also act pastorally toward those in this situation whether Catholics already or seeking full communion in the Church. In this century especially, the relationship between membership of the Church and reception of Holy Communion has been affirmed and appreciated. It is not surprising that, despite reassurances, those who are not permitted to receive Holy Communion find themselves estranged from the family of the Church gathered for the Mass. We are conscious of your deep concern for these couples and their families and your invitation 'to help them experience the charity of Christ ... to trust in God's mercy ... and to find concrete ways of conversion and participation in the life of the community of the Church' (24

January 1997). We are anxious to receive encouragement from you to explore every possible avenue by which we may address this important and sensitive aspect of our pastoral ministry. (*Briefing* 27/11 (20 November 1997): 8)

I think it is fair to say that all the bishops in England and Wales are sympathetic towards the plight of their people, trapped in irreconcilable situations. They are happy to encourage the work of the support groups and some have written pastoral letters in a language and tone unimaginable in bygone days. The most notable example that I am aware of is that of Bishop Ambrose Griffiths of Hexham and Newcastle. His Lenten Pastoral in 2001 included this remarkable passage:

From my heart I speak to you who through separation and divorce feel yourselves cut off from the life of the Church. I recognise the pain you suffer and speak to you as wounded members of the Body of Christ. We are all bound together in the communion of God's love. I ask you to remain in it or return to it so that your sufferings may become part of our common burden. Together we will find a solution to your problems and healing for your pain. Your parish priest and our diocesan counsellors will help you to find a way ahead which is in tune with the truths of the Gospel and with Catholic tradition. (11 March 2001)[9]

I was intrigued that Bishop Ambrose should have spoken so boldly, because I am at a loss to know how he anticipates finding the solution. It seems to me that there remain two major issues that require addressing urgently. The first is how to engage the Roman authorities in a theological dialogue. The second is how to help those whose personal situations seem intractable, not tomorrow or in ten years' time, but now. I am convinced that these are two aspects of the same problem because I believe that only when the theological problem is resolved will the pastoral solution be found to everyone's satisfaction. You see, I am baffled that the German bishops, mentioned above, insist that they have no doctrinal quarrel with Rome, only a dispute over pastoral practice in relation to conscience. It seems to me that the problem is deeply rooted in our understanding of God's redeeming presence among us and how that can and does reach into every human situation. Let me explain further.

The ongoing doctrinal discussion

Since 1990, when first I was engaged by the Marriage and Family Life Committee of the Bishops' Conference, I have sought to unravel the theological impasse which confronts so many separated, divorced and remarried Catholics. Initially I faced the problem of trying to balance my concern over the theological inadequacies with the need to emphasize the pain and suffering of those in pastoral difficulty. In the event I am satisfied that I achieved the balance. Our failure to heed the Pope's call 'to reach out to the divorced' (*Familiaris Consortio*, 84) was not disputed and, as I have indicated above, the climate has changed and continues to change in this regard. However, the complicated theological question surrounding the sacramental consummated bond seems to be as far from resolution as ever. I acknowledge that I was unable to provide a simple definitive solution, but considering the attention the subject has received in current theological debate, I think we can safely assume one does not exist. I mention the attention the subject has received because recently I had occasion to check. A theologian friend, who had been asked to write a chapter on the subject, inquired as to what had been written in recent times. I contacted INTAMS and they provided me with a 36-page bibliography of books and articles written since 1997, the year this book was first published. Theologians continue to chip away from a variety of angles, largely pastoral, but no one has succeeded in forcing a debate on the dogmatic theology itself.

For my part, I do consider that while I may not have been able to offer a simple practical alternative to the present dispensation, I have been able to isolate some of the key questions which require answering, if an official way forward is to be found. And it is here that, four years on, I find myself more than a little frustrated. The reviews of my work have been largely positive. I am especially grateful for the appreciation of my efforts to be sensitive to the dilemma which faces the magisterium. I have resolutely striven not to be provocative and to understand the complexity of the problem, but surely the questions raised deserve a response? It seems that no one, least of all the bishops, denies the fact that the Church's present position is, to say the least, unsatisfactory. I would say it is untenable. The anomalies and injustices which arise out of our present canonical rulings are indefensible, and I think my exposition in chapter 2 and the data of the social research demonstrate this fact. Yet when it comes to furthering the argument we remain locked in a never-ending diplomatic round of seeking further opinion and setting up new committees to present new test cases. For example, in spite of the 1994 report and this thesis, the official line is that we need further research before we can present the Sacred Congregation with a case to be answered. I for one would be grateful for answers to the questions already on the table.

The ongoing pastoral discussion

If it is clear to everyone that the present position is unsatisfactory and maybe untenable – and judging by my conversations and the response, or lack of it, to what I have written, it seems to be – then how can we continue to impose the present strictures? As I have been at pains to explain over and over again, the point at issue is not the sanctity of marriage or even the indissolubility of marriage, but rather our theological way of defining these and the pastoral consequences for people who are suffering. If we cannot be sure that what we are demanding of them is the Lord's will for them, how can they be bound?

I hope it is now clear why I see the dogmatic and pastoral theologies as parts of the one problem. I can appreciate the position of a senior bishop when he says to me that he is in sympathy with what I have written but that he is 'not qualified' to judge the theology, though I want to ask: 'Who *is* qualified?' It is possible that I have missed something which would clarify everything and enable us all to move forward confidently and in peace. If that is so, could someone please come forward and point it out, but to date no one has pointed out any serious flaws in the argument.

My point is that we have reduced our defence of marriage to the defence of the bond as defined in the Scholastic tradition and, as a consequence, in the vast majority of cases we are forced to pursue the annulment process in search of a solution. In this process the Church authorities appoint a 'defender of the bond'. If my thesis is correct, the defender of the bond, far from being a defender of the marriage in question or indeed of marriage itself, may well be reduced to being a defender of the indefensible. The tragedy of all this is that as we continue to go round in ever increasing and more frustrating circles, good people are being left desolate and without hope. The extraordinary thing about all this is that the statistics reveal that even the majority of Catholics are making up their own minds and going their own way in these as in many other matters. So it would seem that we are punishing the few who genuinely want to get it right and receive the official stamp of approval.

Annulments: differing perspectives

From time to time we hear reports of pastoral initiatives, which bring welcome relief to some, but only confirm others in their disillusion. As an example I would instance the pastoral initiative of Bishop Kenneth Untener in Saginaw, a diocese in the United States of America. As a jubilee project for the year 2000 he introduced a streamlining of the annulment process for his people. It was a carefully planned strategy and he left little to chance. Not only did he prepare a pastoral letter for his people, but he also pre-recorded it so that it could be played in all 111 parishes of the diocese. Forty lay auditors were trained and everyone who was in a difficult marriage situation invited to seek help. The process was to be free and efficient. Early in 2001 I contacted the Diocese of Saginaw to inquire how the experiment had gone. I received this gracious reply from the former judicial vicar, Richard Filary:

I will simply state that the reasons the changes were made in our practice was to reach out in a special way during the jubilee holy year to the divorced and/or remarried. Issues surrounding money and the buying of annulments, who can afford them, et cetera, were behind the move no longer to request any fee or offering. This was well received and surfaced many people to re-open a case or to start one: a funny thing as to what money can do or not do! Secondly, we knew that people were overwhelmed with the various forms and questionnaires they received. Parish priests, who were the advocates, did not necessarily have the time or take the time to work with each petitioner. In view of the 'shortage of priests' and wanting to provide the best pastoral care for those petitioning, we decided to train lay people and have them truly walk through this journey with the people. It also dealt with the myth that a priest could not understand, not having been married himself. Lastly, the trained lay person, advocate, was truly to help the person by not giving them the forms but by interviewing them, filling in the information, getting the necessary documents if needed, getting the necessary facts concerning the marriage in question and providing a summary of this for the petitioner to read and sign. In this way, we wanted to make the process a healing process and as 'user friendly,' as I called it, for them in view of the pain and hurt they have experienced with a failed marital relationship and/or based on their misunderstandings or moral inability publicly to be admitted to the sacraments. Many people found things much easier and more healing for them. Word of this spread by mouth and, with the promotion in bulletins and diocesan publications, many came forward. We did not change the procedural canon law that guides what the tribunal does and we were not able necessarily to shorten the time limits. What we did do was clean up the way a person prepared and presented their case to the tribunal and make the process a true ministry of the pastoral care of the divorced and separated. Certainly not all went smoothly but people were satisfied for the most part. The misunderstandings came in people thinking that this would just speed things up and it would be done in no time at all. We knew the potential was great and we could be overwhelmed with a case load. We had no new canonical people in the tribunal and had to seek outside help. We also had no control over the second instance court proceedings as other dioceses in the province also sought to reach out to those in need of a clarification of their status, as I call it, and they (2nd instance) could potentially be overwhelmed. That's all I can think of by way of sharing at this time.

Within the law there is little more that local ordinaries can do and therefore I think Bishop Untener is to be applauded. We can be sure that not only did he bring pastoral relief to many in his diocese, but also his initiative will have helped the wider community to be more understanding and open. However, I hardly need to reiterate my misgivings about the fact that such a pastoral initiative should have been necessary, because there is another story to be heard regarding annulments. Again I turn to the United States to illustrate my point, and it is to a book by Sheila Rauch Kennedy. In *Shattered Faith*,[10] she wrote the story of her struggles with the Boston tribunal over the annulment sought by her husband, Senator Joseph Kennedy, eldest son of Robert F. Kennedy. In summary, her contention was that the annulment process was a contradiction of all she, a compliant Episcopalian, had agreed to when preparing for marriage in the Catholic Church. It was not that she disputed the fact that the marriage had failed and that it was in the interests of all the family that they should have divorced. Rather, she was not willing to participate in a process which, of its very nature, sought to establish that there had been no marriage in the first place. Above all she could not and would not accept that her twin boys had been born in anything other than a sacred union. In my opinion she raises some crucial questions and argues her case well. It is arguable that her former husband was driven more by his desire to be able to remarry without damaging his reputation within the Catholic community, and thereby injuring his political career, than with the justice of his case before the tribunal. Sheila explained her difficulty to him in this reasoned way:

> An annulment says that there was never a true marriage in the eyes of God. I don't know about you, I took our marriage very seriously. And I certainly took the conception and birth of our children seriously. (p. 10)

In his frustration he responded:

> Of course I took our marriage and the children seriously. And of course I think we had a true marriage. But that doesn't matter now. I don't believe this stuff. Nobody actually believes it. It is just Catholic gobbledygook, Sheila. But you just have to say it this way because, well, because that's the way the Catholic Church is. (pp. 10–11)

Towards the end of the book she comes back to this question of why it mattered so much to her to fight, and she wrote this moving statement:

> I realized that even though my reasons for opposing the annulment had remained constant during the two years that I had been defending my marriage, the factors influencing my thinking had broadened. I was still, as I had told Joe, concerned for the boys, but not for their legitimacy. I had always known the boys' legitimacy was protected by American law. I was still concerned that the children know that their birth was the result of great love, commitment, true happiness, and a Christian marriage rather than a non-existent union. They should never have to question that their lives brought immeasurable joy to both of their parents, and neither their father nor his church would ever be able to convince me otherwise. (p. 196)

It is a truly disturbing story and, because of her fierce opposition, it took the Boston tribunal three years before the annulment was granted on the grounds of Joseph's lack of due discretion, Sheila having resisted efforts to establish that she had serious psychological flaws in her character. The book ends with her appealing to the Roman Rota and to the best of my knowledge a decision is still awaited.

I have drawn attention to the contents of this book because I believe that

Sheila Kennedy raises some crucial questions surrounding the present tribunal process and the grounds on which marriages are now annulled. She was stirred to write her story because she was angry, but we must ask whether her anger was justified. Theology has always recognized righteous anger as a God–given response to injustice. One way or another her questions too demand answers. And there is a question I would like to add: In her situation, who was the real defender of the bond of marriage?

The other book to which I would like to draw attention is *Catholic Divorce: The Deception of Annulments*,[11] a compendium of writings, edited by Pierre Hegy and Joseph Martos. Once again the authors have sought to expose the alarming contradiction of the tribunal system operating in the North American Church. Like my own work it contains chapters explaining the sociological experience of the community as well as chapters analysing the theological issues. Unlike my work it is a compilation of writings from a variety of different authors, written over a considerable period of time. What was particularly significant for me was the chapter 'Christian Marriage and the Reality of Complete Marital Breakdown' by Edward Schillebeeckx. Schillebeeckx had written his monumental study, *Marriage: Human Reality and Saving Mystery*, at the time of the Second Vatican Council, and according to a footnote in *Catholic Divorce* the article that forms chapter 4 is a condensation of the chapter written for that major work, but 'either left out of the English translation . . . or deleted from the original before it was published' (p. 107, footnote 15). What is remarkable about this chapter is the clarity of Schillebeeckx's thinking and his analysis of the situation that was emerging at the time of Vatican II, in other words some forty years ago. The tragedy is that all those years ago brilliant and respected theologians like Schillebeeckx (from the dogmatic perspective) and Haring (from the moral perspective) had opened up the theological avenues of thought which could have unlocked the problem for us, yet still we seem no further forward. Just note this passage from the chapter in question:

> Indissolubility cannot mean that a first marriage continues to exist as a prohibition against a second marriage. Such a prohibition would leave indissolubility without any actual meaning; for it says nothing, realistically speaking, about the first marriage in question. If that marriage has in fact completely broken down, then humanly speaking there is no more marriage; there is no longer anything to which 'indissolubility' or 'dissolubility' can be applied. Instead, there is only the reality of a radical failure, regardless of how one might assign guilt

for it; there is the reality of an irrecoverably lost marriage.

Faced with this situation, a Christian can appeal to what Eastern theology calls *oikonomia* (an untranslatable Greek word that can perhaps best be understood as taking everything into account). The Eastern Church is sensitive about not tarnishing the ideal of marriage; it affirms that the intrinsic aim of marriage is an interpersonal relationship, but it also believes that Christians, as Paul says in this context, 'are called by God to freedom' (1 Cor. 7:15).

Now, the practice of Christian churches, especially those whose ecclesial nature is generally recognized, is for Catholics a source of theological information (*locus theologicus*) that can no longer be ignored. These churches, acting with an *oikonomia* that recognizes human failings, do not juridically veto people's desire to remarry, which they regard as a private decision of the two people concerned. This is clearly a pastoral interpretation of a practical problem for which there are models in the New Testament, although in a different cultural context than our own.

If we want to be honest, we have to admit that the practice of *oikonomia* has come into existence in the Catholic church, although for the time being it has to remain underground because it conflicts with the code of canon law. This practice calls into question the legalism of the code, which attempts to safeguard the gospel but does so by translating it into strict legal language that can overstate the proper meaning of the evangelical ideal. We need to reflect on this new practice and on the growing appreciation among Catholics (though not in official circles) for a general Christian consensus with regard to a pastoral practice of recognizing and respecting divorced people's desire to remarry. In this spreading pastoral practice, there is a measure of truth coming to light, albeit indirectly. (pp. 97–8)

So there we have it again: the *oikonomia* of the East provides us with the opening; and what a wonderful description of this mysterious way of understanding the saving presence of God: untranslatable but inviting us to take 'everything into account'. Taking everything into account, then, I believe the time has come to set God's people free from the unnecessary burdens of refusing to consider the possibility of another union after complete marital breakdown and refusing Holy Communion to those caught up in what at present we regard as irregular unions.

A final prayer

Of course I can offer my opinion and shout it from the rooftops and for that matter so can individual bishops and even bishops' conferences, but unless the Roman Magisterium makes a move, these problems will not be resolved. So I end by praying that some progress may be made on this front. Timothy Radcliffe, who recently finished his term as Master General of the Dominicans, has just published a challenging book, *I Call You Friends*.[12] Here he emphasizes the importance of debate, of keeping the dialogue open on all the key issues, reminding us that this is part of the great tradition of his Order which contained some of the giants of the Scholastic tradition. Responding to a question about the Church as *Mater et magistra* (Mother and teacher) he points out that *mater* and *magistra* cannot be in opposition to one another. 'In my view,' he says, 'teaching is a profoundly maternal activity.' Looking back to those great days of theological debate he writes:

> The teacher was someone who instructed his students, but who also listened to them, who challenged them to answer him. The very essence of medieval teaching was the *quaestio disputata*, literally the 'question debated'. (p. 69)

Confronted with a question about those who 'feel excluded by the Church's teaching', and the divorced and remarried are explicitly mentioned, Radcliffe begins by noting that 'the Church, of its very nature, is inclusive'. He goes on to make a profound distinction between those 'whose ideas and attitudes are stamped with hatred' and 'others who have difficulties with the Church not because they hate but because they are living in a relationship that conflicts with the Church's teaching'. His advice unfolds in this way:

> Any love, as love, is good, is God's presence. The essential point of departure is their desire to love. We should recognize this and give it its value. The moral teaching of the Church should never consist in telling people that they should not love someone. It should only invite them to love better. There is no human love that is not in need of healing, which does not need to be led to maturity and fullness ... If we wish to show that the Church's moral teaching is good news, we have to be with people, enter their homes, enjoy their friendship. We

have to understand how they see the world, learn what they have to teach us, see through their eyes, grow in mutual trust. Then we shall find how to express the Church's teaching, with them.

May the debate continue in that spirit and may all those who have been excluded be included without delay.

Notes

1. 1998.2, pp. 221–3.
2. *The Tablet* (14 August 1999), pp. 1111–12.
3. *Crucible* (April–June 1999, pp. 130–2).
4. April 1998 (pp. 157–9).
5. Ibid., p.159.
6. London: Geoffrey Chapman, 1997 (pp. 90–141).
7. Ibid., p.133.
8. Ibid., p.132.
9. Interestingly when I quoted Bishop Ambrose's letter at the National Conference of the ASDC at Newman College, Birmingham, in May 2001, one of the members from the Hexham and Newcastle Diocese reacted strongly. She bemoaned the fact that in the pastoral the Bishop had mentioned neither the Association nor the contribution its members had made in providing much of the text.
10. Dublin: Poolbeg Press, 1997.
11. London: Continuum, 2000.
12. London: Continuum, 2001.

Appendix 1

Sample case history for discussion with support groups

Adrian was 29 when he first approached his parish priest to ask for help in coping with his marriage, which was fast disintegrating. Fr Brian had known Adrian and his wife, Clare, since they were youngsters and he had officiated at their wedding. He already knew things were not going well, because Clare had been to see him, but he felt helpless. They had been married for six years, and at first it had seemed that this was the ideal Catholic marriage. They had been actively involved in the parish all their lives, but now their interest had waned and they had grown apart not only from the parish but from each other. Clare had confided in Fr Brian that she was seeing someone else but explained she had not told Adrian.

Fr Brian was tired on this particular evening and felt sad to think that yet another marriage he knew was crumbling. He felt sorry for himself too. He was in one of those moods when such problems only served to make him question his own vocation, and, with a sigh, he told Adrian that it was a matter between himself and Clare. 'Well what if we do break up – the Church doesn't believe in divorce, does it?' said Adrian. 'Adrian, that is between you and God. Today a lot of people do divorce. The Church is having to accept the fact.' Adrian was furious with Fr Brian's response and stormed out of the presbytery.

The next day Fr Brian felt considerable remorse and contacted Adrian at work, suggesting he might like to contact the CMAC (Catholic Marriage Advisory Council). Adrian was not at his most receptive, but finally agreed. However, when he phoned it was an answerphone. Reluctantly he left a curt message. The following day he was contacted at work by one of the counsellors, who offered him an appointment in six weeks' time.

Long before the six weeks were up, Clare with the two children had left to set up home with the new man in her life, Paul. The appointment with the CMAC was cancelled and all those involved battled with the problems of trying to rebuild their lives. Clare survived a couple of years with Paul but it was not destined to last. A divorce had been obtained after the statutory period of separation and all the arrangements had been amicably settled. Both Adrian and Clare accepted there had been faults on both sides and they wanted to remain good friends. Later Clare met Mike and married him in the register office. Ten years on it seems to be working well and the children are happy. For Clare the Church has long since ceased to have any relevance. By contrast, Adrian has been tormented by the whole experience. He could not bring himself to seek counsel from Fr Brian again, but after a couple of years he did have a chat with the young curate in the neighbouring parish, who reassured him that he was quite entitled to receive the sacraments. The same priest also suggested the possibility of an annulment, but Adrian knew enough about this to realize it would mean questioning the validity of his marriage with Clare, and this he was not prepared to do. Meanwhile, he has faithfully attended Mass each Sunday and gone to Holy Communion, but he has felt a stranger. People have been very kind, but have never spoken about the thing that matters most.

However, recently he met Angela, a vivacious 32-year-old, and he senses that she is rapidly changing his life. She is a divorcee too, having married at 18 and divorced at 19. He is haunted by his fear of God and the Church. Angela has started coming to church with Adrian and is beginning to ask seriously how she should go about taking instruction in the Faith. Adrian does not have the confidence to pose this one even to the friendly curate in the neighbouring parish, but as luck would have it, he has noticed an advertisement for the ASDC/Rainbow/BE in the city centre church, which he sometimes pops into after work. He makes contact and comes to your meeting. What would you want to say to him?

Appendix 2

Sample case history for discussion with clergy groups

Julie arrives at the front door of the presbytery and asks for a chat. You have only just moved to the parish, but already on the two Sundays you have been there you have noticed Julie with the three children. So you make her very welcome.

To begin with her story seems uncomplicated enough. Sandra, her eldest, is in the First Communion class and some of the promptings at the parents' meeting have touched Julie and she has decided to start coming along to church. She had not previously been to church very much since her school days and even then not too regularly. However, you sense that hopefully some real spiritual growth is taking place. It is not just a case of doing the right thing to see through the First Communion programme. Julie wants to know what she should do regarding going back to Holy Communion herself. She knows she ought to go to Confession or 'whatever they call it nowadays', and she understands that this can now be done by private arrangement. You are very impressed not only with Julie but with what the catechetical programme is achieving.

You are gentle and helpful, reminding her that this is undoubtedly the Lord's work. Then you suggest a cup of tea and a continuing chat before actually celebrating the Rite of Reconciliation. It is only during this conversation that you realize that this not quite as simple as you had first anticipated. You ask about the three children and discover that Sandra is the result of a first marriage that had lasted only a few months. You gently check as to whether it was celebrated in a Catholic church and, breathing a sigh of relief, discover that it was not – in fact it had been in the register office. Next you enquire about her present partner and discover that he is much older than Julie: she is 29 and he is 39. However, it is working out really well. Although he is 'Church of England' he is really good about the religion and does not object to the children going to the Catholic school. In fact he has changed quite a lot from the days when they married. She thinks it was mainly his mother's influence that caused him to insist on the wedding taking place in the Anglican Church and the children all being christened there. His first marriage with Betty, a Methodist, had been a disaster and his mother had objected to the fact that they did not get married in a church.

May I just add that it is clear to you that Julie has not the slightest idea about her situation *vis-à-vis* Catholic canon law and you sense that she will be deeply offended if you even hint that she might not be truly married.

You realize that you are up to your neck in this one. How would you respond? Is this different from how you would want to respond?

Selected
bibliography

Bassett, William W. (ed.), *The Bond of Marriage: An Ecumenical and Inter-disciplinary Study* (Notre Dame, IN: University of Notre Dame Press, 1968).

Bernhard, Jean, 'The evolution of matrimonial jurisprudence: the opinion of a French canonist', trans. G. Morrisey OMI and James H. Provost, *The Jurist*, 41 (1981), pp. 105–16.

Brown, Ralph, *Marriage Annulment in the Catholic Church* (3rd edn; Rattlesden: Kevin Mayhew, 1990).

Brunsman, Barry, *New Hope for Divorced Catholics* (San Francisco: Harper & Row, 1989).

Coleman, Gerald D., *Divorce and Remarriage in the Catholic Church* (New York: Paulist Press, 1988).

Congregation for the Doctrine of the Faith, *Letter to the Bishops of the Catholic Church Concerning the Reception of Holy Communion by Divorced and Remarried Members of the Faithful* (Vatican: Libreria Editrice Vaticana, 1994).

Cooke, Bernard, *Sacraments and Sacramentality* (rev. edn; Mystic, CT: Twenty-Third Publications, 1994).

Dalrymple, Jock, *Jack Dominian: Lay Prophet?* (London: Geoffrey Chapman, 1995).

Davey, Theodore, 'The internal forum', *The Tablet* (27 July 1991), pp. 905–6.

de Bono, Edward, *I Am Right — You Are Wrong: From This to the New Renaissance: From Rock Logic to Water Logic* (London: Penguin, 1991).

Dominian, Jack, *Christian Marriage* (London: Darton, Longman and Todd, 1967).

Dominian, Jack, *Passionate and Compassionate Love: A Vision for Christian Marriage* (London: Darton, Longman and Todd, 1991).

Dominian, Jack, Mansfield, Penny, Dormor, Duncan, and McAllister, Fiona, *Marital Breakdown and the Health of the Nation* (London: One Plus One, 1991).

Doogan, Hugh F. (ed.), *Catholic Tribunals: Marriage Annulment and Dissolution* (Newtown, Australia: E.J. Dwyer, 1990).

Dormor, Duncan J., *The Relationship Revolution: Cohabitation, Marriage and Divorce in Contemporary Europe* (London: One Plus One, Marriage and Partnership Research, 1992).

Elliott, Peter J., *What God Has Joined ...: The Sacramentality of Marriage* (New York: Alba House, 1990).

Erickson, J. H., 'Orthodox perspectives on divorce and remarriage' in *The Challenge of Our Past: Studies in Orthodox Canon Law* (New York: St Vladimir's Seminary Press, 1990), pp. 39–51.

Everett, William Johnson, *Blessed Be the Bond: Christian Perspectives on Marriage and Family* (Philadephia: Fortress Press, 1985).

Flannery, Austin, OP (ed.) *Vatican Council II: The Conciliar and Post-Consiliar Documents* (Leominster: Fowler Wright Books, 1988).

Flood, Dom Edmund, *The Divorced Catholic* (London: Collins, 1987).

Genovesi, Vincent J., SJ, *In Pursuit of Love: Catholic Morality and Human Sexuality* (Dublin: Gill and Macmillan, 1987).

Grisez, Germain, Finnis, John and May, William E., 'Indissolubility, divorce and Holy Communion', *New Blackfriars* (June 1994), pp. 321–30.

Haight, Roger, SJ, *The Experience and Language of Grace* (New York: Paulist Press, 1979).

Häring, Bernard, *No Way Out?: Pastoral Care of the Divorced and Remarried* (Slough: St Paul Publications, 1989).

Hegy, Pierre and Martos, Joseph (eds), *Catholic Divorce: The Deception of Annulments* (London: Continuum, 2000).

Hogan, Richard M. and LeVoir, John M., *Covenant of Love: Pope John Paul II on Sexuality, Marriage and Family in the Modern World: With a Commentary on* Familiaris Consortio (2nd edn; San Francisco: Ignatius, 1992).

Hornsby-Smith, Michael P., *Roman Catholics in England: Studies in Social Structure Since the Second World War* (Cambridge: Cambridge University Press, 1987).

Hornsby-Smith, Michael P., *Roman Catholic Beliefs in England: Customary Catholicism and Transformations of Religious Authority* (Cambridge: Cambridge University Press, 1991).

John Paul II, *Familiaris Consortio* (London: CTS, 1981).

John Paul II, *Orientale Lumen* (London: CTS, 1995).

John Paul II, *Ut Unum Sint* (London: CTS, 1995).

Kelly, Kevin T., *Divorce and Second Marriage: Facing the Challenge* (London: Collins, 1982; new edn, London: Geoffrey Chapman, 1996).

Kennedy, Sheila Rauch, *Shattered Faith* (Dublin: Poolbeg Press, 1997).

Kiernan, Kathleen, and Wicks, Malcolm, *Family Change and Future Policy* (London: Family Policy Studies Centre, 1990).

Lawler, Michael G., *Secular Marriage, Christian Sacrament* (Mystic, CT: Twenty-Third Publications, 1985).

Lawler, Michael, *Ecumenical Marriage and Remarriage: Gifts and Challenges to the Churches* (Mystic, CT: Twenty-Third Publications, 1990).

Lawler, Michael G., *Marriage and Sacrament: A Theology of Christian Marriage* (Collegeville, MN: Liturgical Press, 1993).

L'Huillier, Bishop Peter, 'The indissolubility of marriage in Orthodox law and practice', *St Vladimir's Theological Quarterly*, 32 (1988), pp. 199–221.

Lohfink, Gerhard, *Jesus and Community: The Social Dimension of Christian Faith*, trans. John P. Galvin (New York: Paulist Press, 1984).

MacIntyre, Alasdair, *After Virtue: A Study in Moral Theory* (2nd edn; London: Duckworth, 1985).

Mackin, Theodore, SJ, *What Is Marriage? Marriage in the Catholic Church* (New York: Paulist Press, 1982).

Mackin, Theodore, SJ, *Divorce and Remarriage: Marriage in the Catholic Church* (New York: Paulist Press, 1984).

Mackin, Theodore, SJ, *The Marital Sacrament: Marriage in the Catholic Church* (New York: Paulist Press, 1989).

Martin, David and others (eds), *Sociology and Theology: Alliance and Conflict* (New York: St Martin's Press, 1980).

Morgan, David L., *Focus Groups as Qualitative Research* (Sage University Paper Series on Qualitative Research Methods, vol. 16; Beverly Hills, CA: Sage, 1986).

Newman, John Henry, *An Essay on the Development of Christian Doctrine* (London: Longmans, Green and Co., 1900).

Newman, John Henry, *On Consulting the Faithful in Matters of Doctrine*, ed. John Coulson (London: Collins, 1986).

Orsy, Ladislas, 'Intolerable marriage situations: conflict between external and internal forum', *The Jurist*, 30 (1970), pp. 1–14.

Örsy, Ladislas, *The Church: Learning and Teaching, Magisterium, Assent, Dissent, Academic Freedom* (Leominster: Fowler Wright, 1987).

Örsy, Ladislas, SJ, *Marriage in Canon Law: Texts and Comments; Reflections and Questions* (Leominster: Fowler Wright, 1988).

Örsy, Ladislas, SJ, *The Profession of Faith and the Oath of Fidelity: A Theological and Canonical Analysis* (Dublin: Dominican Publications, 1990).

Örsy, Ladislas, SJ, *Theology and Canon Law: New Horizons for Legislation and Interpretation* (Collegeville, MN: Liturgical Press, 1992).

Rabior, William, ACSW, and Wells Bedard, Vicki, *Catholics Experiencing Divorce: Grieving, Healing and Learning to Live Again* (Liguori, MO: Liguori Publications, 1991).

Radcliffe, Timothy, OP, *I Call You Friends* (London: Continuum, 2001).

Ripple, Paula, FSPA, *The Pain and the Possibility: Divorce and Separation Among Catholics* (Notre Dame, IN: Ave Maria Press, 1978).

Roberts, William P. (ed.), *Commitment to Partnership: Explorations of the Theology of Marriage* (New York: Paulist Press, 1987).

Robinson, Geoffrey, *Marriage, Divorce and Nullity* (3rd edn; London: Geoffrey Chapman, 1985).

Rose, Gerry, *Deciphering Sociological Research* (Basingstoke: Macmillan Education, 1982).

Schillebeeckx, E., OP, *Marriage: Secular Reality and Saving Mystery*, trans. N.

D. Smith (London: Sheed and Ward, 1965).

Siegle, Bernard A., TOR, *Marriage: According to the New Code of Canon Law* (New York: Alba House, 1986).

Stone, Lawrence, *Road to Divorce: England 1530–1987* (Oxford: Oxford University Press, 1990).

Vorgrimler, Herbert, *Sacramental Theology*, trans. Linda M. Maloney (Collegeville, MN: Liturgical Press, 1992).

West, Morris and Francis, Robert, *Scandal in the Assembly: A Bill of Complaints and a Proposal for Reform on the Matrimonial Laws and Tribunals of the Roman Catholic Church* (London: Heinemann, 1970).

Wood, Susan, SCL, 'The marriage of baptized nonbelievers: faith, contract, and sacrament', *Theological Studies*, 48 (1987), pp. 279–301.

Young, James J., CSP, *Divorcing, Believing, Belonging* (New York: Paulist Press, 1984).

Zwack, Joseph P., *Annulment: Your Chance to Remarry Within the the Catholic Church* (New York: Harper & Row, 1983).

Index

absolutes 17, 19, 127
adultery 30–2, 35, 38, 39, 43, 45, 46, 53
Albert, St 47, 50
Alexander III, Pope 48, 61
Alphonsus, St 81, 82
Anglican Church 149
annulment 3, 15, 16, 21, 23, 65–7,
74–8, 86, 87, 95, 103, 105, 110, 115,
117, 129, 131, 134, 145, 146, 150, 152,
153, 155–61, 165, 174, 181, 185
Aquinas, St Thomas 42, 47, 51
Aristotle 48
Association of Separated and Divorced
Catholics (ASDC) ix, 23, 86–99,
103–9, 130, 132, 134, 155, 158, 174
Augustine, St 13, 42–9, 56

Basil, St 42
Baum, Gregory 167
Beatitudes, the 43
Beginning Experience (BE) ix, 23, 86,
92–4, 96, 97, 101, 108, 111n, 112n
Benedict XIV, Pope 151
Bernhard, Jean 162, 163
Bonaventure, St 52
bond of marriage 19, 20, 22, 28–30,
32–4, 39–41, 43–50, 52–67, 75, 83, 121,
135, 136, 138, 145, 149, 151, 152, 154,
156, 162–4, 168, 169, 176, 179, 180
dissolution 42, 58, 60, 66, 75, 100,
147, 175
'in favour of the faith' 18, 36, 60
Pauline privilege 35, 58, 59, 75,
150
Petrine privilege 35, 60, 75, 146,
182n
indissoluble 20, 33, 52, 57, 135, 179
natural 28, 32, 52, 57, 59–61, 169
ontological 19, 28, 45, 54, 55, 57, 60,
63, 66, 136, 143, 145, 149, 163, 168,
176, 179
sacramental 19, 44, 46, 50, 57, 58, 61,
63, 66, 135, 179
Bride of Christ 34
Brown, Ralph 84n, 161
Brunsman, Barry 152
Budd, Bishop Christopher 88, 90, 174

Canon Law 6, 10, 17, 22, 47, 51, 71n,
118, 126, 135, 136, 143, 144, 179, 187
Code of 22, 35, 52, 54, 60, 113n, 124,
137, 151, 152, 180
1917 Code 52, 59, 62, 63, 66, 125,
151, 152, 180
1983 Code 54, 59–60, 62, 66–7, 124,
125, 144, 152, 160, 161, 172, 180
canonical form 49, 50, 61, 62, 65–7,
75, 80, 82, 117, 181
Canon Law Society of America 152
Canon Law Society of Great Britain (and
Ireland) 69n, 153
Catechism of the Catholic Church 57–8,
164, 180
'catechism, penny' 49
Catholic Marriage Advisory Council
(CMAC) ix, 113n
Catholic Marriage Care 108, 115
Causas Matrimoniales 152

Chrysostom, St John   42
Commentarium in IV Libros Sententiarum
   51
Congregation for the Doctrine of the
   Faith (CDF)   ix, 60, 127, 128, 137,
   138, 147
conscience   8–10, 15, 26n, 117, 123,
   124, 134, 138, 147, 148, 181
Cooke, Bernard   169, 171
Coulson, John   14
Councils of the Church
   Florence   53
   Second Lateran   52
   Second Vatican   4–7, 15, 29, 115, 120,
      152, 161, 167, 168, 171, 176, 178–80
   Trent   33, 49–51, 53–4, 61, 62, 126,
      151
   Verona   53
counselling   91, 95, 105–8

Davey, Theodore   123, 127, 128, 130
Dei Miseratione   151
de Lubac, Henri   5–6, 7
Denzinger–Schönmetzer   ix, 54
Dispendiosam   151
divorce   1–3, 15, 21, 22, 24, 29–32, 34,
   35, 37, 38, 40–2, 57, 64, 72n, 80, 86,
   87, 99, 100, 102, 108, 109, 112n, 121,
   129, 131, 140n, 144, 157, 158–60, 163,
   164, 172–9, 184, 185
Divorce Reform Act   4, 159
Dominian, Dr Jack   64
Doyle, Thomas P.   54, 55, 58–9, 160,
   161
Duns Scotus   52

Elliott, Peter J.   22, 67
epikeia   124–6, 128
equity   74, 81, 82, 124–6, 128
Erickson, J. H.   173
erwat dabar   32
Eucharist (Holy Communion)   38, 39,
   40, 61, 74, 79, 88–90, 109, 115–18,
   120–2, 126, 128, 129, 131, 133, 134,
   136, 145, 147, 148
external forum   74, 81, 126–8, 137, 145,
   146, 165
extrinsecism   169

Familiaris Consortio   13, 37, 38, 40, 61,
   64, 119, 128, 129, 137, 147, 149, 159

fidelity   20, 39, 44, 46, 49, 51, 52, 58,
   78, 83, 137, 154, 164, 171
Flannery, Austin   11
fornication   39
Francis, Robert   130
fundamentalism   29, 180

Gaudium et Spes   ix, 4–7, 64
Genovesi, Vincent J.   19
German bishops   130, 136–8, 177, 181
Gratian   47, 48, 59
Gregorios, Archbishop of Thyateira and
   Great Britain   174, 175
Gregory II, Pope   89
Gregory of Nyssa   44

Hamer, Archbishop   127
Hamm, Dennis   34
Häring, Bernard   7, 8, 136
Haughton, Rosemary   112n
Heart of the Matter (BBC)   133
Heenan, Cardinal   7–8
Hillel, Rabbi   32
Hornsby-Smith, Michael P.   1, 8–9
Humanae Vitae   8, 9, 11, 19
Hume, Cardinal   12, 87–8

illegitimacy   158
infallibility   13, 18
internal forum   9, 16, 74, 80, 81, 87, 89,
   90, 110, 116, 117, 123–8, 130–4, 136–8,
   146, 181
   conflict cases   126, 128
   hardship cases   126, 128
International Theological Commission
   67

Jerome, St   29, 31, 42, 43
John XXIII, Pope   4, 5, 18
John Paul II, Pope   5, 10, 11, 13, 28, 30,
   37, 61, 64, 78, 79, 89, 128, 176
Jukes, Bishop John   133, 134

Kelly, Kevin T.   179

law
   gradualness of   37
   of gradualness   37
   legalism   117
   natural   17, 18, 20, 51
   Roman   41

Lawler, Michael G. 30, 43, 71n
Lawrence, Susan 155
Lohfink, Gerhard 36, 37
Lombard, Peter 47, 48, 50, 59
Lonergan, Bernard J. F. 17
Lumen Gentium ix, 5, 6, 13, 25n, 149, 171

MacIntyre, Alasdair 17, 21
Mackin, Theodore 30–1, 47, 52, 69–70n
Magee, Fr Luke 112n
magisterium 4, 7, 9–13, 15, 18, 19, 29, 42, 57, 58, 78, 128, 147, 148, 167, 177, 178
marriage
 clandestine 61, 62
 consummation 46, 48, 58, 75, 164
 contract 52, 57, 64, 76, 162, 163, 168, 172, 179
 convalidated 75
 covenant 30, 45, 56, 63, 64, 163, 164, 171, 172
 death of 83
 ends 53
 goods 44, 51
 invalid 1, 75, 76, 120, 126, 127, 160, 163
 irregular 40, 67, 129, 133, 134, 143, 145, 146
 non-consummation 60, 75, 175
 nullity of 75, 76, 89, 121, 152, 153, 155, 156, 160–3
 permanence 28, 41, 44, 46, 58, 77, 110, 136, 168, 172
 ratum et consummatum 48
 sacramental 20, 42, 48, 55, 57, 60, 63, 144, 169, 172
 valid 54, 57, 77, 102, 155, 159, 168
 vows 20
Mills, Fr Joe 134
moral theology 10, 17, 120, 123
Moses 30, 31, 32, 45, 58, 70n, 164
mysterion 172, 177
Mystical Body 9, 34, 41, 170, 178

Ne Temere 62, 66
Newman, Cardinal 13–14, 177, 178

oath of fidelity 10
oikonomia 42, 124–6, 172–7

Orientale Lumen 172, 176
O'Riordan, Sean 131, 133
Örsy, Ladislas 42, 54–6, 60, 125, 126
Orthodox Churches 41, 42, 125, 126, 172–6, 178, 181

pastoral care 5, 9, 15, 17, 22–4, 88, 100, 110, 112n, 115, 116, 119, 123, 132, 134, 136, 148, 176
pastoral problems 2, 3, 20, 21, 23, 28, 29, 42, 58, 62, 117, 150, 168, 179
pastoral solutions 21, 42, 58, 74, 82, 83, 121, 124, 150, 179
pastoral theology 2, 5, 22, 42, 58, 128
Paul, St 5, 20, 33, 36, 37, 41, 43, 58, 59, 129, 150
peace 41, 43, 58–60, 77, 126, 171
Pelagians 44
personalism 117, 119, 120
Pius XII, Pope 60, 62–3
polyandry 60
polygamy 60
Pompedda, Mgr Mario F. 156, 166n
porneia 32
prooftexting 29
Provida Mater 151
psychology 2, 5, 64, 95, 97, 111n

Rahner, Karl 169, 170
Rainbow Groups 23, 86, 90–4, 96–8, 104–9, 155, 185
Ratzinger, Cardinal 89, 123, 128, 137
Redemptorists, the 2, 7, 81
Rite of Christian Initiation of Adults (RCIA) ix, 23–4, 79–82, 143–6, 148, 149, 163
Roman option 148
Roman Rota 16, 28, 161
Rose, Gerry 2

Sacra Virginitas 61
sacrament
 Fundamental 170
 of Reconciliation/Penance 81, 116, 122, 133, 147
 of the Sick 89
 Primordial 170
 seven sacraments 33, 44, 47, 48, 53, 170
sacramentum 44, 45, 47–9, 51

salvation   21, 29, 40, 41, 59, 80, 101,
  169, 171, 174
scandal   19, 78, 81, 83, 101, 110, 117,
  127, 129, 130, 137, 145, 160, 178
Scandinavian bishops   147, 148
Schmemann, Alexander   173, 175, 176
Scholasticism
  esse ad   55, 56
  esse in se   55
  matter and form   169, 171
  opus operantis   50
  opus operatum   50
  substance and accidents   49, 55, 56
Scholastics   18, 19, 33, 42, 45, 47–50,
  54, 56, 67, 169, 170
Scriptures
  Old Testament
  Genesis   28, 29, 30, 32, 33, 39, 47
  Leviticus   31
  Deuteronomy   30, 32, 70n
  Isaiah (Deutero-)   30
  Jeremiah   30
  Ezekiel   30
  Hosea   30
  New Testament
  Synoptic Gospels   35, 101
  Matthew   3, 5, 31, 32, 34–6, 38, 43,
    51, 101
  Mark   3, 30, 31, 32, 34, 36, 37
  Luke   3, 30, 34, 39, 83
  John   37, 40, 83
  Acts of the Apostles   37

Romans   59, 112n
1 Corinthians   5, 20–1, 35, 36, 58, 110,
  129, 144, 150, 170, 174
Ephesians   39, 41, 48, 59, 170
Hebrews   170
Revelation   34
Segnatura Apostolica   16
sensus fidei   13
sensus fidelium   14, 110, 138, 177, 178
sexual relations   30, 42, 44, 48, 49, 98,
  137
Shammai, Rabbi   32
Smith, Bishop Peter   116
sociology   2, 5, 16, 167
Socrates   43
Summa contra Gentiles   51
Summa Theologiae   48
systematic theology   22, 51, 65

Tametsi   50, 61, 73n
tribunals, diocesan   146, 153, 154,
  156–8, 181

Ut Notum Est   60
Ut Unum Sint   176

Veritatis Splendor   5, 7, 10–12, 17–18
vinculum   43, 44, 47, 52, 55, 56, 70n
Vorgrimler, Herbert   170

West, Morris   12, 130
Wrenn, Laurence   151